FAT FREE LIVING COOKBOOK FROM AROUND THE WORLD

* * *

Jyl Steinback

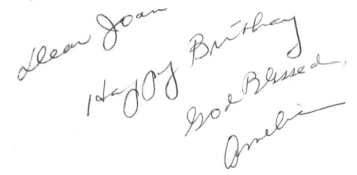

FAT FREE LIVING, INC.

FAT FREE LIVING COOKBOOK
FROM AROUND THE WORLD

Fat Free Living, Inc. 15202 N. 50th Place, Scottsdale, AZ 85254 (602) 996-6300; Fax (602) 996-9897; E-Mail fatfree@dancris.com Visit our Web Site at www.fatfreeliving.com

 Fat Free Living, Inc.

Printed in the United States of America

ISBN 0-963-687-6-7-0

First Printing: January 1999

Cover photos by Elliot Lincis, Camel Studios
Cover design by Michael Swaine, Michael Swaine Design

The recipes in this book were analyzed using the Nutrients III and IV nutrient analysis program. Products not listed on the original data base were added using the nutrition facts section of the product label. All nutrients were rounded to the nearest whole number.
                                                              Debra Kohl, MS.RD

Printed by Jumbo Jack's Cookbooks • A Division of Audubon Media Corporation • 1-800-798-2635

SUCCESS STORIES

Dear Jyl,

I have been cooking "fat free" for 15 years, or so I thought, until I saw one of your books. Despite my not using an egg yolk or butter in my house, I wasn't cooking totally fat-free until I tried your recipes. I work in a bookstore, and a customer told me how great your cookbooks are. Needless to say, I tried a few recipes and am now the grateful owner of all your books.

I also want to thank you for returning my call and answering my questions. You are truly an inspiration to all of us who are dedicated to eating a fat-free diet. I heartily recommend your books to everyone! Keep up the great work and good luck on your next book.

Carol Eidelson-Karol, North Woodmere, NY

Dear Jyl,

My church is using the First Place Program of weight loss. It uses the American Diabetic Association's exchange system. Although I have all six of your cookbooks, and thought I had seen a reference to the ADA, I couldn't find it. My call was to see if the exchanges in your cookbooks fit the First Place Program. To my delight, they do!

But my news gets even better! In four weeks, I have lost 15 pounds using many of the recipes from your cookbooks. I must admit that I have followed a strict program of exercise as well! I am delighted with the results. Thank you for writing your cookbooks. They make eating no-fat possible and delicious!

Kathryn J. French, Ph.D., West Frankfort, IL

Dear Jyl,

Thank you so much for your new cookbook! You make fat-free eating a PLEASURE! I like the information in the front as to where to get information on products you use. Best of luck with your new cookbook and keep up the great work. You're the best! **P.S. Just for the record, for the first time I have lost weight, almost 50 pounds, and kept it off now for almost 3 years!**

Jane Pogorzelski, New Berlin, IL

Dear Jyl,

I have found that cutting fat has made it immensely easier for me to eat healthier, feel and look better. Combining it with exercise is a winning combination. There just is no substitute!

I have all of your books except one and I must add the covers on your books are so appealing. Many thanks!

Mary Beth Williams, Des Moines, IA

Dear Jyl,

I enjoying talking to you last week, after quickly looking through your book, I've decided that my next gift to myself is going to be your set of books! Thanks for writing them!

Mary Howard, Midway, MI

Hi Jyl,

I just have to let you know that last night I made your won tons, they were out of this world, my husband did not believe that I made them and especially that they were FAT FREE! I fed them to my mother and friends and they could not believe it either. This morning I made the French Toast, it was GREAT! Tonight I am making the Stuffed Pasta Shells. Yesterday I went to the book store and bought all of your books, so I am off to a healthy and FAT FREE Lifestyle. I have my whole family starting to eat this way and they can't even tell the difference! I think you should try and go on a TV cooking show. COOKING WITH JYL THAT FAT FREE WAY! I love to watch cooking shows and I am sure it would be a hit. Well I just wanted to say Thanks, and I will keep you posted with my weight loss. I am following your 14 DAY MENU PLAN. Thanks so Much!

Sabrina Neri, Union City, CA

Dear Jyl,

My husband and I really love your **FAT FREE Living Super Cookbook.** Just recently I ordered two more of your cookbooks. They are also terrific! Thanks again!

Eileen Gauck, Astoc, FL

Dear Jyl,

I just wanted to let you know that I am just starting a new life program of eating low fat and was very excited to find your cookbooks. I purchased them and have started to use it and find the recipes so easy to follow, and am very encouraged to start my family on a new way of life in eating. Thank You!

Christina Parks, Oak Harbor, WA

Dear Jyl,

I purchased **The FAT FREE Living FAMILY Cookbook** last weekend. I LOVE IT! There is just two of us at home, working different schedules, liking different things, and yet I have managed to cook all week from this book and have found something each night that we will both eat. I also love the shopping list at the bottom of each page. Sincerely,

Maria Craddock, White Pigeon, MI

Dear Jyl,

I just received your most recent cookbook. I LOVE your cookbooks! I had been looking for a healthy recipe for Red Clam Sauce and I found it in one of your books. I want to be a good example to my son and be healthier. My husband often comments on how good things taste, and how nice it is to know we are eating healthier than ever.

I am a busy mom who works full time and cares for an 18-month-old son and a 41 year old husband. Thanks for helping me out with such tasty recipes - and healthier outlook!

Yvonne Bonsall, Marquette, MI

Dear Jyl,

I am 71 years old, my husband is 72 and my daughter is 53 years old. We started on your wonderful food plan that are in your FAT FREE Living Cookbook. To date, we have all three lost 5 pounds each the first week and now into our second week three more pounds each. The first recipe I made was your Seafood Chowder and we all went crazy about how great it tastes. I had to make it two times because it was so tasty and good. I made the other recipes and they were all so easy and so good! In all my years I never knew almost no fat food was so wonderful! What I like most of all is all the foods are foods we already have in our refrigerator or cupboard. That's a blessing for us old people. Thank you and have a Sunshine Day filled with Peace and Love!

Mrs. Silvanna Amendola, Roseburg, OR

Dear Jyl,

I want to thank you for your unprecedented fat-free cookbooks, I have been a vegetarian for twenty years and I have tried so many things to help my family with a nutritious, yet fat-free life, but to no avail. (They have all been meat and potato lovers!) Finally, I purchased one of your cookbooks and started preparing meals from them. After about two weeks I explained to my family that they had basically been eating fat-free and healthier foods. They love them! Now they, too, share my enthusiasm of getting in the kitchen and preparing wonderful meals. Keep those cookbooks coming! Thanks again.

Jane Hannes, Gracey, KY

Dear Jyl,

When I saw your book, Fat Free Living Desserts, I was excited. A friend and I had recently started a low-fat diet and were looking for recipes to help our cravings. What could be better than sweets? I immediately bought the book and tried several recipes. My family and friend were very surprised with the fact that what they just ate was basically fat-free. My friend immediately ran to the bookstore and found that they had sold out. After visiting every bookstore in Marquette, she had to settle with ordering it. She said it was "well worth the wait". Since buying your dessert book, I have also purchased cookbooks 1 and 2. I haven't been disappointed yet and my family doesn't even realize how healthy they are eating. I love knowing that I am giving them the best diet possible. Thanks for the great books.

Linda Dompierre, Palmer, MI

Dear Jyl,

Thank-you for your wonderful FAT FREE DESSERT Cookbook. All of the recipes that I have tried have been simple to prepare and great tasting. The Sour Cream Pineapple Muffins and Donut Muffins have become staples in our house. My husband and 2 year-old son have loved everything that I have baked, and I have been able to enjoy the desserts without feeling guilty (and staying a size 8). Keep up the good work.

Leslie Price, Evanston, IL

Dear Jyl,

We have enjoyed quite a few of the recipes and found them to be much quicker than our regular methods of cooking. Your program for establishing a fat-free kitchen was most beneficial in making the transition to fat free cooking. Some of our favorites include: Orange Honey Mustard Chicken, Pineapple Baked Beans, Creamy Garlic Chicken Breasts and Ranch-Style Beans. My husband, to date, has lost 32 pounds and loves the results of our new lifestyle.

Brian and Lisa Berch

Dear Jyl,

Just a note of thanks for your Super Cookbook. It has made going fat-free so much easier. I am so glad you've included which recipes can be made ahead and which ones I can make and freeze. We're a family of 7 and some nights I just don't want to cook. So I am glad I can prepare ahead! And your Chicken Enchiladas are the absolute best!! Thanks so much!

Helen Scott, Valdossta, GA

Greetings Jyl,

My husband, I, and another couple are doing your FAT FREE Cookbooks and getting healthy! I never believed that you could eat such good food and lose weight!

Your books have changed me, the way I look at food, now I can eat healthy and it tastes good **TOO!** No more rabbit food!

Because of FAT FREE Living, it has made me to want to get more healthy and to lose weight! My husband and I, and our friends, are going to the YMCA three times a week, playing racquetball and to take water aerobics. I am so excited about my new life changes - I am losing weight and inches and having fun too! I owe it all to you - you are an angel. Jyl, you have saved my life with your cookbooks. Thanks for everything!

Karen Tucker, Nashville, NC

Dear Jyl,

I LOVE your FAT FREE Cookbooks! I saw you on Crook and Chase and I want to get **Roll Yourself Thin in 12 Minutes**. Thanks!

Michelle McKune, Sea Tac, WA

Hi Jyl,

I am learning your **Roll Yourself Thin** exercises and I love them! I am on my sixth day of FAT FREE Living and it is changing my life. Since my first day of living FAT FREE my intense sugar cravings have totally disappeared and I am at peace with food. It's been that way EVERY day! A MIRACLE! Thank you! Potato Bread and Sandwich Subs have the BEST flavor - I can't believe they are FAT FREE! I love Ginger Bread and baked your recipe from the **Super Cookbook** this afternoon- it was WONDERFUL! And with a spoon of FAT FREE Cool Whip it doesn't get better than that! Thank you, Jyl, and God Bless you and your beautiful family!

Joanne Zutz, Norfolk, NE

Hi Jyl,

I love your FAT FREE Breads Cookbook! Even my children (13, 12 and 10 years) eat the whole wheat. My favorites are the fat-free fruit breads. Thank you! Thank you! Thank you! I look forward to getting all your books. Thank you in advance!

Joy Horsman, Canada

Dear Jyl,

I had a car accident in 1979, and was in the hospital, pain and stress center, having taken all kinds of medication. I still have a bad back. Every morning I woke up and I hurt, and most all day it hurt. Since I received your Roll Yourself Thin book I get down and do your exercises. By the time I am finished doing them, the pain and stiffness is gone! My daughter gave me your 1st Recipes for Fat FREE Living Cookbook, which I use often. I am looking forward to getting all your books! Thank you!

Shirley Krafft, Mesa, AZ

Dear Jyl,

I wanted to drop you a note and tell you how much my husband and I are enjoying your book **FAT FREE Living Super Cookbook**. We were recently married, and I am striving to cook healthy and still impress my husband with my cooking abilities. Thanks to your book, I'm succeeding. We enjoy being able to eat flavorful, filling, and yet healthy foods. Thanks!

                    Nancie and Jody Yarbro, Valley Mills, TX

Hi Jyl,

I wanted to take a moment this morning to thank you for your book **The FAT FREE Living FAMILY Cookbook**. Glad to see someone else has found the key to life; fad diets are out - a healthy lifestyle is in. I also like the Exercise section! Roll Yourself Thin in 12 Minutes. I can already see a difference, and my pants are getting loose. Love Ya and keep up the good work!

                    Pat Garrett, Belleview, FL

Dear Jyl,

My husband and I are in our seventies and we are very careful about what we eat because it affects our health. We are especially concerned with heavy fats in our diet. I have every one of your books and use your recipes in our meals. I always look forward to your new books. They help me to manage my weight. Shalom and best wishes to you and your family.

                    Henrietta Kohn, Amarillo, TX

Dear Jyl,

We're enjoying your cookbooks so much. My husband had a heart attack a year ago and four bypasses at age 48. I've looked everywhere for recipes that tastes good. It's hard! But NOT WITH YOUR BOOKS! I've been telling all my friends. Thank you so much!

                    Barbara Franks, Amarillo, TX

ACKNOWLEDGMENTS

FAT FREE LIVING COOKBOOK From AROUND THE WORLD is here! I love spreading the FAT FREE and healthy word! It's my mission in life! Thank You ALL for making it possible. Be healthy always! Love, Jyl.

You've heard it all--cut calories, forget, exercise to lose weight. We all know what to do, but how do we get there? Regardless of genetic background or past weight struggles, you can take CONTROL. You have to BELIEVE in YOURSELF. Change the vision of destiny by removing yourself from a state of despair to one of self-discipline and power. Once you believe...discover happiness beyond the numbers on your scale...and increase your sense of self-respect, self-love, and confidence...weight loss will surely follow. Stop looking to others for the answers to all your dieting questions and needs--look inside yourself and take charge! Don't forget to *COUNT ALL YOUR BLESSINGS!*

Gary, celebrating our 18th anniversary is a wonderful miracle. Thank you for the **best** years of my life. I love you so very much! You are my soul mate and I am extremely lucky to have you in my life. I count my blessings every day and you are *always #1 on my list.* Let's go for it all! We always do!

Jamie, you are 13 now, and what a beautiful lady you have become. Both inside and out! I admire you, Jam, you set your goals, go after each and every one, and succeed! You have a <u>heart of gold</u> and know the true meaning of "unconditional love". I love you so much, Jamie, more than life! Thank you, thank you for YOU! *You are one of my best blessings.* Lucky me!

Scott, you are already 5 and I love you! You are smart, witty, adorable, "all boy" and have <u>tons</u> of energy with the very best smiling eyes I've ever seen, and I love every inch of you. Thanks for being in my life. I love you, Scott, more than life! *You are one of my special blessings.*

Mom and Dad, Only you two would go to a bookstore and hand out my flyers, type all my labels and keep on typing with each new batch that I send to you, fly from St. Louis to Scottsdale to baby-sit your grandkids at a drop of a hat, walk the malls and stop at every store to make sure there are enough books on the shelves, go to the warehouse clubs to report how many books are left and rearrange them so FAT FREE Living is right up front, and only you two would love me unconditionally all of my life. You are two of my lucky blessings! I love you both very much! Thank you!

Jacie, You're the best sister. Motivating, persistent, loving, giving and caring! Thank you for you! I Love You lots!

Jeff and Diane, Alex, and Casey, I say it every time, but you are amazing and you motivate me to keep on going with new and creative ideas all the time. Thanks for always being there for all of us! I love you very much! Your mission is to change the world to a better place and with your passion and mine I think we might just do it!

Snooky and Harlan, Happy 50th Anniversary! Congratulations! We have beautiful memories, a fabulous trip, and a lot more to celebrate. I love you very much. Thank You!

Grandma, I Love You!

I am extremely thankful for the opportunity and pleasure to work with each one of you. You are a blessing in my life! Thank you all! This book wouldn't be possible without YOU!

Mikki Eveloff, You are Amazing! You are Extremely Talented! Creative! Positive! and a Beautiful Person! Thank you for working with me and being such a fabulous friend. I love you lots, Mikki, Thank you!

Debbie Kohl, We did it again. You are the best! Debra Kohl is a Registered Dietitian with a master's degree in Nutrition and Dietetics and you can reach her services at (602) 266-0324. Thanks, Deb, for being such a special friend and making FAT FREE Living Nutritionally Perfect!

Elliot Lincis, You are an extraordinary friend and an awesome photographer. I love you, El. Thanks for always going the extra mile and making it _perfect_. I always say, "It only takes two" and you always give me way and above. These were some fabulous shots! This one was FUN!

Mike Swain, The covers are your best! I love the "world" and how you designed and dressed us all. You are talented, creative, and always give that extra-special touch! Thanks, Mike, for working with us and making FAT FREE Living From Around The World, the very _best_ yet! These front and back covers are dedicated to your dad. God Bless.

Alan Skversky, It truly has been a pleasure to work with both you and Sandee. Thanks a million for helping make this book possible!

Kim Clausen, thank you for being such a special friend and for all of your beautiful costumes that make our front and back cover so picture perfect!

CONTENTS

AMERICAN

AMERICAN

What's more American than tips
for healthy living?
33 more healthy living tips!

1. **Do** eat three meals a day. Skipping meals will leave you feeling hungry and increase your chances of snacking on the "wrong" foods.
2. **Don't** put yourself last. Even if you're busy taking care of others, take the time to take care of yourself. Your happiness will have a positive effect on those around you.
3. **Don't** plan to diet. Gradually change your eating and exercise habits.
4. **Don't** think of food as your enemy. Think of it as fuel, supplying your body with energy.
5. **Don't** think further ahead than today! Monitor healthy eating one day at a time and make healthy eating a lifestyle.
6. **Do** set one goal at a time and take it slow!
7. **Do** plan your meals and snacks.
8. **Do** try to eat at regular intervals to feel satisfied without feeling stuffed, and avoid overeating.
9. **Do** throw leftovers from other plates away-immediately! Better in the trash than on your hips or waistline.
10. **Do** divide your plate into healthy sections. Fill up 3/4 of your plate with vegetables, whole-grains, fruits and beans while the remaining portion holds low-fat meat or dairy products for protein.
11. **Don't** go to the table with a half-filled plate. Fill up any extra space on your plate with "free" vegetables! It will provide added vitamins and minerals, fiber, and fill you up without filling you out!
12. **Do** wait 10 minutes before indulging in the need to binge. Suck on a slice of lemon that can fight the urge to splurge. Ask yourself, "Do I really want this?" before indulging.
13. **Don't** think of these changes as a chore...keep it fun!
14. **Don't** go shopping on an empty stomach when you will be more likely to stock up on high-calorie foods or be tempted by special offers.
15. **Do** write out a shopping list and stick to it!

1

16. **Don't** give yourself too many choices at mealtimes. We are tempted to eat more when presented with an array of different smells, colors, textures and shapes.

17. **Do** play slow, relaxing music while you eat - you will eat slower and give your mind time to register you're full, before feeling overstuffed.

18. **Don't** eat while watching television. It's too easy to become distracted and consume a day's worth of calories through one TV sitcom.

19. **Do** place your food on a smaller plate so serving sizes look more substantial.

20. **Do** get in touch with your feelings of hunger and **don't** depend on the clock to tell you when it's time to eat.

21. **Don't** give up snacking - just make it part of your daily food plan with healthier choices.

22. **Do** wait 20 minutes between your main course and dessert.

23. **Do** spice it up! Add flavor without fat to fill you up!

24. **Do** have someone else clear the table so you will be less likely to pick at leftovers.

25. **Do** make sure you get enough sleep. Research has shown that appetite increases when you're feeling tired.

26. **Do** have a glass of water at the first sign of hunger. Many people mistake thirst for hunger.

27. **Do** exercise for at least 20 minutes each day. This can be as simple as taking the stairs instead of the elevator, parking far away and walking to your destination, taking the dog for a walk, or biking with your kids.

28. **Don't** choose an exercise activity you don't enjoy. If you force yourself to do it, chances are you won't.

29. **Do** drink lots of water!

30. **Don't** eat standing up.

31. **Do** learn to accept compliments! These can be more rewarding than a chocolate bar!

32. **Do** eat the same way when you're alone as you do when you're with others, and eat the same way with others as you do when you're alone. This makes for a healthy and HONEST lifestyle change.

33. **Don't** be tempted by magical foods, herbs or medicines. There is no such thing as a quick and easy shortcut to HEALTHY LIVING!

CHILI-SPICED POTATO SKINS

EASY

ingredients: 1/3 cup fat-free bread crumbs
1 tsp. chili powder
1/2 tsp. ground cumin
1/2 tsp. salt
4 baking potatoes, baked and cooled
1/4 cup fat-free mayonnaise
fat-free cheese, fat-free sour cream or
    salsa for topping (optional)

directions: Preheat oven to 425 degrees.
Lightly spray cookie sheet with nonfat cooking spray. Combine bread crumbs, chili powder, cumin and salt on waxed paper.
Cut potatoes lengthwise into quarters.
Scoop out potato pulp, leaving 1/4-inch-thick shells. Brush shells with mayonnaise, then roll in crumb mixture to coat.
Bake in cookie sheet for 25 minutes.
Turn over and bake 25 minutes longer, or until crisp.
Top with fat-free cheese, fat-free sour cream or salsa, if desired.

Serves: 4

Nutrition per Serving		Exchanges
Calories	168	2 starch
Carbohydrate	38 grams	
Cholesterol	0 milligrams	
Dietary Fiber	4 grams	
Fat	< 1 gram	
Protein	3 grams	
Sodium	405 milligrams	

Shopping List: 4 baking potatoes, 2 ounces fat-free mayonnaise, fat-free bread crumbs, chili powder, ground cumin, salt, optional toppings (fat-free cheese, fat-free sour cream or salsa)

CHICKEN ROSEMARY CONSOMMÉ WITH FRESH VEGETABLES

DIFFICULT

ingredients:
6 cups fat-free chicken broth
3 rosemary sprigs
Ground pepper
1/2 medium red onion, julienned
1 red bell pepper, julienned
1 Italian zucchini
1 yellow squash
1 large carrot

directions:
Boil chicken broth with rosemary and a pinch of pepper.
Shave 1/8-inch-thick pieces of zucchini, squash and carrot skins; julienne thinly.
Warm soup bowls in the oven; arrange all the vegetables (onion, bell pepper, zucchini, squash and carrot) in colorful mix.
Pour hot broth over vegetables to blanch; serve immediately.

Serves: 4

Nutrition per Serving		Exchanges
Calories	39	1 1/2 vegetable
Carbohydrate	8 grams	
Cholesterol	0 milligrams	
Dietary Fiber	2 grams	
Fat	< 1 gram	
Protein	1 gram	
Sodium	909 milligrams	

Shopping List: 48 ounces fat-free chicken broth, 1 yellow squash, 1 Italian zucchini, 1 carrot, red onion, red bell pepper, rosemary sprigs, ground pepper

CHILLED BEET SOUP

AVERAGE - DO AHEAD

ingredients:
2 medium beets, cooked and peeled
2 cups fat-free sour cream
1/2 cup seasoned rice wine vinegar
Salt and pepper, to taste

directions:
Boil beets and peel with fingers as you rinse. (Protect hands with plastic gloves as beet juice will stain.) Submerge in ice bath to cool. Finely dice or julienne one-half of one beet and reserve for garnish.

Chop remaining beets into small pieces.

Combine beets, 1 1/2 cups sour cream, rice wine vinegar, salt and pepper in a food processor or blender; purée until smooth.

Chill soup in refrigerator 10 minutes.

Serve in chilled bowls with diced or julienned beet garnish and a spoonful of sour cream.

Serves: 4

Nutrition per Serving		Exchanges
Calories	118	1 vegetable
Carbohydrate	17 grams	1 milk
Cholesterol	0 milligrams	
Dietary Fiber	1 gram	
Fat	< 1 gram	
Protein	8 grams	
Sodium	97 milligrams	

Shopping List: 2 medium beets, 16 ounces fat-free sour cream, seasoned rice wine vinegar, salt, pepper

CHILLED CARROT SOUP WITH GARDEN HERBS

AVERAGE - DO AHEAD

ingredients:
5 large carrots, sliced thin
1 large white onion, sliced thin
1 tsp. fresh thyme, chopped
1 tsp. brown sugar
1/2 tsp. ground nutmeg
5 cups fat-free chicken broth
1/4 cup orange juice
2 tsp. chopped chives

directions:
Lightly spray large nonstick skillet with nonfat cooking spray and heat over medium-high heat. Add sliced carrots and onions; cook, stirring frequently, 5-6 minutes. Add thyme, brown sugar and nutmeg; cook 5 minutes. Pour chicken broth into skillet and cook, uncovered, 20 minutes. Pour mixture into food processor or blender and purée until smooth. Add orange juice and mix well. Chill in refrigerator about 40 minutes and serve in chilled bowls. Garnish with chives and serve immediately.

Serves: 4

Nutrition per Serving
Calories   71
Carbohydrate   16 grams
Cholesterol   0 milligrams
Dietary Fiber   4 grams
Fat   < 1 gram
Protein   2 grams
Sodium   371 milligrams

Exchanges
1 vegetable
2/3 fruit

Shopping List: 5 large carrots, 1 large white onion, 40 ounces fat-free chicken broth, 2 ounces orange juice, fresh thyme, brown sugar, ground nutmeg, chives

CHILLED CUCUMBER SOUP

AVERAGE - DO AHEAD

ingredients:
2 large cucumbers, peeled and seeded
1 clove garlic, minced
1 cup fat-free plain yogurt
6 fresh dill sprigs
1/2 cup seasoned rice wine vinegar
Salt and pepper, to taste

directions:
Peel and seed cucumbers by cutting in half length-wise and scooping out seeds. Neatly dice 1 piece (one-half) of cucumber and set aside for garnish. Chop the remaining pieces and combine with garlic, yogurt, vinegar and 2 dill sprigs in a food processor or blender; purée until smooth.
Season with salt and pepper. Chill and pour soup into chilled glass soup bowls.
Garnish with a spoonful of yogurt, diced cucumber and dill sprig.
Serve immediately.

Serves: 4

Nutrition per Serving		Exchanges
Calories	55	2 vegetable
Carbohydrate	10 grams	
Cholesterol	1 milligram	
Dietary Fiber	2 grams	
Fat	< 1 gram	
Protein	4 grams	
Sodium	47 milligrams	

Shopping List:
2 large cucumbers, 8 ounces fat-free plain yogurt, 4 ounces seasoned rice wine vinegar, garlic, dill sprigs, salt, pepper

CREAM OF TOMATO AND RICE SOUP

EASY - DO AHEAD

ingredients: 28 oz. can diced tomatoes
14 oz. can fat-free chicken broth
1 cup nonfat dry milk
2 cups cooked rice
1/4 tsp. pepper
1 tsp. dried parsley flakes
1 tsp. salt

directions: Process tomatoes in blender for 10 seconds.
Combine broth and dry milk in a medium sauce-pan. Heat over medium heat and whisk until thoroughly blended.
Add tomatoes, rice, pepper, parsley and salt. Cook until heated through.

Serves: 6

Nutrition per Serving		Exchanges
Calories	131	2 vegetable
Carbohydrate	26 grams	1 starch
Cholesterol	2 milligrams	
Dietary Fiber	2 grams	
Fat	< 1 gram	
Protein	6 grams	
Sodium	906 milligrams	

Shopping List: 28-ounce can diced tomatoes, 14-ounce can fat-free chicken broth, nonfat dry milk, fat-free rice, pepper, dried parsley flakes, salt

POTATO STEW

EASY

ingredients:
3 lb. all-purpose potatoes, peeled and cubed
3 1/2 cups fat-free chicken broth
1 cup chopped onions
3/4 cup chopped carrots
3/4 cup chopped celery
1 1/2 tsp. minced garlic
1/4 tsp. thyme
1/4 tsp. pepper
10 oz. frozen asparagus spears, thawed
    and drained
2 tbsp. chopped chives

directions:
Combine potatoes, broth, onion, carrots, celery, garlic, thyme and pepper in a Dutch oven and bring to a boil over medium-high heat.
Reduce heat to low, cover and simmer 25-30 minutes, until potatoes are tender.
Add asparagus spears and cook over medium-high heat 1 minute.
Sprinkle with chives and serve immediately.

Serves: 4

Nutrition per Serving		Exchanges
Calories	370	5 1/2 vegetable
Carbohydrate	84 grams	3 starch
Cholesterol	0 milligrams	
Dietary Fiber	11 grams	
Fat	< 1 gram	
Protein	10 grams	
Sodium	498 milligrams	

Shopping List:
3 pounds all-purpose potatoes, 32 ounces fat-free chicken or vegetable broth, 8-ounce package chopped onions, 1 carrot, celery, 10-ounce package frozen asparagus spears, chives, minced garlic, thyme, pepper

AMERICAN

SPICY APPLE SOUP

EASY - DO AHEAD

ingredients: 6 Granny Smith apples, cored,
peeled and chopped
1/2 cup sugar
2 tsp. paprika, divided
1/2 tsp. cayenne pepper
Pinch of ground cloves
Pinch of cinnamon
Pinch of nutmeg
2 1/2 cups fat-free chicken broth
1/2 cup fat-free sour cream

directions: Combine apples, sugar, 1 1/2 teaspoons paprika, cayenne pepper, cloves, cinnamon, nutmeg and chicken broth in a medium saucepan; cook over medium heat until apples are tender.
Purée mixture in food processor or blender; chill several hours.
Add sour cream and blend with wire whisk until smooth.
Serve in chilled bowls and garnish with remaining 1/2 teaspoon paprika.

Serves: 4

Nutrition per Serving		Exchanges
Calories	238	4 fruit
Carbohydrate	59 grams	
Cholesterol	0 milligrams	
Dietary Fiber	5 grams	
Fat	< 1 gram	
Protein	3 grams	
Sodium	247 milligrams	

Shopping List: 6 Granny Smith apples, 20 ounces fat-free chicken broth, 4 ounces fat-free sour cream, sugar, paprika, cayenne pepper, ground cloves, cinnamon, nutmeg

WHITEFISH SOUP

EASY - DO AHEAD

ingredients:
8 oz. cod
1 large onion, finely chopped
2 parsnips, finely chopped
2 1/2 cups water (or fish stock)
2 1/2 cups skim milk
Salt and pepper, to taste
Lemon wedges (optional)

directions:
Remove bones and skin from fish and cut into bite-sized pieces.
Combine all ingredients in a saucepan; bring to a boil over high heat and season to taste.
Reduce heat to low and simmer 20 minutes. Serve hot, garnished with lemon wedges.

Serves: 4

Nutrition per Serving		Exchanges
Calories	179	4 vegetable
Carbohydrate	26 grams	1/2 milk
Cholesterol	27 milligrams	1 meat
Dietary Fiber	4 grams	
Fat	< 1 gram	
Protein	17 grams	
Sodium	118 milligrams	

Shopping List: 8 ounces cod, 1 large onion, 2 parsnips, 20 ounces skim milk, lemon wedges, salt, pepper

CARROT SALAD

EASY - DO AHEAD

ingredients: 3 cups grated carrots
1/2 cup raisins
1 cup fat-free plain yogurt
1/4 cup orange juice
1 1/2 tsp. lemon juice

directions: Combine carrots and raisins in a large bowl. Combine yogurt, orange juice and lemon juice in a small bowl and blend well.
Toss dressing with carrot mixture.
Cover and refrigerate 2 hours; serve cold.

Serves: 6

Nutrition per Serving

Calories	86
Carbohydrate	19 grams
Cholesterol	1 milligram
Dietary Fiber	2 grams
Fat	< 1 gram
Protein	3 grams
Sodium	50 milligrams

Exchanges
1/2 vegetable
1/2 fruit
1/2 milk

Shopping List: 8-ounce package grated carrots, raisins, 8 ounces fat-free plain yogurt, 2 ounces orange juice, lemon juice

CREAMY SHRIMP SALAD

EASY - DO AHEAD

ingredients:
1 lb. fat-free cooked shrimp, cleaned and
    chilled
1 1/4 cups chopped celery
2 tsp. finely-chopped onions
1/2 cup fat-free Russian dressing
4 cups shredded romaine lettuce

directions:
Combine shrimp, celery and onions in a large bowl; mix lightly.
Add dressing and toss until coated evenly.
Cover and chill at least 20 minutes.
Evenly divide lettuce among 4 plates.
Top each with shrimp mixture. Serve chilled.

Serves: 4

Nutrition per Serving		Exchanges
Calories	128	4 vegetable
Carbohydrate	21 grams	1 meat
Cholesterol	10 milligrams	
Dietary Fiber	2 grams	
Fat	< 1 gram	
Protein	10 grams	
Sodium	867 milligrams	

Shopping List: 1 pound fat-free cooked shrimp, celery, onion, fat-free Russian salad dressing, romaine lettuce

CUCUMBER AND RED ONION SALAD

EASY - DO AHEAD

ingredients: 2 tbsp. red wine vinegar
1 tbsp. mustard
1 tbsp. fresh parsley, snipped
1 tsp. fat-free mayonnaise
1/2 tsp. black pepper
2 cucumbers, thinly sliced
1 red onion, thinly sliced
Lettuce leaves

directions: Combine red wine vinegar, mustard, parsley, mayonnaise and pepper in a medium bowl and whisk until blended smooth.
Add cucumbers and onions; toss lightly.
Line bowls with lettuce leaves. Scoop salad into center and chill at least 1 hour before serving.

Serves: 4

Nutrition per Serving		Exchanges
Calories	40	1 1/2 vegetable
Carbohydrate	8 grams	
Cholesterol	0 milligrams	
Dietary Fiber	2 grams	
Fat	< 1 gram	
Protein	1 gram	
Sodium	64 milligrams	

Shopping List: 2 cucumbers, 1 red onion, lettuce, red wine vinegar, mustard, fresh parsley, fat-free mayonnaise, black pepper

LENTIL, RED PEPPER AND POTATO SALAD

AVERAGE - DO AHEAD

ingredients:
2 cups cooked lentils
1 cup cooked potatoes, diced
1/2 cup cooked fresh or frozen green peas
1/2 cup finely-chopped red bell pepper
1/4 cup chopped red onion
1/4 cup chopped celery
1 tbsp. finely-chopped fresh Italian parsley
1 tbsp. finely-chopped fresh basil
2 tbsp. red wine vinegar
Salt and pepper, to taste

directions:
Combine lentils, potatoes, peas, red bell peppers, red onion, celery, parsley and basil in a large bowl. Combine vinegar, salt and pepper in a small bowl and whisk until blended.
Add dressing to lentil mixture; toss and serve.

Serves: 6

Nutrition per Serving		Exchanges
Calories	114	1 1/2 vegetable
Carbohydrate	22 grams	1 starch
Cholesterol	0 milligrams	
Dietary Fiber	5 grams	
Fat	< 1 gram	
Protein	7 grams	
Sodium	38 milligrams	

Shopping List: lentils, potatoes, peas, red bell pepper, red onion, celery, parsley, basil, red wine vinegar, salt, pepper

RASPBERRY SPINACH SALAD

AVERAGE

ingredients: 1/2 cup raspberry vinegar
1/4 cup sugar
1/4 cup whole raspberries
1 jalapeño pepper, halved and seeded
Black pepper
2 large button mushrooms, washed, dried and julienned
1 small red onion, peeled and julienned
1 large carrot, peeled and julienned
1/2 lb. bag baby spinach, stems removed
3/4 cup fat-free seasoned croutons

directions: Combine raspberry vinegar, sugar, raspberries and seeded jalapeño in a small saucepan; cook over medium heat until liquid is reduced by half. Pour mixture into food processor or blender and purée until smooth.
Season with pepper and refrigerate at least 20 minutes until chilled.
Combine baby spinach, julienned vegetables, prepared dressing and croutons in a large bowl.
Toss and serve immediately.

Serves: 4

Nutrition per Serving

		Exchanges
Calories	86	2 vegetable
Carbohydrate	24 grams	1 fruit
Cholesterol	0 milligrams	
Dietary Fiber	2 grams	
Fat	< 1 gram	
Protein	3 grams	
Sodium	72 milligrams	

Shopping List: 1/2 pound bag baby spinach, 1 carrot, 2 large button mushrooms, 1 red onion, raspberries, 4 ounces raspberry vinegar, jalapeño pepper, sugar, fat-free seasoned croutons, pepper

16

BAKED WHITE FISH
EASY

ingredients: 1 lb. cod
2 tsp. fat-free Italian salad dressing
1 onion, sliced thin
Juice of 1 lime
2 cups fat-free finely-shredded Cheddar cheese

directions: Preheat oven to 350 degrees.
Lightly spray 8x12-inch baking pan with nonfat cooking spray; arrange cod in pan.
Pour salad dressing over fish; top with sliced onion and sprinkle with lime juice.
Bake 20 minutes in preheated oven; top with cheese and bake 5 minutes, until cheese is melted.

Serves: 4

Nutrition per Serving		Exchanges
Calories	194	1 vegetable
Carbohydrate	7 grams	5 meat
Cholesterol	49 milligrams	
Dietary Fiber	<1 gram	
Fat	< 1 gram	
Protein	36 grams	
Sodium	602 milligrams	

Shopping List: 1 pound cod, fat-free Italian salad dressing, 1 onion, 1 lime, 8 ounces fat-free finely-shredded Cheddar cheese

SOLE WITH A HEART

AVERAGE

ingredients: 1 1/2 lb. fillets of sole, cut in 6 pieces
1/8 tsp. pepper
4 tbsp. fat-free melted margarine, divided
1 cup minced onions
2 red bell peppers, sliced thin
16 oz. can chopped tomatoes, undrained
1/8 tsp. red chili pepper
1/8 tsp. salt (optional)

directions: Preheat broiler on high heat.
Line baking sheet with foil and lightly spray with nonfat cooking spray. Arrange sole on baking sheet; sprinkle with pepper and brush with 2 tablespoons melted margarine.
Broil 5 inches from heat, 5 to 8 minutes. Pour remaining melted margarine into medium non-stick skillet and heat over medium heat. Add onions and bell pepper; cook, stirring frequently, about 4 minutes, until tender.
Add tomatoes, chili pepper and salt; reduce heat to low and simmer 10 minutes, stirring occasionally. Spoon sauce over fish and serve immediately.

Serves: 6

Nutrition per Serving		Exchanges
Calories	90	1 vegetable
Carbohydrate	6 grams	2 meat
Cholesterol	35 milligrams	
Dietary Fiber	1 gram	
Fat	< 1 gram	
Protein	14 grams	
Sodium	226 milligrams	

Shopping List: 1 1/2 pounds sole fillets, fat-free margarine, minced onion, 2 red bell peppers, 16-ounce can chopped tomatoes, red chili pepper, pepper, salt

HAWAIIAN BAKED CHICKEN
EASY

ingredients: 1/4 cup fat-free margarine, melted
1 cup all-purpose flour
3 tsp. salt, divided
1/4 tsp. pepper
2 tsp. paprika
2 1/2 lb. fat-free chicken breasts
1 tsp. ginger
1 tbsp. cornstarch
3/4 cup light brown sugar
3/4 cup pineapple juice
1 cup pineapple chunks, drained
1/3 cup vinegar
2 tbsp. soy sauce

directions: Preheat oven to 400 degrees.
Lightly spray 9x13-inch baking dish with nonfat cooking spray; cover bottom of dish with melted margarine.
Combine flour, 2 teaspoons salt, pepper and paprika in a resealable plastic bag; add chicken and shake until coated. Arrange chicken in baking dish, turning to coat with melted margarine. Bake 15 minutes. Combine ginger, 1 teaspoon salt, cornstarch and brown sugar in a small saucepan. Add the pineapple juice, pineapple chunks, vinegar and soy sauce; mix well. Cook over medium heat, stirring constantly, until slightly thickened. Remove chicken from oven and turn over. Reduce oven temperature to 350 degrees. Spoon sauce over chicken and bake 30-35 minutes, until chicken is cooked through.

Serves: 6

Nutrition per Serving		Exchanges
Calories	409	6 meat
Carbohydrate	153 grams	3 1/2 fruit
Cholesterol	93 milligrams	
Dietary Fiber	1 gram	
Fat	< 1 gram	
Protein	47 grams	
Sodium	1850 milligrams	

Shopping List: 2 1/2 pounds fat-free chicken breasts, fat-free margarine, 6 ounces pineapple juice, 8 ounces pineapple chunks in juice, brown sugar, vinegar, soy sauce, flour, salt, pepper, paprika, ginger, cornstarch

GRILLED AND ROASTED VEGGIE WRAP

AVERAGE - DO AHEAD

ingredients:
1 medium zucchini, sliced thin
1 medium yellow squash, sliced thin
1 red bell pepper, seeded and sliced thin
1 green pepper, seeded and sliced thin
1 yellow bell pepper, seeded and sliced thin
2 portabello mushrooms, sliced thin
1 cup fat-free cream cheese, softened
1/2 cup sun-dried tomatoes (not oil-packed)
1/4 cup chopped green onions
1/2 tsp. garlic powder
Salt and pepper, to taste
4 fat-free flour tortillas

directions:
Preheat oven to 400 degrees. Line baking sheet(s) with foil and lightly spray with nonfat cooking spray. Arrange vegetables in a single layer; lightly spray vegetables with cooking spray and bake 15-20 minutes until browned.

Combine cream cheese, tomatoes, green onions, garlic, salt and pepper in a medium bowl and mix until completely blended smooth. Spread 2 tablespoons cream cheese mixture on each tortilla.

Add 1/2 cup julienned vegetables; fold in sides of tortilla. Roll up and serve.

Serves: 4

Nutrition per Serving		Exchanges
Calories	203	5 vegetable
Carbohydrate	39 grams	1 starch
Cholesterol	0 milligrams	
Dietary Fiber	5 grams	
Fat	< 1 gram	
Protein	14 grams	
Sodium	707 milligrams	

Shopping List: 1 zucchini, 1 yellow squash, 1 red bell pepper, 1 green bell pepper, 1 yellow bell pepper, 2 portabello mushrooms, 8 ounces fat-free cream cheese, sun-dried tomatoes (not oil-packed), green onions, garlic powder, salt, pepper, fat-free flour tortillas

GRILLED VEGGIE SANDWICH

AVERAGE - DO AHEAD

ingredients:
1 cup sun-dried tomatoes (not oil-packed)
1 tbsp. minced garlic
2 to 3 T. fat-free vegetable broth or water
3 tbsp. fat-free Parmesan cheese
2 medium portabello mushrooms
1 medium zucchini, sliced thin
1 medium yellow squash, sliced thin
1 small eggplant, sliced thin
1 red bell pepper, quartered and seeded
8 slices fat-free bread (French, Italian,
    multi-grain)

directions:
Combine sun-dried tomatoes, garlic, vegetable broth and Parmesan cheese in a food processor or blender and process until pasty.
Remove stems and "lungs" from mushrooms.
Lightly spray all the veggies with nonfat cooking spray and grill until lightly browned on both sides.
Spread tomato mixture on bread slices and top with grilled veggies.

Serves: 4

Nutrition per Serving		Exchanges
Calories	235	3 vegetable
Carbohydrate	48 grams	2 starch
Cholesterol	0 milligrams	
Dietary Fiber	4 grams	
Fat	< 1 gram	
Protein	10 grams	
Sodium	387 milligrams	

Shopping List: 1 zucchini, 1 yellow squash, 1 eggplant, 2 portabello mushrooms, 1 red bell pepper, 1 cup sun-dried tomatoes (not oil-packed), minced garlic, vegetable broth, fat-free Parmesan cheese, fat-free bread

AU GRATIN VEGETABLES AND NOODLES

AVERAGE

---

ingredients:
2 tbsp. chicken broth
2 onions, sliced
2 green peppers, seeded and diced
1 yellow squash, sliced
4 ripe tomatoes, skinned and chopped
2 cloves garlic, peeled and crushed
2 tbsp. chili sauce
1 tsp. salt
1 tsp. thyme
12 oz. yolk-free noodles, cooked and drained
1 cup fat-free Parmesan cheese

directions:
Pour chicken broth into large saucepan and heat over medium-high heat. Cook onion in hot broth until translucent.

Add green peppers, squash, tomatoes, garlic, chili sauce, salt and thyme to pan and mix well. Reduce heat to low, cover and simmer 10-15 minutes. Uncover and simmer an additional 15 minutes. Preheat oven to 425 degrees.

Lightly spray 8-inch baking dish with nonfat cooking spray; place half the noodles in bottom of dish. Cover with vegetable mixture; top with remaining noodles and sprinkle with cheese. Bake 10 minutes until browned.

Serves: 6

Nutrition per Serving

		Exchanges
Calories	221	3 vegetable
Carbohydrate	42 grams	2 starch
Cholesterol	0 milligrams	
Dietary Fiber	4 grams	
Fat	< 1 gram	
Protein	13 grams	
Sodium	588 milligrams	

Shopping List: fat-free chicken broth, 2 onions, 2 green bell peppers, 1 yellow squash, 4 tomatoes, whole garlic, chili sauce, 12 ounces yolk-free noodles, 4 ounces fat-free Parmesan cheese, salt, thyme

BAKED APPLES
AND CARROTS

EASY

ingredients:	6 tbsp. sugar
	2 tbsp. all-purpose flour
	salt to taste
	5 apples, peeled, cored and thinly sliced
	2 cups carrots, cooked and sliced lengthwise
	3/4 cup orange juice

directions: Preheat the oven to 350 degrees.
Lightly spray 9x13-inch baking dish with nonfat cooking spray.
Combine sugar, flour and salt in a small bowl and mix until blended.
Alternate layers of apples and carrots in baking dish, sprinkling each layer with sugar/flour mixture. Repeat layering with remaining ingredients. Pour orange juice over top and bake 20-30 minutes. Stir every 10 minutes while baking.

Serves: 6

Nutrition per Serving		**Exchanges**
Calories	147	1 vegetable
Carbohydrate	37 grams	2 fruit
Cholesterol	0 milligrams	
Dietary Fiber	4 grams	
Fat	< 1 gram	
Protein	1 gram	
Sodium	119 milligrams	

Shopping List: 5 apples, 16-ounce package frozen sliced carrots, 6 ounces orange juice, flour, sugar, salt

BAKED PINEAPPLE RICE

EASY

ingredients:
1 cup fat-free rice, uncooked
3 1/2 cups cubed pineapple (fresh)
5 1/2 tbsp. fat-free margarine, melted
3/4 cup brown sugar
3/4 cup pineapple juice

directions:
Cook rice according to package directions.
Preheat oven to 350 degrees. Lightly spray 8-inch baking dish with nonfat cooking spray.
Place 1/3 of rice in baking dish; cover with 1/2 the pineapple cubes.
Combine margarine and brown sugar in a small cup and mix well; spoon 1/2 of the sugar mixture over pineapple.
Repeat layers, ending with sugar mixture; pour pineapple juice over top and bake, uncovered, 30 minutes.

Serves: 6

Nutrition per Serving

		Exchanges
Calories	281	1 starch
Carbohydrate	67 grams	3 1/3 fruit
Cholesterol	0 milligrams	
Dietary Fiber	1 gram	
Fat	< 1 gram	
Protein	3 grams	
Sodium	94 milligrams	

Shopping List: fat-free rice, fresh pineapple, 6 ounces pineapple juice, brown sugar, fat-free margarine

CREAM CHEESE CORN
EASY - DO AHEAD

ingredients:
2 (16 oz.) pkg. frozen corn kernels
1 cup fat-free cream cheese
1 (4 oz.) can chopped green chilies
1/4 cup reconstituted Butter Buds

directions:
Combine all ingredients in a medium saucepan and cook over medium heat until cheese is melted; mix well and serve hot.
Corn casserole can also be microwaved on HIGH heat until ingredients are melted and blended.

Serves: 8

Nutrition per Serving		Exchanges
Calories	119	2 vegetable
Carbohydrate	26 grams	1 starch
Cholesterol	0 milligrams	
Dietary Fiber	3 grams	
Fat	< 1 gram	
protein	7 grams	
Sodium	394 milligrams	

Shopping List:
2 (16 ounce) packages frozen corn kernels, 8-ounce package fat-free cream cheese, 4-ounce can chopped green chilies, Butter Buds

HONEY-BAKED ONIONS
EASY

ingredients: 3 large red onions, peeled and cut in half
1/4 cup water
1/3 cup honey
3 tbsp. fat-free margarine, melted
1 tsp. paprika
1 tsp. ground coriander
1/2 tsp. salt
1/8 tsp. cayenne pepper

directions: Preheat oven to 350 degrees.
Arrange onions, cut-side down, in ungreased baking dish.
Sprinkle with water, cover with foil and bake 30 minutes.
Combine honey, margarine, paprika, coriander, salt and cayenne pepper in a small bowl and mix well.
Remove the onions from oven, turn cut-side up and spoon half the honey mixture over top.
Return to oven and bake, uncovered, 15 minutes.
Baste with remaining honey mixture and bake an additional 15-20 minutes, until onions are tender.
Serve hot or at room temperature.

Serves: 6

Nutrition per Serving

		Exchanges
Calories	93	1 vegetable
Carbohydrate	22 grams	1 fruit
Cholesterol	0 milligrams	
Dietary Fiber	1 gram	
Fat	< 1 gram	
Protein	1 gram	
Sodium	226 milligrams	

Shopping List: 3 large red onions, honey, fat-free margarine, paprika, ground coriander, salt, cayenne pepper

RED BEETS WITH ORANGE SAUCE

EASY

ingredients:	4 medium red beets 1/3 cup orange juice 1 tsp. grated orange peel 1 tsp. Lighter Bake 1 clove garlic, minced 1/8 tsp. salt 1/8 tsp. ground black pepper
directions:	Trim the beets, leaving 3/4-inch of the stems and taproots (the long, thin bottom roots). Place them in a medium saucepan with enough water to cover. Cover with lid and bring to a boil over high heat. Reduce heat to low and simmer until beets are tender-crisp, about 45 minutes. Rinse the cooked beets under cold running water and rub them between your hands to slip off the skins and stems. Slice the beets and arrange them in a serving dish. Combine remaining ingredients in a small bowl and mix until blended. Pour over beets and serve hot or at room temperature.

Serves: 4

Nutrition per Serving		Exchanges
Calories	29	1 vegetable
Carbohydrate	7 grams	
Cholesterol	0 milligrams	
Dietary Fiber	1 gram	
Fat	< 1 gram	
Protein	1 gram	
Sodium	92 milligrams	

Shopping List: 4 medium beets, orange juice, orange peel, Lighter Bake, garlic, salt, pepper

RED ONION SAUCE

AVERAGE

ingredients: 3 cloves garlic, minced
2 medium red onions, peeled and julienned
1 cup red cooking wine
1/3 cup sugar
Salt and pepper

directions: Lightly spray large nonstick skillet with nonfat cooking spray and heat over medium-high heat.
Add minced garlic and onions; cook, stirring frequently, until translucent.
Add red wine and sugar, cooking over medium heat until nearly dry.
Remove from heat and pour contents into blender or food processor.
Purée until smooth, and season with salt and pepper.
If mixture is too thick, add a little water to desired consistency.
Serve over cooked chicken.

Serves: 4

Nutrition per Serving   **Exchanges**
Calories   136   5 vegetable
Carbohydrate   24 grams
Cholesterol   0 milligrams
Dietary Fiber   2 grams
Fat   < 1 gram
Protein   2 grams
Sodium   6 milligrams

Shopping List: fresh garlic, 2 medium red onions, sugar, red cooking wine, salt, pepper

SUGARED ASPARAGUS

EASY

ingredients:
3 tbsp. fat-free margarine
2 tbsp. brown sugar
2 lb. fresh asparagus, cut into 2-inch pieces
1 cup fat-free chicken broth

directions:
Melt butter in a skillet over medium-high heat. Add the sugar and cook until it dissolves. Add the asparagus and sauté for 2 minutes.

Stir in the chicken broth. Bring to a boil; reduce the heat, cover and simmer 8-10 minutes, until asparagus is tender-crisp.

Transfer the asparagus to a serving dish and keep warm. Cook the sauce until it is reduced by half. Pour over the asparagus and serve immediately.

Serves: 4

Nutrition per Serving		Exchanges
Calories	86	3 vegetable
Carbohydrate	16 grams	
Cholesterol	0 milligrams	
Dietary Fiber	0 grams	
Fat	< 1 gram	
Protein	6 grams	
Sodium	270 milligrams	

Shopping List:
fat-free margarine, brown sugar, 2 pounds fresh asparagus, 8 ounces fat-free chicken broth

TOMATOES IN SOUR CREAM

EASY

---

ingredients: 6 medium tomatoes
Salt
Pepper
1/4 cup fat-free margarine
1 onion, finely chopped
1/2 cup fat-free sour cream
Fresh parsley, finely chopped

directions: Cut the tomatoes into thick slices and season with salt and pepper. Melt margarine in frying pan and sauté onion until translucent.
Add tomatoes and cook over a low-medium heat for 3-4 minutes.
Stir in sour cream and heat thoroughly, for 1 to 2 minutes.
Arrange on a serving dish and garnish with parsley.

Serves: 6

Nutrition per Serving		Exchanges
Calories	53	2 vegetable
Carbohydrate	9 grams	
Cholesterol	0 milligrams	
Dietary Fiber	2 grams	
Fat	< 1 gram	
Protein	3 grams	
Sodium	85 milligrams	

Shopping List: 6 medium tomatoes, 1 onion, fat-free margarine, 4 ounces fat-free sour cream, salt, pepper, fresh parsley

WILD RICE WITH WHITE CORN

AVERAGE

ingredients: 2 cups + 1 tbsp. fat-free chicken broth, divided
1/2 onion, chopped
1 large stalk celery, chopped
1/2 tsp. minced garlic
1/2 tsp. minced jalapeño pepper
1/4 lb. wild rice
1 bay leaf
2 ears white corn, husked, and kernels cut
from cob

directions: Pour 1 tablespoon chicken broth into large pot and heat over medium-high heat.
Add onion, celery, garlic and jalapeño pepper, and cook 2 minutes until softened.
Add wild rice, bay leaf and remaining chicken broth to pot and bring to a boil over high heat.
Reduce heat to low, cover and simmer 1 1/4 hours.
Add corn to pot and cook, uncovered, until all the liquid is absorbed.
Discard bay leaf and serve.

Serves: 4

Nutrition per Serving		Exchanges
Calories	164	2 starch
Carbohydrate	34 grams	
Cholesterol	0 milligrams	
Dietary Fiber	2 grams	
Fat	< 1 gram	
Protein	7 grams	
Sodium	438 milligrams	

Shopping List: 16 ounces fat-free chicken broth, onion, celery, jalapeño pepper, 2 ears white corn, 1/4 pound wild rice, bay leaf, minced garlic

APPLE PIZZA
EASY - DO AHEAD

ingredients: 1 cup fat-free cream cheese, softened
1/2 cup sugar
1/8 tsp. cinnamon
1/8 tsp. nutmeg
1 tsp. vanilla
1 fat-free pizza crust*
2 apples, cored and sliced thin
2 tbsp. lite Hershey's chocolate syrup
1 tbsp. powdered sugar

directions: Combine cream cheese, sugar, cinnamon, nutmeg and vanilla; blend until smooth. Spread evenly over pizza crust and top with apple slices.
Bake until crust is golden, about 10-15 minutes.
Drizzle with chocolate syrup and dust with powdered sugar.
Serve immediately.

Serves: 6

Nutrition per Serving		Exchanges
Calories	275	2 1/2 starch
Carbohydrate	59 grams	1 1/3 fruit
Cholesterol	0 milligrams	
Dietary Fiber	2 grams	
Fat	< 1 gram	
Protein	9 grams	
Sodium	418 milligrams	

Shopping List: 8 ounces fat-free cream cheese, 2 apples, sugar, vanilla, cinnamon, nutmeg, lite chocolate syrup, powdered sugar, ingredients for pizza crust (*or fat-free frozen bread dough, thawed)

APPLE RINGS

EASY

ingredients: 3 large apples, cored and sliced into rings
3 tbsp. fat-free margarine
1 tbsp. powdered sugar
2 tbsp. water
1 tsp. cinnamon

directions: Heat margarine in nonstick skillet; place apple rings in single layer in skillet and sprinkle with powdered sugar.
Add water, cover skillet and simmer apples over low heat until tender.
Uncover skillet and brown apple rings on both sides.
Sprinkle with cinnamon before serving.
Serve immediately.

Serves: 4

Nutrition per Serving   **Exchanges**
Calories   102   1 2/3 fruit
Carbohydrate   26 grams
Cholesterol   0 milligrams
Dietary Fiber   3 grams
Fat   < 1 gram
Protein   < 1 gram
Sodium   69 milligrams

Shopping List: 3 large apples, fat-free margarine, powdered sugar, cinnamon

PINEAPPLE-BERRY RELISH

EASY - DO AHEAD

ingredients:　　20 ounce can crushed pineapple, drained
2 (16 ounces) cans whole cranberry sauce
16 ounce package frozen whole strawberries,
thawed and drained

directions:　　Combine all ingredients in a large bowl and mix
well.
Cover and refrigerate several hours before serving.

Yields: 6 1/2 cups (serving size = 1/4 cup)

Nutrition per Serving		Exchanges
Calories	78	1 1/3 fruit
Carbohydrate	20 grams	
Cholesterol	0 milligrams	
Dietary Fiber	1 gram	
Fat	< 1 gram	
Protein	< 1 gram	
Sodium	11 milligrams	

Shopping List:　　20-ounce can crushed pineapple, 2 (16-ounce) cans whole
cranberry sauce, 16-ounce package whole strawberries

PINEAPPLE SORBET

EASY - DO AHEAD

ingredients:
2/3 cup sugar
2/3 cup water
1 1/2 lb. very ripe pineapple, peeled, cored
and cut into chunks
2 tbsp. dark rum
2 tsp. vanilla extract

directions:
Combine sugar and water in a small saucepan; heat to boiling over high heat, stirring until the sugar is completely dissolved.

Remove from heat, cover and refrigerate.

Place pineapple chunks in food processor or blender and process until smooth.

Combine pineapple, sugar mixture, rum and vanilla; mix well. Process in ice cream maker following manufacturer's instructions, or follow freezer instructions.

For a granita-style sorbet, pour the mixture into a shallow container. Freeze until an ice crystal begins to form, then stir vigorously with a fork to break them up.

Repeat the freezing and stirring until the mixture is thoroughly frozen, but slushy.

Let freeze several hours; remove from freezer 15 minutes before ready to serve.

Serves: 6

Nutrition per Serving		Exchanges
Calories	151	2 1/2 fruit
Carbohydrate	36 grams	
Cholesterol	0 milligrams	
Dietary Fiber	1 gram	
Fat	< 1 gram	
Protein	1 gram	
Sodium	1 milligram	

Shopping List: 1 1/2 pound ripe pineapple, sugar, vanilla extract, dark rum

POACHED APPLES

EASY

ingredients: 2 large Golden Delicious apples, peeled,
halved and cored
1/4 cup light brown sugar
1/3 cup golden raisins
2 tbsp. fat-free margarine, cut into small pieces
1/4 cup water

directions: Arrange apples, cored-sides up, in a shallow, 8-inch square, microwave-safe baking dish. Sprinkle apples with brown sugar and raisins; dot with margarine. Add water, cover with lid or vented plastic wrap, and microwave on HIGH 6 to 8 minutes, until tender. Turn apples and baste with sauce halfway through cooking.
Serve warm.

Serves: 4

Nutrition per Serving		Exchanges
Calories	171	3 fruit
Carbohydrate	44 grams	
Cholesterol	0 milligrams	
Dietary Fiber	4 grams	
Fat	< 1 gram	
Protein	1 gram	
Sodium	52 milligrams	

Shopping List: 2 large Golden Delicious apples, light brown sugar, golden raisins, fat-free margarine

STRAWBERRY-ORANGE SPREAD

AVERAGE

ingredients: 2 (10-ounce) packages frozen strawberries, thawed
1 3/4 oz. package powdered fruit pectin
1 tbsp. grated orange peel
1/2 cup orange juice
3 1/2 cups sugar

directions: Combine strawberries, pectin, orange peel and orange juice in a medium saucepan; cook over medium heat until pectin is dissolved.
Increase heat to high and cook, stirring constantly, until mixture comes to a rolling boil, about 2 minutes.
Add sugar. Bring to a boil, stirring constantly; remove from heat. Skim foam off top.
Immediately pour mixture into hot, sterilized jars, glasses or freezer containers.
Cover tightly and cool.
Refrigerate or freeze up to 3 months.

Yields: 4 1/2 pints (2 tablespoons per serving).

Nutrition per Serving		Exchanges
Calories	44	2/3 fruit
Carbohydrate	12 grams	
Cholesterol	0 milligrams	
Dietary Fiber	1 gram	
Fat	< 1 gram	
Protein	0 grams	
Sodium	1 milligram	

Shopping List: 2 (10-ounce) packages frozen strawberries, 1 3/4- ounce package powdered fruit pectin, grated orange peel, 4 ounces orange juice, sugar

VERY BERRY COBBLER

EASY

ingredients:
21 oz. can cherry pie filling
10 oz. package frozen blueberries, thawed
10 oz. package frozen raspberries, thawed
2 tbsp. cornstarch
1/4 cup + 2 tbsp. sugar, divided
2 cups all-purpose flour
1 tbsp. baking powder
3/4 tsp. salt
1/2 cup cold fat-free margarine
1 cup skim milk

directions:
Preheat oven to 375 degrees.
Combine pie filling, blueberries, raspberries, cornstarch and 2 tablespoons sugar in a 9x13-inch baking pan.
Combine flour, remaining sugar, baking powder and salt in a medium bowl.
Cut in margarine with a pastry blender or 2 knives until mixture is crumbly.
Add the milk and mix lightly with a fork.
Drop by spoonfuls onto the fruit mixture.
Bake in preheated oven 35-40 minutes, until lightly browned and bubbly.

Serves: 8

Nutrition per Serving		Exchanges
Calories	293	2 starch
Carbohydrate	67 grams	2 1/3 fruit
Cholesterol	1 milligram	
Dietary Fiber	4 grams	
Fat	< 1 gram	
Protein	5 grams	
Sodium	437 milligrams	

Shopping List: 21-ounce can cherry pie filling, 10-ounce package frozen blueberries, 10-ounce package frozen raspberries, 8 ounces skim milk, fat-free margarine, flour, cornstarch, sugar, baking powder, salt

ASIAN

ASIAN

Chinese, Japanese, Szechwan, Hunan, and more--Asian cooking covers a diverse spectrum, with the main emphasis on seasoned foods and natural flavors. The essence of Chinese cuisine is the balance of five flavors--*butter, salt, sour, hot and sweet.* Foods are presented all at one time (hot or cold) and may include soups, steamed breads, noodles, dim sum, a choice of fish, meat or poultry, vegetables, and cold or hot salads. The traditional meal begins when the host or family head raises his chopsticks. The Japanese consider cooking an art form and take pride in the presentation of food, garnishing their plates with everything from carved fruits and vegetables to pine needles. The most common ingredient in Asian cuisine--**RICE!**

Common Asian Ingredients

- *bok choy (Chinese chard):* Chinese white cabbage used in soups and stir-fries
- *cassia/cinnamon:* Commonly used spice that originated in Indonesia, China and Vietnam
- *cayenne pepper/chili powder:* Type of chili used in "spicy hot" dishes
- *cilantro/Chinese parsley:* One of the few herbs used in Chinese cooking; resembles parsley but has a sharp, citrus-like flavor
- *cornstarch:* Used in Asian cooking to bind and thicken sauces; blend with cold water to form a smooth paste before adding to any sauce
- *daikon radish:* Large Asian radish with a sweet, slightly hot and spicy flavor
- *five-spice powder:* A mixture of star anise, Szechwan peppercorns, fennel, cloves and cinnamon
- *garlic:* Essential part of Chinese cuisine used whole, chopped, crushed or minced
- *ginger (shoyu):* Pungent, spicy flavoring used to enhance soups, fish, sauces and vegetable dishes
- *hoisin sauce:* Made from soybeans, vinegar, sugar, spices and their flavorings, this thick sauce adds a sweet and spicy flavor
- *karashi:* <u>Very</u> hot yellow mustard (use sparingly!)
- *leeks:* Vegetable that resembles overgrown green onions with a

mild onion flavor
- *lemon grass:* A member of the mint family (also known as citronella), the leaves are used in cooking but removed before serving.
- *mirin:* Sweet rice wine that is low in alcohol
- *miso:* High-protein bean paste made of fermented soybeans and grains
- *noodles:* Used in stir-fry dishes and soups
  - *cellophane noodles:* Made from ground mung beans
  - *soba noodles:* Thin noodles made with a combination of buckwheat and wheat flours, served hot or cold
  - *udon noodles:* Thick, round noodles that should be served *al denté*
- *sake:* Japanese rice wine used to enhance flavors, counteract strong odors and cover excess saltiness (not to be used as a substitute for mirin)
- *shallots:* Small, mild-flavored members of the onion family
- *snow peas (snap beans):* Vegetable used in many Asian dishes with a crisp, tender texture and sweet flavor
- *star anise:* Main ingredient in Chinese five-spice powder; extremely fragrant with a licorice flavor
- *oyster sauce:* Popular Asian condiment or cooking seasoning (made of oysters, brine and soy sauce)
- *wasabi:* Japanese horseradish available as a paste or powder
- *wok:* Most commonly used cooking tool in Asian cooking, used for stir-frying, steaming, stewing and "baking"

7 Best Cooking Tips for Asian Cooking:
1. *Read* the entire recipe to make sure you understand instructions and have all ingredients on hand.
2. *Chop, slice and cut* all ingredients to a uniform size **before** you start cooking.
3. *Prepare* all sauces, thickeners, pastes and other ingredients before you start cooking.
4. *Freeze* any leftover broth or stock in ice cube trays for future use. 1 cube = 2 tablespoons broth.
5. *Always* mix cornstarch with cold liquid to prevent lumps before adding to hot sauce or other food.
6. *DO NOT OVERCOOK* vegetables!
7. *Substitute* fat-free broth, juice, or wine for oil for low-fat stir-fry!

BROCCOLI-SHOOT APPETIZER

EASY - DO AHEAD

ingredients:
2 cups chopped broccoli
1/2 cup alfalfa sprouts
1/2 cup sliced bamboo shoots, drained
1/4 cup rice vinegar
2 tbsp. water
1 tsp. soy sauce
1 garlic clove, crushed
1 tomato, cut in wedges (optional)

directions:
Boil broccoli for 2 minutes; drain well.
Combine broccoli, alfalfa sprouts and bamboo shoots in a medium bowl.
In a separate bowl, combine rice vinegar, water, soy sauce and garlic; mix well. Pour sauce over vegetables and toss to coat evenly.
Serve with cut tomato, if desired.

Serves: 4

Nutrition per Serving		Exchanges
Calories	27	1 vegetable
Carbohydrate	6 gm	
Cholesterol	0 mg	
Dietary fiber	2 gm	
Fat	< 1 gm	
Protein	2 gm	
Sodium	102 mg	

Shopping List: 1 pound head broccoli, alfalfa sprouts, 6-ounce can bamboo shoots, rice vinegar, soy sauce, crushed garlic, tomato (optional)

CHINESE EGG ROLLS

DIFFICULT - DO AHEAD - FREEZE

ingredients:
2 tbsp. low-sodium soy sauce
1 tsp. cornstarch
1/2 tsp. dry mustard
3/4 tsp. garlic powder, divided
1/4 tsp. pepper
2 tsp. fat-free chicken broth
1 cup chopped celery
1/4 cup chopped green onions
1 cup shredded Chinese cabbage
3/4 cup chopped mushrooms
1 cup chopped fresh spinach
1/2 tsp. onion powder
1/2 tsp. ground ginger
12 egg roll skins
3/4 cup sweet and sour sauce
3 tbsp. Chinese mustard

directions:
Combine soy sauce, cornstarch, dry mustard, 1/4 teaspoon garlic powder and pepper in a small bowl and blend until cornstarch is completely dissolved; set aside. Lightly spray large nonstick skillet or wok with nonfat cooking spray; add chicken broth and heat over medium-high heat. Add celery, green onions, cabbage, mushrooms and spinach to skillet; sprinkle with ginger, 1/2 teaspoon garlic powder and onion powder. Stir-fry vegetables 2-3 minutes until vegetables are tender-crisp. Stir in soy sauce mixture; toss with vegetables and cook, stirring constantly, 1 minute, until sauce thickens and vegetables are coated. Remove from heat. To form egg rolls: place 3-4 tablespoons vegetable mixture into center of egg roll wrapper. Fold side corners over top; roll egg roll to the open corner. Moisten corner of wrapper with water and seal when rolled. Repeat with remaining egg roll wrappers. Lightly spray large nonstick skillet with nonfat cooking spray and heat over medium-high heat. Add egg rolls to skillet and cook until lightly browned on all sides. Serve with sweet and sour sauce and hot mustard.

Serves: 6

Nutrition per Serving		Exchanges
Calories	101	1 vegetable
Carbohydrate	22 grams	1 starch
Cholesterol	< 1 milligram	
Dietary Fiber	1 gram	
Fat	< 1 gram	
Protein	3 grams	
Sodium	416 milligrams	

Shopping List: 1 package egg roll wrappers, low-sodium soy sauce, fat-free chicken broth, green onions, celery, 4 ounces shredded Chinese cabbage, 3 ounces mushrooms, fresh spinach, sweet and sour sauce, Chinese mustard, onion powder, ground ginger, garlic powder, pepper, dry mustard, cornstarch

GARLIC-CHEESE WONTON CHIPS

EASY - DO AHEAD

ingredients: 24 wonton wrappers, cut in half
1 tbsp. garlic powder
1/4 cup fat-free Parmesan cheese
Sweet and sour sauce (optional)

directions: Preheat oven to 350 degrees.
Line baking sheet(s) with foil and lightly spray with nonfat cooking spray.
Stack wonton wrappers; cut in half diagonally to form triangles. Arrange wontons in a single layer on baking sheet(s). Lightly spray wontons with cooking spray. Immediately sprinkle with garlic powder and Parmesan cheese.
Bake in preheated oven 7-8 minutes, until golden brown and crisp.
Serve with sweet and sour sauce, if desired.

Serves: 6

Nutrition per Serving		Exchanges
Calories	95	1 1/3 starch
Carbohydrate	19 grams	
Cholesterol	0 milligrams	
Dietary Fiber	0 grams	
Fat	< 1 gram	
Protein	4 grams	
Sodium	158 milligrams	

Shopping List: wonton wrappers, 1 ounce fat-free Parmesan cheese, garlic powder, sweet and sour sauce (optional).

ASIAN-STYLE CHICKEN SOUP

AVERAGE - DO AHEAD

ingredients:
1 lb. fat-free chicken tenders, cut into strips
6 1/4 cups fat-free chicken broth, divided
2 tsp. ground ginger
1 tsp. garlic powder
1 slice lemon
1/2 tsp. coriander seed
1/4 tsp. cumin seed
1/8 tsp. pepper
1/2 tsp. anise seed
1 bunch green onions, shredded

directions:
Place chicken tenders in medium saucepan; pour enough chicken broth (about 3/4 cup) over chicken to cover. Bring to a boil over high heat. Reduce heat to low, cover and simmer 5-6 minutes until chicken is cooked through. Place chicken in colander and drain, discarding broth. Pour 5 1/2 cups chicken broth into large soup pot. Add ginger, garlic, lemon, coriander, cumin, anise seed and pepper to broth; bring to a boil over medium-high heat. Reduce heat to low, cover and simmer 30-45 minutes. Add green onions and chicken to broth and heat over medium heat 5-6 minutes, until chicken is heated through.

Serves: 6

Nutrition per Serving		Exchanges
Calories	99	3 meat
Carbohydrate	2 grams	
Cholesterol	37 milligrams	
Dietary Fiber	< 1 gram	
Fat	< 1 gram	
Protein	21 grams	
Sodium	964 milligrams	

Shopping List: 4 (16-ounce) cans fat-free chicken broth, 1 pound fat-free chicken tenders, 1 bunch green onions, ground ginger, garlic powder, lemon, coriander seeds, cumin seeds, anise seeds, pepper

CHINESE CHICKEN AND WATERCRESS SOUP

EASY

ingredients: 6 cups fat-free chicken broth, divided
1/2 lb. fat-free chicken tenders, cut into 1"
  pieces
3/4 tsp. garlic powder
3/4 tsp. ground ginger
3/4 cup chopped green onions
1 tbsp. dry sherry
1 1/2 tsp. low-sodium soy sauce
3/4 cup fat-free cooked rice
1 1/3 cups watercress sprigs

directions: Lightly spray large nonstick skillet with nonfat
cooking spray; pour 2 tablespoons chicken broth
into skillet and heat over medium-high heat. Add
chicken tenders to skillet; sprinkle with garlic powder and ginger. Cook, stirring constantly, until
chicken is no longer pink. Remove skillet from heat.
Pour remaining broth into large soup pot. Add
cooked chicken, green onions, sherry, soy sauce
and rice to broth. Bring to a boil over high heat.
Reduce heat to low, cover and simmer 3-5 minutes. Stir watercress into hot soup. Remove pot
from heat and let stand until watercress begins to
wilt, about 1 minute. Serve immediately.

Serves: 6

Nutrition per Serving		Exchanges
Calories	73	2 vegetable
Carbohydrate	9 grams	1 meat
Cholesterol	24 milligrams	
Dietary Fiber	< 1 gram	
Fat	< 1 gram	
Protein	9 grams	
Sodium	1045 milligrams	

Shopping List: 1/2 pound fat-free chicken tenders, 48 ounces fat-free
chicken broth, 1 bunch green onions, dry sherry, low-
sodium soy sauce, fat-free white rice, watercress sprigs,
garlic powder, ground ginger

EGG DROP SOUP
EASY - DO AHEAD - FREEZE

ingredients:　　8 cups fat-free chicken broth
3 tbsp. cornstarch
3 tbsp. water
1/3 cup chopped green onions
3 large egg whites
1/8 tsp. pepper

directions:　　Pour chicken broth into large soup pot and bring to a boil over high heat.
Combine cornstarch and water in a small cup; mix until cornstarch is dissolved. Add cornstarch mixture to soup and cook, stirring frequently, until soup becomes thick. Add green onions to soup and mix well; cook 1-2 minutes.
Remove pot from heat.
Gradually pour egg whites into hot soup and break apart with a fork. Sprinkle with pepper and serve.
Soup can be frozen for up to 2 months.

Serves: 6

Nutrition per Serving		Exchanges
Calories	35	1/3 starch
Carbohydrate	35 grams	
Cholesterol	0 milligrams	
Dietary Fiber	< 1 gram	
Fat	< 1 gram	
Protein	2 grams	
Sodium	1228 milligrams	

Shopping List:　　64 ounces fat-free chicken broth, 3 eggs, green onions, cornstarch, pepper

HOT AND SOUR
SCALLOP SOUP

EASY

ingredients:
4 cups fat-free chicken broth
1 cup sliced mushrooms
1/4 cup bamboo shoots
1/2 lb. fat-free scallops
1 tsp. soy sauce
1/4 tsp. white pepper
2 tbsp. cornstarch
2 tbsp. warm water
1/4 cup egg substitute
3 tbsp. rice vinegar
1/3 c. thinly-sliced green onions

directions:
Combine chicken broth, mushrooms and bamboo shoots in a large saucepan; bring to a boil over high heat. Reduce heat to low and simmer 5 minutes. Rinse scallops under cold running water. Add scallops, soy sauce and pepper to saucepan; bring to a boil over high heat.

Dissolve cornstarch in warm water; add to soup mixture and cook, stirring frequently, until mixture thickens.

Gradually pour in beaten egg substitute; remove saucepan from heat. Stir in rice vinegar and sprinkle with green onions.

Serves: 4

Nutrition per Serving		Exchanges
Calories	96	2 meat
Carbohydrate	8 grams	1 vegetable
Cholesterol	19 milligrams	
Dietary Fiber	1 gram	
Fat	< 1 gram	
Protein	14 grams	
Sodium	981 milligrams	

Shopping List: 1/2 pound scallops, 32 ounces fat-free chicken broth, 2 ounces egg substitute, 1/2 pound sliced mushrooms, green onions, 6-ounce can sliced bamboo shoots, soy sauce, rice vinegar, cornstarch, white pepper

HOT AND SOUR
SOUP WITH SHRIMP

EASY - DO AHEAD

ingredients: 6 cups fat-free chicken broth
1/3 cup rice wine vinegar
3 tbsp. sugar
1/2 tsp. crushed red pepper
1/2 tsp. ground ginger
1 1/2 lb. fat-free frozen, uncooked shrimp,
     thawed and drained
1 1/2 cups sliced water chestnuts
1 cup chopped green onions
1 1/2 cups frozen, chopped spinach, thawed and
     drained

directions: Pour chicken broth into large saucepan or soup pot; bring to a boil over high heat. Add vinegar, sugar, red pepper and ginger; mix well. Add shrimp; cook 3-4 minutes, just until shrimp turn pink. Remove pan from heat. Stir in water chestnuts, green onions and spinach. Cover pan and let stand 3-5 minutes before serving.

Serves: 6

Nutrition per Serving		Exchanges
Calories	190	6 vegetable
Carbohydrate	32 grams	1 meat
Cholesterol	6 milligrams	
Dietary Fiber	1 gram	
Fat	< 1 gram	
Protein	15 grams	
Sodium	1399 milligrams	

Shopping List: 48 ounces fat-free chicken broth, 2 (8-ounce) cans sliced water chestnuts, 1 1/2 pounds small shrimp, 1 bunch green onions, 10 ounces frozen chopped spinach, rice wine vinegar, sugar, crushed red pepper, ground ginger

MUNG BEAN SOUP
EASY - DO AHEAD

ingredients: 1 can mung beans, wash and soak overnight
Water to soak beans
4 cups water
2 cups fat-free vegetable broth
1 tbsp. onion powder
1 cup chopped celery
1 cup chopped tomatoes, drained
1 1/2 tsp. minced garlic
1/4 tsp. pepper
1/4 tsp. ground turmeric
1/4 cup chopped cilantro
2 tbsp. lemon juice
1/2 cup fat-free sour cream

directions: Soak beans overnight in water; drain, rinse, and drain beans again.
Combine 4 cups water and vegetable broth in a large saucepan. Add beans and bring to a boil over high heat. Cook 10 minutes, skimming top frequently. Add onion powder, celery, tomatoes, garlic, pepper and turmeric; bring to a boil over high heat. Reduce heat to medium-low, cover and cook 30-35 minutes; reduce heat to low and simmer 15-20 minutes until beans are soft. Add cilantro and lemon juice; mix well and remove from heat. Top each serving with a dollop of sour cream.

Serves: 6

Nutrition per Serving		Exchanges
Calories	69	1 vegetable
Carbohydrate	12 grams	
Cholesterol	0 milligrams	
Dietary Fiber	1 gram	
Fat	< 1 gram	
Protein	4 grams	
Sodium	398 milligrams	

Shopping List: whole mung beans, 16-ounce can fat-free vegetable broth, celery, 14 1/2-ounce can chopped tomatoes, 4 ounces fat-free sour cream, onion powder, minced garlic, ground turmeric, pepper, fresh cilantro, lemon juice

CHINESE
VEGETABLE SALAD
EASY - DO AHEAD

ingredients: 2 tsp. sesame seeds
2 tabsp. fat-free chicken broth
2 1/2 tbsp. rice vinegar
1 1/2 tbsp. honey
1 1/2 tbsp. low-sodium soy sauce
2 tsp. garlic powder
3 cups frozen green beans, thawed and drained
3 cups frozen cauliflower florets, thawed and drained
3 cups broccoli florets, thawed and drained
6 ounces sliced water chestnuts, drained
6 cups shredded lettuce

directions: Lightly spray nonstick skillet with nonfat cooking spray. Add sesame seeds to skillet and cook, stirring constantly, 1-2 minutes, until toasted. Remove skillet from heat. Add chicken broth, vinegar, honey, soy sauce and garlic powder; mix until blended. Combine green beans, cauliflower, broccoli and water chestnuts in medium bowl; mix lightly. Pour broth over vegetables and toss until well coated. Cover and refrigerate 5-6 hours or overnight. Serve over shredded lettuce.

Serves: 6

Nutrition per Serving		Exchanges
Calories	92	4 vegetable
Carbohydrate	18 grams	
Cholesterol	0 milligrams	
Dietary Fiber	7 grams	
Fat	< 1 gram	
Protein	6 grams	
Sodium	396 milligrams	

Shopping List: 3 (8-ounce) packages shredded lettuce, 16 ounces frozen green beans, 16 ounces frozen cauliflower florets, 16 ounces broccoli florets, 6-ounce can sliced water chestnuts, 2 ounces fat-free chicken broth, rice vinegar, honey, low-sodium soy sauce, garlic powder, sesame seeds

MANDARIN CABBAGE SALAD

EASY - DO AHEAD

ingredients:
10 oz. shredded red and green cabbage
6 oz. can water chestnuts, chopped fine
8 oz. can hearts of palm, cut into 1-inch pieces
1 1/2 cups mandarin oranges in juice, drained
1/2 cup fat-free honey-Dijon salad dressing

directions:
Combine all ingredients except salad dressing in a large bowl and mix well. Toss with salad dressing; refrigerate several hours before serving.

Serves: 4

Nutrition per Serving		Exchanges
Calories	118	1/2 fruit
Carbohydrate	27 grams	3 1/2 vegetable
Cholesterol	0 milligrams	
Dietary Fiber	3 grams	
Fat	< 1 gram	
Protein	4 grams	
Sodium	190 milligrams	

Shopping List: 10-ounce package shredded cabbage, 6-ounce can water chestnuts, 8-ounce can hearts of palm, 10-ounce can mandarin oranges in juice, 4 ounces fat-free honey-dijon salad dressing

51

THAI-STYLE SLAW

EASY - DO AHEAD

ingredients: 8 cups shredded red and green cabbage
2 cups shredded carrots
2 tsp. chili garlic sauce*
6 1/2 tbsp. lime juice
1/4 cup low-sodium soy sauce

directions: Combine shredded cabbage and carrots in a large bowl.
Combine chili garlic sauce, lime juice and soy sauce in a sealed container. Shake until mixture is completely blended. Pour dressing over cabbage mixture and toss until well mixed.
Refrigerate 1 hour before serving.

Serves: 6

Nutrition per Serving		Exchanges
Calories	50	2 vegetable
Carbohydrate	12 grams	
Cholesterol	0 milligrams	
Dietary Fiber	3 grams	
Fat	< 1 gram	
Protein	2 grams	
Sodium	452 milligrams	

Shopping List: 3 (8-ounce) packages shredded green and red cabbage mix, 8-ounce package shredded carrots, lime juice, low-sodium soy sauce, chili garlic sauce*

*Look for Huy Fong Foods Chili Garlic Sauce in the Asian cooking section of your supermarket.

THAI-STYLE VEGETABLE SLAW

EASY - DO AHEAD

ingredients:
1/3 cup red wine vinegar
1/3 cup water
1/3 cup low-sodium soy sauce
1/8 tsp. cayenne pepper
3 cups shredded cabbage mix
1 1/2 cups bok choy, shredded
1 cup mung bean sprouts
1 cup shredded carrots
1 cup shredded zucchini
1 cup chopped green onions

directions:
Combine vinegar, water, soy sauce and cayenne pepper in a sealed container; shake mixture until blended.
Combine cabbage, bok choy, sprouts, carrots, zucchini and green onions in a large bowl; toss until mixed. Pour dressing over vegetables and toss until coated and mixed.
Cover and refrigerate 1-2 hours before serving.

Serves: 6

Nutrition per Serving

		Exchanges
Calories	40	2 vegetable
Carbohydrate	9 grams	
Cholesterol	0 milligrams	
Dietary Fiber	2 grams	
Fat	< 1 gram	
Protein	3 grams	
Sodium	551 milligrams	

Shopping List: 12-ounce package shredded cabbage mix, 1/2-3/4 pound bok choy, mung bean sprouts, 8-ounce package shredded carrots, 1 large zucchini, green onions, red wine vinegar, low-sodium soy sauce, cayenne pepper

SCALLOPS YAKATORI WITH PEACHES

AVERAGE - DO AHEAD

ingredients:
1 lb. scallops
2 peaches, cut in 1-inch cubes
2 zucchini, sliced
1 onion, cut in chunks
1/2 cup water
1/4 cup lite soy sauce
1/4 cup white wine vinegar
3 tbsp. sugar
1 tbsp. cornstarch
1 tsp. grated ginger root

directions:
Alternate scallops, peaches, zucchini and onions on 8 metal skewers. Arrange skewers in shallow baking dish in a single layer.

Combine remaining ingredients in a medium saucepan and cook over medium-high heat, stirring constantly, until mixture comes to a boil and becomes thick. Pour mixture over skewers and marinate in refrigerator 2-3 hours.

Prepare a medium-hot grill; cook scallop skewers 5-6 minutes per side, brushing with sauce while cooking.

Serves: 4

Nutrition per Serving		Exchanges
Calories	188	1 fruit
Carbohydrate	24 grams	1 vegetable
Cholesterol	41 milligrams	3 meat
Dietary Fiber	2 grams	
Fat	< 1 gram	
Protein	23 grams	
Sodium	1113 milligrams	

Shopping List: 1 pound scallops, 2 peaches, 2 zucchini, 1 onion, lite soy sauce, white wine vinegar, sugar, cornstarch, grated ginger root

SHRIMP AND SCALLOP FRIED RICE

EASY

ingredients:	1 tbsp. fat-free Oriental broth
	8 medium fat-free shrimp
	8 fat-free sea scallops
	2 cups fat-free cooked rice
	3 tbsp. lite soy sauce
	1 onion, chopped
	1/4 cup sliced mushrooms
	1/2 cup chopped green onions
	1/4 cup sugar snappeas
	1/4 cup bamboo shoots
	1/4 cup bean sprouts
	1/4 cup grated carrots

directions: Lightly spray large nonstick skillet with nonfat cooking spray; add chicken broth and heat over medium-high heat. Add shrimp and scallops to skillet and cook, stirring frequently, until cooked through. Add cooked rice and soy sauce; mix well. Stir in remaining ingredients and toss until mixed. Cook until rice mixture is heated through.

Serves: 4

Nutrition per Serving		**Exchanges**
Calories	199	1 meat
Carbohydrate	36 grams	1 starch
Cholesterol	29 milligrams	3 1/2 vegetable
Dietary Fiber	2 grams	
Fat	< 1 gram	
Protein	11 grams	
Sodium	850 milligrams	

Shopping List: 8 medium fat-free shrimp, 8 sea scallops, fat-free rice, lite soy sauce, sliced mushrooms, 1 onion, green onions, sugar snappeas, canned bamboo shoots, bean sprouts, shredded carrots, fat-free Oriental broth

CHICKEN AND SOBA NOODLES

EASY - DO AHEAD - FREEZE

ingredients:
4 cups fat-free chicken broth
1/2 lb. fat-free chicken tenders
1 tbsp. onion powder
8 oz. soba noodles, cooked and drained
1 tsp. tahini
1 1/2 tbsp. sugar
2 tbsp. low-sodium soy sauce
1/2 tsp. pepper
6 oz. fresh spinach, washed and chopped
2 tbsp. chopped green onions

directions:
Combine chicken broth, chicken tenders and onion powder in a large saucepan and bring to a boil over high heat. Reduce heat to low, cover and simmer 20-25 minutes. Remove chicken from soup; shred or thinly slice chicken and return to soup. Add cooked noodles, tahini, sugar, soy sauce, pepper and spinach to soup. Cook over medium-high heat until spinach is wilted and soup is heated through. Sprinkle green onions on top of soup just before serving.

Serves: 6

Nutrition per Serving

		Exchanges
Calories	197	2 vegetable
Carbohydrate	34 grams	1 1/2 starch
Cholesterol	24 milligrams	1 meat
Dietary Fiber	1 gram	
Fat	< 1 gram	
Protein	6 grams	
Sodium	1135 milligrams	

Shopping List:
32 ounces fat-free chicken broth, 1/2 pound fat-free chicken tenders, 8 ounces soba noodles, 6 ounces fresh spinach, tahini, sugar, low-sodium soy sauce, green onions, pepper, onion powder

CHICKEN CHOW MEIN
AVERAGE

ingredients: 12 oz. fat-free angel hair pasta
4 1/2 tbsp. fat-free chicken broth
4 1/2 T. low-sodium soy sauce
1 1/2 tsp. cornstarch
12 oz. fat-free chicken tenders
1 tbsp. onion powder
2 tsp. garlic powder
1/8 tsp. pepper
3 cups shredded cabbage
1 1/2 cups sliced mushrooms
3/4 cup bamboo shoots
1 cup shredded carrots
1/2 cup chopped green onions
1/2 cup sliced water chestnuts, drained

directions: Cook pasta according to package directions and drain well. Lightly spray pasta with nonfat cooking spray and toss lightly.
Combine chicken broth, soy sauce and cornstarch in a small bowl and mix until cornstarch is dissolved; set aside. Lightly spray large nonstick skillet or wok with nonfat cooking spray and heat over medium-high heat. Add chicken to skillet. Sprinkle with onion powder, garlic powder and pepper; toss until coated. Cook, stirring frequently, 4-5 minutes, until chicken is no longer pink. Remove from skillet and keep warm. Remove wok or skillet from heat and respray with cooking spray; heat over medium-high heat. Add remaining ingredients and stir-fry 2-3 minutes, until vegetables are tender-crisp. Remove vegetables from skillet and set aside. Add cooked pasta to skillet and stir-fry over medium-high heat 2-3 minutes. Add reserved broth mixture, vegetables and chicken to pasta and cook, stirring constantly, 2-3 minutes, until sauce thickens and mixture is coated. Serve immediately.

Serves: 6

Nutrition per Serving		Exchanges
Calories	258	2 vegetable
Carbohydrate	42 grams	2 starch
Cholesterol	28 milligrams	1 1/2 meat
Dietary Fiber	4 grams	
Fat	< 1 gram	
Protein	22 grams	
Sodium	628 milligrams	

Shopping List: 12 ounces fat-free angel hair pasta, fat-free chicken broth, low-sodium soy sauce, 12 ounces fat-free chicken tenders, 12-ounce package shredded cabbage, 8-ounce package shredded carrots, 4 ounces sliced mushrooms, green onions, 8-ounce can bamboo shoots, 8-ounce can sliced water chestnuts, cornstarch, onion powder, garlic powder, pepper

CHICKEN CHOP SUEY
EASY - DO AHEAD

ingredients:　　1 1/2 lb. fat-free chicken tenders
1/2 tsp. ground ginger
1 1/2 cups bok choy, sliced
1 1/2 cups chopped fresh spinach
3 stalks celery, chopped
3/4 cup shredded carrots
3/4 cup chopped green onions
8 oz. stir-fry sauce
6 cups fat-free cooked rice

directions:　　Cut chicken tenders in thin strips.
Lightly spray large nonstick skillet or wok with nonfat cooking spray and heat over medium-high heat. Add chicken to skillet and sprinkle with ginger. Stir-fry 3-4 minutes, until chicken is no longer pink. Remove chicken from skillet and set aside.
Respray skillet with cooking spray and heat over medium-high heat. Add bok choy, spinach, celery, carrots and green onions to skillet; stir-fry 2-3 minutes, until vegetables are tender-crisp. Add stir-fry sauce and chicken to vegetables; mix well. Stir-fry 2-3 minutes until heated through. Serve with cooked rice.

Serves: 6

Nutrition per Serving		Exchanges
Calories	342	5 vegetable
Carbohydrate	52 grams	2 meat
Cholesterol	56 milligrams	2 starch
Dietary Fiber	2 grams	
Fat	< 1 gram	
Protein	32 grams	
Sodium	488 milligrams	

Shopping List:　　1 1/2 pounds fat-free chicken tenders, 8 ounces fat-free stir-fry sauce, bok choy, fresh spinach, celery, packaged shredded carrots, green onions, fat-free rice, ground ginger

CHICKEN WITH CURRY SAUCE
AVERAGE

ingredients:
1 1/2 lb. fat-free chicken tenders, cut into 1-inch pieces
1 small onion, finely chopped
2 cloves garlic, pressed
1/2 tsp. garlic salt
1/4 cup chopped celery
1 medium apple, peeled and finely chopped
1 banana, diced
2 tbsp. curry powder
1 cup fat-free chicken broth
1/2 cup stewed, diced tomatoes
2 tsp. dry Butter Buds
1/2 cup golden raisins
4 cups cooked rice

directions: Lightly spray large nonstick skillet with nonfat cooking spray and heat over medium-high heat. Cook chicken and onion until browned. Add garlic and garlic salt; cook until garlic is browned. Add celery, apple, banana and curry powder to skillet and cook 1 minute. Add chicken broth, tomatoes and Butter Buds; mix well. Simmer over low heat for 15 minutes. Add raisins during the last 5 minutes of cooking time. Serve over cooked rice.

Serves: 6

Nutrition per Serving		Exchanges
Calories	328	1 vegetable
Carbohydrate	46 grams	1 1/2 starch
Cholesterol	64 milligrams	3 1/2 meat
Dietary Fiber	4 grams	1 fruit
Fat	< 1 gram	
Protein	34 grams	
Sodium	640 milligrams	

Shopping List: 1 1/2 pounds fat-free chicken tenders, 1 small onion, garlic, celery, 1 medium apple, 1 banana, 8 ounces fat-free chicken broth, stewed diced tomatoes, Butter Buds, curry powder, garlic salt, golden raisins, fat-free rice

CHINESE CHICKEN STEW

EASY

ingredients: 7 cups fat-free chicken broth
1 cup white wine
1/4 cup low-sodium soy sauce
6 ounces fat-free angel hair pasta
7 ounces straw mushrooms, drained
1 cup baby corn, cut in half
10 oz. frozen pea pods, thawed and drained
1 lb. fat-free chicken tenders, cut into 1-inch
    pieces
1/2 cup chopped green onions
16 oz. package frozen Oriental-style mixed
    vegetables

directions: Combine chicken broth, wine and soy sauce in a
large soup pot; break pasta into pot. Add mush-
rooms, corn, pea pods, chicken, green onions and
Oriental vegetables to broth mixture; bring to a
boil over high heat. Reduce heat to medium-low
and cook, stirring occasionally, until chicken is no
longer pink and vegetables are tender. Serve immediately.

Serves: 6

Nutrition per Serving		Exchanges
Calories	265	1 vegetable
Carbohydrate	35 grams	2 meat
Cholesterol	47 milligrams	2 starch
Dietary Fiber	5 grams	
Fat	< 1 gram	
Protein	23 grams	
Sodium	1763 milligrams	

Shopping List: 4 (16-ounce) cans fat-free chicken broth, 8 ounces white
wine, low-sodium soy sauce, 6 ounces angel hair pasta,
7-ounce can straw mushrooms, 7-ounce can baby corn,
10 ounces frozen pea pods, 1 pound fat-free chicken
tenders, 16-ounce package frozen Oriental vegetables,
green onions

CHINESE TUNA AND CHIPS

EASY - DO AHEAD

ingredients:
16 whole wonton wrappers
1/2 tsp. onion powder
1/4 tsp. cayenne pepper
1 1/2 cups fat-free tuna, drained and flaked
1/2 cup fat-free mayonnaise
1/4 cup chopped water chestnuts
1 stalk celery, chopped fine
1 medium cucumber, seeded and chopped
1/8 tsp. pepper
1/4 tsp. dried dill weed

directions:
Preheat oven to 375 degrees.
Lightly spray 2 baking sheets with nonfat cooking spray. Arrange wonton wrappers in a single layer on baking sheet and cut in half. Lightly spray with nonfat cooking spray. Immediately sprinkle with onion powder and cayenne pepper. Bake in preheated oven 5-7 minutes, until lightly browned and crisp. Remove from oven and cool at room temperature.
Combine tuna, mayonnaise, water chestnuts, celery, cucumber, pepper and dill in a medium bowl; mix well. Serve tuna with wonton chips.

Serves: 8

Nutrition per Serving		Exchanges
Calories	114	1 vegetable
Carbohydrate	13 grams	1/2 starch
Cholesterol	8 milligrams	1 1/2 meat
Dietary Fiber	< 1 gram	
Fat	< 1 gram	
Protein	14 grams	
Sodium	326 milligrams	

Shopping List: wonton wrappers, 2 (6-ounce) cans fat-free tuna, 4 ounces fat-free mayonnaise, 6 ounces canned water chestnuts, celery, 1 cucumber, onion powder, cayenne pepper, pepper, dill weed

EGG FOO YUNG

EASY

ASIAN

ingredients:
1 1/4 cups egg substitute
12 ounces fat-free cooked frozen shrimp,
    thawed and drained
3/4 cup chopped water chestnuts
3/4 cup chopped bean sprouts
1/3 cup chopped green onions
1/4 tsp. ground ginger
1/8 tsp. cayenne pepper
1/4 cup Chinese mustard

directions:
Combine all the ingredients, except Chinese mustard, in a medium bowl and mix until ingredients are blended.
Lightly spray large nonstick skillet with nonfat cooking spray and heat over medium-high heat. Spoon 2-3 tablespoons egg mixture into skillet to form each pancake; cook 2-3 minutes, until bottom is set and slightly browned. Turn pancake over and cook 2-3 minutes, until browned and cooked through. Remove from skillet and keep warm. Repeat with remaining batter. Serve with Chinese mustard.

Serves: 6

Nutrition per Serving
Calories	103
Carbohydrate	14 grams
Cholesterol	4 milligrams
Dietary Fiber	1 gram
Fat	< 1 gram
Protein	10 grams
Sodium	501 milligrams

Exchanges
3 vegetable
1 meat

Shopping List:
10 ounces egg substitute, 12 ounces fat-free frozen cooked shrimp, 8-ounce can sliced water chestnuts, canned bean sprouts, green onions, ground ginger, cayenne pepper, Chinese mustard

GINGER MANGO CHICKEN
EASY

ingredients: 1 1/2 lb. fat-free chicken breasts
3/4 cup flour
Salt and pepper, to taste
3 tbsp. fat-free margarine
2 tsp. freshly-grated ginger
1 clove garlic, finely chopped
16 oz. can sliced mangoes

directions: Rinse the chicken and pat dry; set aside.
Combine flour, salt and pepper in a medium bowl and mix well; dredge chicken in seasoned flour.
Lightly spray large nonstick skillet with nonfat cooking spray. Add 2 tablespoons margarine to skillet and cook until melted; add chicken to skillet and cook until golden brown. Drain chicken on paper towels.
Melt remaining margarine in skillet; sauté ginger and garlic over low heat for 5-6 minutes. Add mangos with juice and cook over low heat 7-8 minutes, until chicken is tender. (If desired, thicken sauce with cornstarch mixture--1 teaspoon cornstarch mixed with several drops of water.)

Serves: 4

Nutrition per Serving		Exchanges
Calories	286	6 meat
Carbohydrate	22 grams	1 1/2 fruit
Cholesterol	96 milligrams	
Dietary Fiber	3 grams	
Fat	< 1 gram	
Protein	47 grams	
Sodium	456 milligrams	

Shopping List: 1 1/2 pounds fat-free chicken breasts, 16-ounce can sliced mango, fresh ginger, garlic, fat-free margarine, flour, salt, pepper

63

ORANGE CHICKEN

EASY - DO AHEAD

ingredients:
1 1/2 cups mandarin oranges in juice
1 1/2 tbsp. cornstarch
1 1/2 cups frozen pepper strips
2 tsp. orange peel
1/4 cup chopped green onions
3/4 tsp. ground ginger
1 1/2 tsp. garlic powder
1/8 tsp. red pepper flakes
1 1/4 lb. fat-free chicken tenders, cut into 1-inch pieces
1 1/2 tbsp. low-sodium soy sauce
4 cups fat-free cooked rice

directions: Drain mandarin oranges and reserve juice. Combine cornstarch and 3 tablespoons reserved juice in a small bowl; mix until cornstarch is dissolved. Lightly spray large nonstick skillet or wok with nonfat cooking spray and heat over medium-high heat. Add peppers, orange peel and green onions to skillet. Sprinkle with ginger, garlic and red pepper; stir-fry mixture 2 minutes. Add chicken to skillet and stir-fry 5-6 minutes, until no longer pink and cooked through. Add remaining juice, oranges, soy sauce and cornstarch mixture to skillet and cook over medium-high heat, stirring constantly, until sauce becomes thick and bubbly. Coat chicken and vegetables with sauce. Serve over cooked rice.

Serves: 6

Nutrition per Serving		Exchanges
Calories	263	2 vegetable
Carbohydrate	42 grams	1 starch
Cholesterol	59 milligrams	1 fruit
Dietary Fiber	2 grams	2 meat
Fat	< 1 gram	
Protein	23 grams	
Sodium	379 milligrams	

Shopping List: 16 ounces frozen pepper strips, 1 1/4 pounds fat-free chicken tenders, 16 ounces mandarin oranges in juice, fat-free rice, green onions, low-sodium soy sauce, cornstarch, red pepper flakes, garlic powder, ground ginger, orange peel

SESAME CHICKEN

EASY

ingredients:
1/4 cup egg substitute
1/2 cup skim milk
1/2 cup flour
1 tbsp. sesame seeds
1 tsp. baking powder
2 tsp. paprika
1 tsp. garlic powder
1 tsp. salt
2 lb. fat-free chicken breasts
1/2 cup fat-free margarine, melted

directions:
Preheat oven to 400 degrees.
Lightly spray 9x13-inch baking dish with nonfat cooking spray.
Combine egg substitute and milk in medium bowl; mix until blended.
Combine flour, sesame seeds, baking powder, paprika, garlic powder and salt in a ziploc plastic bag and shake to mix.
Dip chicken breasts into egg mixture; place in plastic bag and shake until well coated with flour mixture. Arrange chicken in baking dish and drizzle with melted margarine. Bake 35-40 minutes, until tender and cooked through.

Serves: 6

Nutrition per Serving		Exchanges
Calories	254	6 1/2 meat
Carbohydrate	10 grams	1/2 starch
Cholesterol	93 milligrams	
Dietary Fiber	< 1 gram	
Fat	< 1 gram	
Protein	47 grams	
Sodium	926 milligrams	

Shopping List: 2 pounds fat-free chicken breasts, 4 ounces skim milk, 2 ounces egg substitute, flour, sesame seeds, baking powder, paprika, garlic powder, salt, fat-free margarine

SIMPLE TERIYAKI CHICKEN
EASY - DO AHEAD

ingredients:
6 fat-free chicken breasts (about 2 lb.)
2 tsp. garlic powder
1 tbsp. onion powder
1 1/2 cups low-sodium teriyaki sauce, divided
16 oz. frozen pepper strips, thawed and drained
1 medium onion, sliced thin
6 cups fat-free cooked rice

directions:
Place chicken breasts in a 9x13-inch baking dish; sprinkle both sides with garlic and onion powder. Pour 1 cup teriyaki sauce over chicken and turn to coat. Cover and refrigerate 3-4 hours.
Preheat broiler on high heat. Line broiler pan with foil and lightly spray with nonfat cooking spray. Remove chicken from marinade and discard marinade; arrange chicken in a single layer on broiler pan. Arrange peppers and onions around chicken; pour remaining teriyaki sauce over chicken and vegetables. Broil chicken 6-7 minutes; turn chicken over and broil 4-6 minutes, until chicken is no longer pink and is cooked through. Serve over rice.

Serves: 6

Nutrition per Serving		Exchanges
Calories	496	3 vegetable
Carbohydrate	90 grams	5 starch
Cholesterol	71 milligrams	1 meat
Dietary Fiber	2 grams	
Fat	< 1 gram	
Protein	32 grams	
Sodium	1556 milligrams	

Shopping List:
2 pounds fat-free chicken breasts, 12 ounces low-sodium teriyaki sauce, 16-ounce package frozen pepper strips, 1 medium onion, fat-free rice, garlic powder, onion powder

SPICY SZECHWAN CHICKEN
AVERAGE - DO AHEAD

ingredients:
3 tbsp. egg substitute
2 1/4 tbsp. cornstarch
1 1/2 lb. fat-free chicken tenders
16 oz. frozen pepper strips, thawed and drained
1/2 cup chopped green onions
1/2 cup chopped bean sprouts
1/2 cup bamboo shoots
3/4 cup sliced mushrooms
1 1/4 tsp. minced garlic
1/4 tsp. ground ginger
1/2 cup fat-free Szechwan stir-fry sauce
6 oz. fat-free angel hair pasta, cooked and drained

directions:
Combine egg substitute and cornstarch in a shallow baking dish; mix well. Add chicken tenders and toss with mixture until chicken is coated.
Lightly spray large nonstick skillet or wok with nonfat cooking spray and heat over medium-high heat. Add chicken to skillet and cook, stirring constantly, 3-5 minutes, until chicken is no longer pink. Remove chicken from skillet and set aside.
Remove skillet or wok from heat and respray with cooking spray; heat over medium-high heat. Add peppers, green onions, bean sprouts, bamboo shoots and mushrooms to skillet. Sprinkle with ginger and garlic. Toss mixture and stir-fry 2-3 minutes, until vegetables are tender-crisp. Add chicken to skillet and mix lightly. Pour stir-fry sauce over chicken-vegetable mixture and stir-fry 1-2 minutes, until heated through. Serve over cooked angel hair pasta, if desired.

Serves: 6

Nutrition per Serving		Exchanges
Calories	228	2 vegetable
Carbohydrate	27 grams	1 starch
Cholesterol	71 milligrams	3 meat
Dietary Fiber	3 grams	
Fat	< 1 gram	
Protein	28 grams	
Sodium	395 milligrams	

Shopping List: 1 1/2 pounds fat-free chicken tenders, 4 ounces Szechwan stir-fry sauce, 16 ounces frozen pepper strips, green onions, bean sprouts, canned bamboo shoots, 4 ounces sliced mushrooms, 6 ounces fat-free angel hair pasta, egg substitute, cornstarch, minced garlic, ground ginger

STIR-FRY PINEAPPLE CHICKEN

EASY

ASIAN

ingredients:
4 cups fat-free cooked rice
1/2 cup pineapple juice
1/3 cup orange juice
2 tsp. cornstarch
1/4 tsp. crushed red pepper
1 1/2 tbsp. fat-free chicken broth
1 1/2 cups frozen pepper strips, thawed and drained
6 green onions, chopped
1 1/2 tsp. garlic powder
1 lb. fat-free chicken tenders
2 cups pineapple chunks in juice, drained
1/2 cup sliced water chestnuts

directions:
Cook rice according to package directions; keep warm. Combine pineapple juice, orange juice, cornstarch and red pepper in a small bowl; mix well and set aside. Lightly spray large nonstick skillet or wok with nonfat cooking spray; pour chicken broth into skillet and heat over medium-high heat. Add peppers, green onions, and garlic powder to skillet and cook, stirring constantly, 1-2 minutes, until tender. Remove vegetables from skillet and set aside. Add chicken to skillet and cook, stirring constantly, 3-4 minutes, until chicken is no longer pink. Add pineapple sauce mixture to skillet and cook, stirring constantly, until mixture becomes thick and bubbly. Return vegetables to skillet and mix with chicken and sauce. Stir in pineapple chunks and water chestnuts. Cook, stirring constantly, 1-2 minutes, until heated through. Serve over cooked rice.

Serves: 6

Nutrition per Serving		Exchanges
Calories	360	3 vegetable
Carbohydrate	70 grams	3 starch
Cholesterol	47 milligrams	1 meat
Dietary Fiber	1 gram	1 fruit
Fat	< 1 gram	
Protein	21 grams	
Sodium	199 milligrams	

Shopping List: 1 pound fat-free chicken tenders, 4 ounces pineapple juice, 3 ounces orange juice, fat-free rice, cornstarch, fat-free chicken broth, 16 ounces frozen pepper strips, 1 bunch green onions, 20 ounces pineapple chunks in juice, canned sliced water chestnuts, garlic powder, crushed red pepper

TANDORI TURKEY BREAST

AVERAGE - DO AHEAD

ingredients:
2 cups fat-free plain yogurt
2 tbsp. freshly-grated ginger root
1 1/2 tbsp. paprika
1 tbsp. minced garlic
1 tbsp. ground coriander
1 tbsp. ground cumin
2 tsp. salt
2 tsp. ground cayenne pepper
1/4 tsp. ground cinnamon
1/8 tsp. ground cloves
3 lb. fat-free, boneless turkey breast

directions:
Combine all ingredients except turkey in a large food storage bag. Make several 1-inch-deep slits in the underside of turkey breast and place in bag. Press out air, seal and turn to coat turkey. Refrigerate 8-24 hours. Preheat oven to 375°. Line broiler pan with foil and lightly spray with nonfat cooking spray. Place turkey on pan and bake 40 minutes, turning once. Remove turkey from oven; turn broiler on high heat. Broil turkey 4-6 inches from heat source for 30-40 minutes, turning once, until a meat thermometer inserted in the thickest part registers 165-175 degrees or until juices run clear when the meat is pierced. Let stand 15 minutes before serving.

Serves: 6

Nutrition per Serving		Exchanges
Calories	259	4 meat
Carbohydrate	16 grams	1 1/4 milk
Cholesterol	82 milligrams	
Dietary Fiber	0 grams	
Fat	< 1 gram	
Protein	37 grams	
Sodium	3283 milligrams	

Shopping List: 16 ounces fat-free plain yogurt, 3 pounds fat-free boneless turkey breast, fresh ginger root, paprika, minced garlic, ground coriander, ground cumin, salt, ground cayenne pepper, ground cinnamon, ground cloves

TERIYAKI CHICKEN AND NOODLES

AVERAGE

ingredients:
12 oz. fat-free angel hair pasta
24 oz. package broccoli slaw mixture
3/4 cup + 1 1/2 tbsp. fat-free chicken broth, divided
1 lb. fat-free chicken tenders
3 tbsp. chopped green onions
2 tsp. minced garlic
1 tbsp. cornstarch
1/4 cup + 1 1/2 tsp. tamari soy sauce
1/4 tsp. red pepper flakes

directions:
Cook pasta 3-4 minutes in boiling water, just until tender; add broccoli slaw mix and boil 1-2 minutes until softened. Drain well and set aside.
Lightly spray large nonstick skillet or wok with nonfat cooking spray. Add 1 1/2 tablespoons chicken broth and heat over medium-high heat. Add chicken; stir-fry 5-6 minutes, until chicken is cooked through and no longer pink. Push chicken to side of skillet. Add green onions and garlic. Stir-fry over medium-high heat 1 minute until vegetables are tender. Combine 3 tablespoons chicken broth with cornstarch in a small cup and mix until cornstarch is dissolved and mixture is blended. Add mixture to skillet with remaining broth, tamari sauce and red pepper flakes. Cook 2-3 minutes, stirring constantly, until mixture thickens and comes to a boil. Return pasta mixture to skillet and toss with chicken, vegetables and sauce until coated. Serve immediately.

Serves: 6

Nutrition per Serving		Exchanges
Calories	267	2 vegetable
Carbohydrate	40 grams	2 starch
Cholesterol	47 milligrams	2 meat
Dietary Fiber	4 grams	
Fat	< 1 gram	
Protein	26 grams	
Sodium	1084 milligrams	

Shopping List:
12 ounces fat-free angel hair pasta, 24-ounce package broccoli slaw mix, 1 pound fat-free chicken tenders, 16-ounce can fat-free chicken broth, green onions, minced garlic, cornstarch, tamari sauce, red pepper flakes

CHINESE STYLE EGGPLANT

EASY - DO AHEAD

ingredients:
2 lb. eggplant, cut into 1/2-inch slices
3/4 tsp. Chinese Five Spice Powder
1/2 cup fat-free stir-fry sauce
3/4 cup fat-free chicken broth
1 cup chopped green onions

directions:
Preheat oven to 375 degrees. Line baking sheet with foil and lightly spray with nonfat cooking spray. Arrange eggplant slices on baking sheet; sprinkle with spice powder and stir-fry sauce. Pour chicken broth over eggplant and bake in preheated oven 20-25 minutes, until tender. Top with green onions and bake 5 minutes.

Serves: 6

Nutrition per Serving		Exchanges
Calories	44	2 vegetable
Carbohydrate	10 grams	
Cholesterol	0 milligrams	
Dietary Fiber	4 grams	
Fat	< 1 gram	
Protein	1 gram	
Sodium	227 milligrams	

Shopping List: 2-pound eggplant, 4 ounces fat-free stir-fry sauce, Chinese Five-Spice Powder, fat-free chicken broth, green onions

MUSHROOMS ORIENTAL

EASY

ingredients: 1 1/2 cups sliced mushrooms
1 1/2 tbsp. soy sauce
2 tsp. crushed garlic
1/4 cup fat-free chicken broth
2 tbsp. thinly-sliced green onions
1/8 tsp. grated ginger root
1/8 tsp. sugar

directions: Lightly spray large nonstick skillet with nonfat cooking spray and heat over medium-high heat. Add all ingredients to skillet and bring to a boil; cover and cook for 2 minutes. Uncover skillet and cook, stirring occasionally, about 2-3 minutes.

Serves: 4

Nutrition per Serving		Exchanges
Calories	13	Free
Carbohydrate	2 grams	
Cholesterol	0 milligrams	
Dietary Fiber	< 1 gram	
Fat	< 1 gram	
Protein	1 gram	
Sodium	436 milligrams	

Shopping List: 12 ounces sliced mushrooms, soy sauce, fat-free chicken broth, crushed garlic, green onions, ginger root, sugar

ORIENTAL VEGETABLE STIR-FRY WITH SOBA NOODLES

AVERAGE

ingredients:
3 tbsp. cold water
1 1/2 tbsp. cornstarch
12 oz. soba noodles, cooked and drained
1/4 cup + 2 tbsp. low-sodium soy sauce
1/4 cup + 2 tbsp. fat-free chicken broth
2 tsp. minced garlic
3/4 tsp. ground ginger
1/4 tsp. crushed red pepper
3 large carrots, peeled and sliced
1 cup broccoli florets
1 cup cauliflower florets
3/4 lb. mushrooms, quartered
1 1/2 cups chopped green onions

directions: Combine cold water and cornstarch in a small cup; mix until cornstarch is dissolved and mixture is blended. Set aside.

Cook noodles according to package directions. Drain well and toss with 3 tablespoons soy sauce. Lightly spray nonstick skillet or wok with nonfat cooking spray. Pour 1/4 cup chicken broth into skillet and heat over medium-high heat. Add garlic, ginger, red pepper, carrots, broccoli and cauliflower to skillet and cook, stirring constantly, 5-6 minutes, until vegetables are tender-crisp. Push vegetables to side of skillet. Add 2 tablespoons chicken broth to skillet and heat over medium-high heat. Add mushrooms and green onions; stir-fry 4-5 minutes until tender. Add cornstarch mixture to skillet and cook, stirring constantly, until mixture becomes thick. Cook the vegetables until vegetables are coated; stir in noodles and toss lightly. Serve immediately.

Serves: 6

Nutrition per Serving		Exchanges
Calories	173	4 vegetable
Carbohydrate	37 grams	1 starch
Cholesterol	0 milligrams	
Dietary Fiber	2 grams	
Fat	< 1 gram	
Protein	9 grams	
Sodium	738 milligrams	

Shopping List: 12 ounces soba noodles, 3 large carrots, broccoli florets, cauliflower florets, green onions, 3/4 pound mushrooms, fat-free chicken broth, low-sodium soy sauce, cornstarch, minced garlic, ground ginger, crushed red pepper

SHRIMP FRIED RICE
EASY

ingredients:
3 green onions, chopped
1/2 cup egg substitute
3 cups cooked fat-free rice
1/4 lb. cooked baby shrimp
3 tbsp. soy sauce

directions:
Lightly spray large nonstick skillet with nonfat cooking spray and heat over medium-high heat. Add onions and stir-fry 30 seconds. Add egg substitute and scramble until cooked through. Stir in rice, shrimp and soy sauce; cook, stirring frequently, until heated through.

Serves: 6

Nutrition per Serving		Exchanges
Calories	115	1/2 vegetable
Carbohydrate	19 grams	1 starch
Cholesterol	29 milligrams	1 meat
Dietary Fiber	1 gram	
Fat	< 1 gram	
Protein	8 grams	
Sodium	572 milligrams	

Shopping List: 1/4 pound cooked baby shrimp, 4 ounces egg substitute, green onions, fat-free rice, soy sauce

VEGETABLE LO-MEIN

AVERAGE - DO AHEAD

ingredients: 16 ounces fat-free angel hair pasta, cooked and drained
2 cups fat-free chicken broth
1/2 cup lite soy sauce
2 carrots, sliced on bias 1/8" thick
2 cups broccoli florets
1/2 lb. snow peas
1/4 cup scallions, sliced thin
1/2 cup julienned red bell pepper
1/2 cup julienned yellow bell pepper
1 cup julienned shiitake mushrooms
4 oz. can sliced water chestnuts, drained
4 oz. can bamboo shoots, drained
1 tbsp. grated ginger
1/2 tbsp. minced garlic

directions: Prepare pasta according to package directions; drain well and keep warm.
Pour chicken broth and soy sauce into large non-stick skillet or wok and bring to a boil over high heat. Add carrots and stir-fry 2 minutes. Add broccoli and stir-fry 1-2 minutes. Add snowpeas, scallions, bell peppers, mushrooms, water chestnuts, bamboo shoots, ginger and garlic; cook, stirring frequently, until vegetables are tender-crisp. Serve over cooked noodles.

Serves: 8

Nutrition per Serving		Exchanges
Calories	217	1 1/2 starch
Carbohydrate	45 grams	4 vegetable
Cholesterol	0 milligrams	
Dietary Fiber	4 grams	
Fat	< 1 gram	
Protein	10 grams	
Sodium	854 milligrams	

Shopping List: 1 pound fat-free angel hair pasta, 1 head broccoli, 2 carrots, 1/2 pound snow peas, scallions, 1 red bell pepper, 1 yellow bell pepper, 8 ounces shiitake mushrooms, 4-ounce can sliced water chestnuts, 4-ounce can bamboo shoots, 16 ounces fat-free chicken broth, lite soy sauce, ginger, minced garlic

VEGETABLE MEDLEY STIR-FRY

AVERAGE - DO AHEAD

ingredients:
2 tsp. sesame seeds
4 tbsp. fat-free chicken broth, divided
1 cup shiitake mushrooms, stems removed
16 oz. frozen pea pods, thawed and drained
1 cup carrots, sliced diagonally
3/4 tsp. minced garlic
1/2 cup canned bamboo shoots, drained
2 tbsp. low-sodium soy sauce
1/2 tsp. cornstarch
1/2 tsp. Dijon mustard

directions:
Lightly spray large nonstick skillet or wok with nonfat cooking spray and heat over medium-high heat. Add sesame seeds to skillet and cook, stirring constantly, until lightly browned. Remove from skillet and set aside. Remove skillet from heat and respray with cooking spray; add 1 tablespoon chicken broth to skillet and heat over medium-high heat. Add mushrooms, pea pods, carrots, garlic and bamboo shoots to skillet and stir-fry 2-3 minutes, until tender-crisp. Combine 3 tablespoons chicken broth, soy sauce, cornstarch and mustard in a small bowl and mix until cornstarch is dissolved and mixture is blended smooth. Add mixture to skillet and cook, stirring constantly, until mixture thickens. Toss with chicken and vegetables until coated. Sprinkle sesame seeds into skillet and toss lightly, just before serving.

Serves: 6

Nutrition per Serving		Exchanges
Calories	60	2 1/2 vegetable
Carbohydrate	12 grams	
Cholesterol	0 milligrams	
Dietary Fiber	2 grams	
Fat	< 1 gram	
Protein	3 grams	
Sodium	436 milligrams	

Shopping List: 16 ounces frozen pea pods, 1/3 pound carrots, 6-ounce can bamboo shoots, shiitake mushrooms, minced garlic, low-sodium soy sauce, Dijon mustard, cornstarch, fat-free chicken broth, sesame seeds

GINGER PINEAPPLE AND BANANA DESSERT

EASY

ingredients:
2 tsp. Baking Healthy (Smucker's)
3 tbsp. brown sugar
1 tsp. ground ginger
1 cup pineapple chunks in juice, drained
4 large bananas, cut into 1/2-inch slices
2 cups fat-free frozen yogurt*
1/4 cup maraschino cherries

directions:
Lightly spray large nonstick skillet with nonfat cooking spray and heat over medium heat. Add Baking Healthy; quickly stir in brown sugar and ginger. Cook, stirring constantly, until sugar is dissolved. Immediately add pineapple and cook 1-2 minutes, until coated and softened.
Divide sliced bananas among 4 dessert dishes. Top each with 1/2 cup frozen yogurt; drizzle with pineapple mixture. Place cherry on top.

Serves: 4

Nutrition per Serving		Exchanges
Calories	269	3 3/4 fruit
Carbohydrate	63 grams	1/2 milk
Cholesterol	0 milligrams	
Dietary Fiber	2 grams	
Fat	< 1 gram	
Protein	5 grams	
Sodium	76 milligrams	

Shopping List:
8-ounce can pineapple chunks in juice, 16 ounces fat-free frozen yogurt (*flavor of choice), 4 large bananas, brown sugar, Baking Healthy (Smucker's), ginger, maraschino cherries

GLAZED FRUIT TARTS

AVERAGE - DO AHEAD

ASIAN

ingredients:
12 wonton skins
1/4 cup frozen apple juice concentrate
1 tsp. cornstarch
2 cups chopped apples
1/2 cup fat-free vanilla yogurt*

directions:
Press wonton skins between 2 muffin tins; press together firmly. Cut away the excess dough, using a sharp knife. Place the muffin tins on a baking sheet and bake in 375 degree oven for 10 minutes. Remove the top tin and return to oven; bake 3-5 minutes, until lightly browned. Remove from oven and place on wire rack to cool.

Combine apple juice and cornstarch in a small saucepan; bring to a boil over high heat. Reduce heat to low and simmer 1 1/2 minutes, stirring frequently. Remove saucepan from heat.

Place apples in a medium bowl and top with apple glaze; toss to coat.

Just before serving, spoon fruit into baked wonton shells. Top with yogurt and serve.

Serves: 12

Nutrition per Serving		Exchanges
Calories	45	2/3 fruit
Carbohydrate	10 grams	
Cholesterol	0 milligrams	
Dietary Fiber	< 1 gram	
Fat	< 1 gram	
Protein	1 gram	
Sodium	39 milligrams	

Shopping List: wonton wrappers, 2 large apples, 4 ounces fat-free yogurt (*flavor of choice), frozen apple juice concentrate, cornstarch

MANGO SORBET

EASY - DO AHEAD - FREEZE

ingredients:
1 1/4 cups sugar
3 tbsp. rum (optional)
1/2 cup fresh lemon juice
1 tsp. minced fresh lemon zest
2 cups water
2 pints mangoes (about 3)

directions:
Combine sugar, rum, lemon juice, lemon zest and water in a medium saucepan and cook over medium heat; stir to dissolve sugar. Increase heat to high and bring mixture to a boil; boil for 10 minutes. Remove from heat and cool mixture (it will look like syrup).
Peel, slice and purée mangoes; add to cooled mixture. Place mango mixture in ice cream machine and follow manufacturer's instructions. If ice cream machine is not available, place mixture in a shallow pan and freeze; break up with a wooden spoon when completely frozen, blend in a food processor and freeze again.

Yields: 1 1/2 quarts (8 servings)

Nutrition per Serving		Exchanges
Calories	180	3 fruit
Carbohydrate	45 grams	
Cholesterol	0 milligrams	
Dietary Fiber	2 grams	
Fat	< 1 gram	
Protein	1 gram	
Sodium	2 milligrams	

Shopping List: 3 mangoes, 3 lemons, sugar, rum

ORANGE-GINGER COOKIES

EASY - DO AHEAD

ASIAN

ingredients:
1 cup fat-free margarine, softened
2/3 cup sugar
1/4 cup egg substitute
1 tbsp. grated orange peel
1 1/2 tsp. ginger
1 tsp. vanilla
1/4 tsp. salt
2 1/4 cups flour

directions:
Preheat oven to 350 degrees.
Combine margarine, sugar, egg substitute, orange peel, ginger, vanilla and salt in a large bowl; mix well. Stir in flour and mix to form dough into a ball. Press dough into desired shapes, using a cookie press or cutters, and decorate as desired. Place cookies on ungreased cookie sheet and bake 8-10 minutes, until set, but not brown. Cool and serve.

Serves: 16

Nutrition per Serving

		Exchanges
Calories	68	1 starch
Carbohydrate	15 grams	
Cholesterol	0 milligrams	
Dietary Fiber	< 1 gram	
Fat	< 1 gram	
Protein	1 gram	
Sodium	89 milligrams	

Shopping List: fat-free margarine, 2 ounces egg substitute, sugar, flour, orange peel, ginger, vanilla, salt

FRENCH

FRENCH

French cooking evokes images of culinary masterpieces, perfectly planned, prepared, and presented. Ever since the French Revolution, Americans have enjoyed the flavors of French cuisine. Thomas Jefferson hired a French chef for his White House and introduced Americans to the sophisticated flavors of French cuisine. The culinary diversity of French cooking comes from the many geographical regions. The fertile soil and temperate climate of France produces a variety of meats, fish, seafood, poultry, fruits and vegetables. French cuisine also encompasses a wide range of cooking styles, from "gourmet elegant" to good old "home cooking."

- *Haute Cuisine* (or classic cuisine) is the oldest form of cooking. Based on five sauces, *haute cuisine* is carefully planned, cooked to perfection, and presented with the utmost care. Haute cuisine is served in relatively small portions in order to appreciate the flavor and presentation of the food.
- *Cuisine Bourgeoise* (or provincial cooking) is best described as high-quality home cooking; this type of cooking is also meticulously planned, prepared, and presented, but relies on local ingredients and simple recipes. The cuisine of the "people," this version of French cooking appeals to those without highly technical cooking skills.
- *Nouvelle Cuisine* is a more contemporary version of haute cuisine, with lighter sauces and simple presentation. Started in the 1970's, nouvelle cuisine often includes exotic ingredients.

You no longer have to avoid the elegance of French cuisine in order to adapt to a "healthier" lifestyle. Substituting, innovating, and experimenting are the keys to keeping your French cuisine "healthy." As tradition rules, the French eat three meals a day, usually at the same hour. Just about every French meal is served with bread, wine and water; sodas and iced teas are rarely found on a French table. Garlic is one of the favored foods, as it finds its way into almost every dish except desserts. **The Healthiest French Habit for Americans to Adopt** — follow the portion sizes, usually much less generous than those served in the United States.

Petit Déjeuner (breakfast) usually consists of *le pain* (bread—leave off the butter and go with the preserves) and *café crème* (expresso with hot, foamy milk—stick with skim milk). *Déjeuner* (lunch) is usually the main meal of the day and is enjoyed between the hours of noon and 2:00 p.m. *Dîner* (dinner) is rarely served before 8:00 p.m., but is a lighter meal. *Déjeuner* and *dîner* traditionally include:

- *Apértif*: alcoholic drink, such as Kir, a pastis, a Suze or a Vermouth
- *Entrée:* an appetizer usually consisting of soup, egg dishes, small salads (not greens) or charcuterie (cured or prepared meats)
- *Plat:* entrée or main course, including meat or fish served with a sauce and accompanied by rice, beans, potatoes or vegetables
- *Salade verte:* green salad
- *Fromage:* cheese
- *Dessert:* usually includes tarts, cakes, mousses, ice cream or fruit
- *Coffee* with a *digestif:* after-meal alcoholic drink (such as cognac, armagnac, or other local specialities) to help digestion

Most popular herbs and spices used in French cooking:
anise seeds, bay leaf, caraway, chervil, chives, cloves, coriander seed, cumin, fennel seed, juniper berry, marjoram, mint, oregano, parsley, rosemary, sage, savory, thyme.
Dried herb mixtures:
- crushed bay leaves, oregano, rosemary, savory, and thyme
- anise seeds, marjoram, rosemary, sage, savory, and thyme
- basil, fennel seeds, marjoram, rosemary, sage, savory, and thyme

CHEESE FONDUE

EASY - DO AHEAD

ingredients: 6 oz. fat-free finely-shredded Mozzarella cheese
6 oz. fat-free finely-shredded Cheddar cheese
1/4 c. white wine
1/2 tsp. garlic powder
3/4 lb. fat-free French bread, cut into cubes

directions: Lightly spray medium saucepan with nonfat cooking spray.
Combine all ingredients except bread in pan; cook over low heat, stirring constantly, until cheese is completely melted and blended.
Transfer to fondue pot and keep warm. Serve with French bread cubes.

Serves: 6

Nutrition per Serving		Exchanges
Calories	256	2 meat
Carbohydrate	34 grams	2 1/3 starch
Cholesterol	0 milligrams	
Dietary Fiber	2 grams	
Fat	< 1 gram	
Protein	22 grams	
Sodium	755 milligrams	

Shopping List: 6 ounces fat-free finely-shredded Mozzarella cheese, 6 ounces fat-free finely shredded Cheddar cheese, 2 ounces white wine, garlic powder, 3/4 pound fat-free French bread

EGGPLANT CAVIAR

EASY - DO AHEAD

ingredients: 1 1/2 lb. eggplant
3 tbsp. lemon juice
1 1/2 tsp. garlic powder
1/4 tsp. cayenne pepper
1/8 tsp. pepper

directions: Preheat oven to 400 degrees.
Wrap whole eggplant(s) in foil, place on baking sheet and bake 1 hour, until very soft.
Remove from oven, unwrap and let cool 15 minutes.
Cut eggplant in half; scoop pulp from shell and place in food processor or blender.
Add remaining ingredients and process until smooth.
Transfer to a bowl, cover and refrigerate 2-4 hours, before serving with fat-free crackers or French bread slices.

Serves: 6

Nutrition per Serving		Exchanges
Calories	30	1 vegetable
Carbohydrate	7 grams	
Cholesterol	0 milligrams	
Dietary Fiber	3 grams	
Fat	< 1 gram	
Protein	1 gram	
Sodium	3 milligrams	

Shopping List: 1 1/2 pound eggplant, lemon juice, garlic powder, cayenne pepper, pepper

ROASTED GARLIC BREAD WITH CHEESE

EASY - DO AHEAD

ingredients: 6 heads garlic, trimmed
1 cup + 2 tbsp. fat-free chicken broth
3/4 tsp. dried thyme
1/8 tsp. pepper
6 slices fat-free French bread
1/2 cup fat-free Parmesan cheese

directions: Preheat oven to 400 degrees.
Trim garlic heads so tops of cloves are exposed.
Arrange garlic heads in a shallow baking dish;
pour chicken broth over garlic and sprinkle with
thyme and pepper.
Cover pan with foil and bake in preheated oven 1
hour, until cloves are soft.
Line baking sheet with foil; arrange bread slices on
sheet.
Mash garlic heads and spread on bread slices.
Sprinkle with Parmesan cheese.
Return to oven and bake 5-6 minutes, until cheese
is lightly browned and bread is toasted.

Serves: 6

Nutrition per Serving		Exchanges
Calories	135	1 2/3 starch
Carbohydrates	26 grams	
Cholesterol	0 milligrams	
Dietary Fiber	1 gram	
Fat	< 1 gram	
Protein	7 grams	
Sodium	346 milligrams	

Shopping List: whole garlic, 10 ounces fat-free chicken broth, fat-free
French bread, 2 ounces fat-free Parmesan cheese, dried
thyme, pepper

FRENCH-STYLE CHILLED CUCUMBER SOUP

EASY - DO AHEAD

FRENCH

ingredients:
3 cups fat-free chicken broth
1 1/2 tbsp. onion powder
2 medium baking potatoes, peeled and cut into 1-inch pieces
5 medium cucumbers, peeled, seeded and chopped
1 1/8 cups fat-free sour cream, divided
3/4 cup fat-free yogurt
1/4 tsp. pepper
2 tbsp. chopped chives

directions:
Pour chicken broth into large soup pot; add onion powder and potatoes.
Bring to a boil over high heat. Reduce heat to low and simmer 15-20 minutes, until potato is tender.
Place cucumbers and soup in food processor; process until blended.
Gradually add 3/4 cup sour cream and yogurt and mix until blended.
Season with pepper.
Store in sealed container and refrigerate 3-6 hours before serving. Serve with additional sour cream and chives, if desired.

Serves: 6

Nutrition per Serving		Exchanges
Calories	132	1/2 milk
Carbohydrate	23 grams	1/2 starch
Cholesterol	1 milligram	2 vegetable
Dietary Fiber	3 grams	
Fat	< 1 gram	
Protein	8 grams	
Sodium	451 milligrams	

Shopping List:
2 medium baking potatoes, 5 medium cucumbers, 24 ounces fat-free chicken broth, 9 ounces fat-free sour cream, 6 ounces fat-free yogurt, onion powder, pepper, chives

CREAM OF CARROT SOUP

(SOUPE DE CRECY)
AVERAGE - DO AHEAD

FRENCH

ingredients: 32 oz. fat-free chicken broth, divided
1 cup chopped onion
3/4 lb. baking potatoes, cut into 1-inch pieces
1 1/2 lb. carrots, peeled & cut into 1-inch pieces
1 1/2 cups skim milk
1/4 tsp. pepper
1/2 cup frozen carrot slices, thawed and drained

directions: Pour 2 tablespoons chicken broth into large sauce-pan and heat over medium-high heat.
Add onion and cook, stirring frequently, until onions are tender.
Add potatoes, carrots and remaining broth to pan. Bring to a boil over high heat.
Reduce heat to low, cover and simmer 25-30 minutes.
Transfer soup mixture to food processor or blender and process until smooth. Return soup to sauce-pan; stir in milk and pepper and cook over medium heat, stirring constantly, until blended. Add thawed carrot slices and heat 1 minute.

Serves: 6

Nutrition per Serving   **Exchanges**
Calories   145   3 vegetable
Carbohydrate   29 grams   1/4 milk
Cholesterol   1 milligram   1/2 starch
Dietary Fiber   5 grams
Fat   < 1 gram
Protein   7 grams
Sodium   574 milligrams

Shopping List: 32 ounces fat-free chicken broth, 1 large onion, 2 medium baking potatoes, 1 1/2 pounds carrots, 12 ounces skim milk, pepper, frozen carrot slices

CREAM OF VEGETABLE SOUP

EASY - DO AHEAD - FREEZE

ingredients:
2 cups fat-free vegetable broth
1 large baking potato, cut into 1-inch pieces
1 cup chopped onions
1/2 tsp. curry powder
1/8 tsp. pepper
1 cup frozen broccoli florets
1 cup frozen carrot slices
1 cup sliced mushrooms
1 cup frozen cauliflower florets
1 cup skim milk

directions:
Pour vegetable broth into large saucepan; add potato, onions, curry powder and pepper. Bring to a boil over high heat. Reduce heat to medium-low and cook 15 to 20 minutes, until potato is softened. Bring to a boil over high heat; add broccoli, carrots, mushrooms and cauliflower and cook 5-7 minutes, until vegetables are cooked through. Remove 1 cup of the cooked vegetables and set aside. Pour half of the vegetable mixture into blender and process until smooth; pour mixture into bowl. Repeat blending with remaining mixture. Return soup to saucepan; gradually add milk and cook, stirring constantly, 5-6 minutes, until mixture becomes thick and heated through. Stir in reserved vegetables and heat through.

Serves: 4

Nutrition per Serving		Exchanges
Calories	133	1 vegetable
Carbohydrate	27 grams	1/4 milk
Cholesterol	1 milligram	1 starch
Dietary Fiber	6 grams	
Fat	> 1 gram	
Protein	7 grams	
Sodium	302 milligrams	

Shopping List:
16 ounces fat-free vegetable broth, 1 large potato, 8-ounce package chopped onions, frozen broccoli florets, frozen carrot slices, 4 ounces sliced mushrooms, frozen cauliflower florets, 8 ounces skim milk, curry powder, pepper

CREAMY VEGETABLE SOUP
EASY - DO AHEAD - FREEZE

ingredients: 29 oz. + 1 tbsp. fat-free chicken broth, divided
1 cup chopped onions
1 1/2 cups shredded carrots
1 large potato, peeled and chopped
1 large leek, cut into 1-inch pieces
1 large parsnip, peeled and chopped
1 cup skim milk
1/4 tsp. pepper

directions: In a large saucepan, heat 1 tablespoon chicken broth over medium-high heat. Add onions and carrots and cook until vegetables are tender, about 10 minutes. Add potato, leek, parsnip and remaining broth to pan and bring to a boil over high heat. Reduce heat to low, cover and simmer 25-30 minutes. Transfer soup mixture to food processor or blender and process until smooth. Return soup to saucepan; stir in milk and pepper and cook over medium heat, stirring constantly, until blended.

Serves: 8

Nutrition per Serving		Exchanges
Calories	150	3 vegetable
Carbohydrate	32 grams	
Cholesterol	1 milligram	
Dietary Fiber	5 grams	
Fat	< 1 gram	
Protein	5 grams	
Sodium	971 milligrams	

Shopping List: 2 (16 ounce) cans fat-free chicken broth, chopped onions (frozen or packaged fresh), 8-ounce package shredded carrots, 1 large potato, 1 large leek, 1 large parsnip, 8 ounces skim milk, pepper

FRENCH ONION SOUP

EASY - DO AHEAD - FREEZE

ingredients:
1 1/2 cups yellow onions, sliced thin
1 1/2 cups red onions, sliced thin
3 tbsp. Butter Buds, reconstituted
6 1/4 cups fat-free beef broth
1 1/2 tbsp. Worcestershire sauce
6 slices fat-free French bread
12 oz. fat-free sliced Swiss cheese

directions:
Combine onions and Butter Buds in a large soup pot and heat over medium heat; cook, stirring occasionally, 10-15 minutes, until onions are tender.

Add broth and Worcestershire sauce to onions and mix well. Bring to a boil over high heat. Reduce heat to low, cover and simmer 25-30 minutes.

Preheat oven to 350 degrees. Line baking sheet with foil. Cut bread slices in half and arrange in single layer on baking sheet. Bake in preheated oven 5-10 minutes, until lightly browned. Turn bread over and bake 5-6 minutes, until bread is crisp. Remove from oven and turn broiler to high heat. Place one slice of bread in the bottom of each soup bowl; top with one slice of cheese. Spoon soup into bowl to fill to the top; top each bowl with cheese. Place bowls on baking sheet and cook under broiler until cheese is completely melted.

Serves: 6

Nutrition per Serving		Exchanges
Calories	230	1 starch
Carbohydrate	32 grams	3 vegetable
Cholesterol	0 milligrams	2 meat
Dietary Fiber	2 grams	
Fat	< 1 gram	
Protein	23 grams	
Sodium	1769 milligrams	

Shopping List: 3/4 pound yellow onions, 3/4 pound red onions, 48 ounces fat-free beef broth, 12 ounces fat-free Swiss cheese slices, fat-free French bread, Butter Buds, Worcestershire sauce

PISTOU SOUP
AVERAGE - DO AHEAD

ingredients:
1 (28 oz.) can crushed tomatoes
1 tbsp. garlic powder
1 tbsp dried basil
3 tbsp. fat-free Parmesan cheese
1 1/2 + 2 tbsp. fat-free chicken broth, divided
2 medium potatoes, peeled and diced
10 oz. frozen carrot slices, thawed and drained
1/2 cup chopped green onions
1 cup canned fat-free red kidney beans, drained
1 cup frozen peas, thawed and drained
1 tsp. dried parsley

directions:
Combine tomatoes, garlic powder, basil and cheese in a food processor or blender and process until smooth; set aside. Lightly spray Dutch oven with nonfat cooking spray.
Pour 1 1/2 tablespoons chicken broth into pan and heat over medium-high heat. Add potatoes, carrots and green onions to pan and cook 3-4 minutes, stirring constantly, until tender. Add tomato mixture, remaining broth and beans to pan and bring to a boil over high heat. Reduce heat to low, cover and simmer 20-25 minutes, until potatoes are tender. Add peas and parsley to soup; cook until heated through.

Serves: 8

Nutrition per Serving

		Exchanges
Calories	132	1 starch
Carbohydrate	28 grams	2 1/2 vegetable
Cholesterol	0 milligrams	
Dietary Fiber	5 grams	
Fat	< 1 gram	
Protein	6 grams	
Sodium	492 milligrams	

Shopping List:
1 (28-ounce) can crushed tomatoes, 10 ounces frozen carrot slices, 15 ounces fat-free chicken broth, canned red kidney beans, frozen peas, green onions, 2 medium potatoes, dried parsley, fat-free Parmesan cheese, garlic powder, dried basil

POTATO AND LEEK SOUP

(VICHYSSOISE)
EASY - DO AHEAD

ingredients:
1 1/2 lb. leeks, cut into 1-inch pieces
1 lb. potatoes, peeled and quartered
1/2 lb. celery, sliced thin
1 tbsp. onion powder
6 cups fat-free chicken broth
2 cups skim milk
1 cup evaporated skim milk
1/4 tsp. white pepper

directions:
Combine leeks, potatoes, celery, onion powder and chicken broth in a large soup pot. Bring to a boil over high heat.
Reduce heat to low and simmer, uncovered, 45-60 minutes, until vegetables are tender. Pour 3/4 of the soup into a large bowl; divide into 2-3 batches and process until smooth, in food processor or blender.
Return puréed soup to pot. Add milk and evaporated milk to soup. Cook over medium heat until soup is heated through (do not boil). Serve warm.

Serves: 6

Nutrition per Serving		Exchanges
Calories	214	1/2 vegetable
Carbohydrate	43 grams	1/2 milk
Cholesterol	3 milligrams	2 starch
Dietary Fiber	4 grams	
Fat	1 gram	
Protein	10 grams	
Sodium	1050 milligrams	

Shopping List: 1 1/2 pounds leeks, 1 pound potatoes, 1/2 pound celery, 40 ounces fat-free chicken broth, 16 ounces skim milk, 8 ounces evaporated skim milk, onion powder, white pepper

SWEET VICHYSSOISE

EASY - DO AHEAD

ingredients:
1 1/2 cups fat-free chicken broth
1 1/2 cups sweet potatoes, peeled and cubed
1 tbsp. onion powder
2 cups chopped celery
3 cups skim milk
1/4 tsp. pepper
2 drops Tabasco sauce
1 1/2 tbsp. fat-free ricotta cheese

directions:
Combine chicken broth, sweet potatoes, celery and onion powder in a food processor or blender and process until smooth.

Pour mixture into large soup pot and bring to a boil over medium-high heat. Reduce heat to medium-low and simmer 30 minutes.

Remove soup from heat. Combine milk, pepper, Tabasco and cheese in a food processor or blender and process until smooth.

Gradually add milk mixture to broth and mix well. In separate batches, blend soup in food processor or blender. Refrigerate soup several hours before serving.

Serves: 6

Nutrition per Serving

		Exchanges
Calories	102	1/2 milk
Carbohydrate	18 grams	3/4 starch
Cholesterol	3 milligrams	
Dietary Fiber	2 grams	
Fat	< 1 gram	
Protein	7 grams	
Sodium	328 milligrams	

Shopping List: 12 ounces fat-free chicken broth, 2 medium sweet potatoes, celery, 24 ounces skim milk, pepper, Tabasco sauce, fat-free ricotta cheese, onion powder

TARRAGON BROCCOLI SOUP

EASY

FRENCH

ingredients: 3 cups + 2 tsp. fat-free chicken broth, divided
1/2 cup chopped onions
1/2 tsp. garlic powder
1 medium red potato, peeled and diced
2 tsp. dried parsley
1/2 tsp. dried tarragon
2 cups frozen broccoli florets
1/4 cup fat-free sour cream

directions: Lightly spray a large saucepan with nonfat cooking spray and heat over medium-high heat.
Add 2 teaspoons chicken broth, onions and garlic powder; cook, stirring frequently, until onions are tender.
Pour remaining chicken broth into pan; add potato, parsley and tarragon and bring to a boil over medium-high heat.
Reduce heat to medium and simmer 7-8 minutes, until potatoes are tender.
Increase heat to medium-high; add frozen broccoli florets and cook 2-3 minutes, until tender. Remove from heat and stir in sour cream.

Serves:4

Nutrition per Serving		Exchanges
Calories	88	1/3 starch
Carbohydrate	17 grams	2 1/2 vegetable
Cholesterol	0 milligrams	
Dietary Fiber	5 grams	
Fat	< 1 gram	
Protein	5 grams	
Sodium	719 milligrams	

Shopping List: 1 red potato, 1 onion, 2 (16-ounce) cans fat-free chicken broth, 16-ounce package frozen broccoli florets, fat-free sour cream, garlic powder, dried parsley, dried tarragon

CRAB LOUIS SALAD

EASY - DO AHEAD

ingredients: 1/2 cup fat-free mayonnaise
1/2 cup fat-free plain yogurt
1/2 cup fat-free sour cream
3 tbsp. skim milk
3/8 cup chili sauce
1/3 cup frozen pepper strips, thawed and drained
1/3 cup chopped green onions
1 1/2 tbsp. lemon juice
3 tbsp. sliced green olives
6 cups shredded lettuce
18 oz. canned crabmeat, drained

directions: Combine mayonnaise, yogurt, sour cream, milk, chili sauce, peppers, onions, lemon juice and olives in a medium bowl and mix until all ingredients are blended. Cover and refrigerate at least 30 minutes.
Place 1 cup shredded lettuce in each salad bowl. Add crabmeat to salad dressing and toss until well mixed.
Spoon crab salad over shredded lettuce and serve. Great with crusty French bread!

Serves: 6

Nutrition per Serving		Exchanges
Calories	146	3 vegetable
Carbohydrate	212 grams	1 meat
Cholesterol	10 milligrams	1/2 milk
Dietary Fiber	1 gram	
Fat	< 1 gram	
Protein	13 grams	
Sodium	890 milligrams	

Shopping List: 4-ounces fat-free mayonnaise, 4-ounces fat-free plain yogurt, 4-ounces fat-free sour cream, skim milk, chili sauce, frozen pepper strips, green onions, green olives, 3 (6-ounce) cans fat-free crabmeat, 2 (8-ounce) packages shredded lettuce, lemon juice

FRENCH

FRENCH DIJON DRESSING
EASY - DO AHEAD

ingredients: 1/3 cup fat-free plain yogurt
1/3 cup fat-free sour cream
2 tbsp. honey
2 tbsp. Dijon mustard
2 tsp. dried tarragon
1 tsp. garlic powder

directions: Combine all ingredients in a food processor or
blender and process until smooth.
Transfer to bowl, cover and refrigerate several
hours before serving.
Great over assorted greens!

Serves: 6

Nutrition per Serving:		Exchanges
Calories	56	2/3 starch
Carbohydrate	11 grams	
Cholesterol	< 1 milligram	
Dietary Fiber	0 milligrams	
Fat	< 1 gram	
Protein	2 grams	
Sodium	94 milligrams	

Shopping List: 3 ounces fat-free plain yogurt, 3 ounces fat-free sour
cream, honey, Dijon mustard, dried tarragon, garlic
powder

HONEY-DIJON POTATO SALAD

EASY - DO AHEAD

ingredients:
1 1/2 lb. red potatoes, sliced
1/2 cup chopped red onions
1/3 cup diced celery
1/4 tsp. pepper
2 tsp. dried parsley
1/2 cup + 2 tbsp. fat-free honey dijon
    dressing
Paprika

directions:
Place potatoes in a medium saucepan; cover with water and bring to a boil over high heat.
Reduce heat to medium and cook 6-8 minutes, just until potatoes are tender.
Drain potatoes and place in a large mixing bowl.
Add onions, celery, pepper and parsley.
Pour dressing over top and toss lightly to coat.
Cover and refrigerate several hours before serving.
Sprinkle with paprika just before serving.

Serves: 6

Nutrition per Serving		Exchanges
Calories	121	2 vegetable
Carbohydrate	28 grams	1 starch
Cholesterol	0 milligrams	
Dietary Fiber	2 grams	
Fat	< 1 gram	
Protein	2 grams	
Sodium	112 milligrams	

Shopping List: 1 1/2 pounds red potatoes, celery, 1 small red onion, 5 ounces fat-free honey-dijon salad dressing, pepper, dried parsley, paprika

97

PICKLED BEETS AND RED ONIONS

EASY - DO AHEAD

ingredients:
4 medium beets (about 3/4 lb.)
1/4 cup raspberry vinegar
1 1/2 tsp. sugar
1 large red onion, peeled and sliced

directions:
Cut the roots and stems from beets. Arrange in microwave-safe baking dish and cover with plastic wrap.

Microwave on High heat 7 minutes. Rotate plate and cook 8-10 minutes longer, until beets are tender.

Cool beets slightly; remove skins and cut into cubes. Combine vinegar and sugar in a small bowl and mix until sugar is dissolved.

Combine onions and beets in a medium bowl; pour vinegar dressing over top and mix well.

Cover and refrigerate 3-4 hours or overnight before serving.

Serves: 6

Nutrition per Serving		Exchanges
Calories	24	1 vegetable
Carbohydrate	6 grams	
Cholesterol	0 milligram	
Dietary Fiber	1 gram	
Fat	<1 gram	
Protein	1 gram	
Sodium	17 milligrams	

Shopping List:
1 large red onion, 4 medium beets (about 3/4 pound), 2 ounces raspberry vinegar, sugar

RASPBERRY SALAD

EASY - DO AHEAD

ingredients: 2 cups curly endive lettuce, torn into bite-size
pieces
2 cups bibb lettuce, torn into bite-size pieces
2 cups romaine lettuce, torn into bite-size pieces
3/4 cup fat-free raspberry vinaigrette salad
dressing
1 1/2 cups fresh raspberries

directions: Combine salad greens in a large mixing bowl; toss
with raspberry dressing.
Add raspberries to salad and mix lightly.

Serves: 6

Nutrition per Serving		Exchanges
Calories	44	1 vegetable
Carbohydrate	9 grams	1/2 fruit
Cholesterol	0 milligrams	
Dietary Fiber	2 grams	
Fat	< 1 gram	
Protein	1 gram	
Sodium	127 milligrams	

Shopping List: curly endive lettuce, bibb lettuce, romaine lettuce, 6
ounces fat-free raspberry vinaigrette salad dressing, 1
pint fresh raspberries

RED CABBAGE-CARROT SLAW

EASY - DO AHEAD

FRENCH

ingredients:
1 lb. shredded cabbage
2 cups shredded carrots
1/2 cup raspberry vinegar
2 1/2 tbsp. sugar
3 tbsp. lemon juice
1 tsp. crushed caraway seed
1/8 tsp. cinnamon
1/4 tsp. pepper

directions: Combine cabbage and carrots in a large bowl and mix well. Combine remaining ingredients in a food processor or blender and process until blended. Pour vinegar blend over cabbage mixture and toss until well mixed. Cover and refrigerate 3-4 hours or overnight before serving.

Serves: 6

Nutrition per Serving		Exchanges
Calories	56	2 1/2 vegetable
Carbohydrate	15 grams	
Cholesterol	0 milligrams	
Dietary Fiber	3 grams	
Fat	< 1 gram	
Protein	1 gram	
Sodium	27 milligrams	

Shopping List: 16-ounce package shredded red cabbage, 8-ounce package shredded carrots, 4 ounces raspberry vinegar, lemon juice, sugar, caraway seed, cinnamon, pepper

SALADE NICOISE
EASY - DO AHEAD

ingredients: 24 oz. frozen green beans, thawed and drained
1 small red bell pepper, sliced thin
1 small green bell pepper, sliced thin
1 1/2 cups chopped celery
3 medium red potatoes, cooked and sliced
1 1/2 cups cherry tomatoes
14 oz. fat-free tuna
2 tbsp. sliced black olives
1 medium red onion, sliced thin
2 tsp. dried basil
3 tbsp. chopped green onions
3/4 cup fat-free red wine vinegar salad dressing

directions: Arrange green beans, red and green bell pepper slices, celery, sliced potatoes and cherry tomatoes on platter.
Alternate vegetables on platter to fill to center.
Flake tuna over vegetables; top with sliced olives, red onion, basil and green onions.
Serve with fat-free red wine vinaigrette salad dressing.

Serves: 6

FRENCH

Nutrition per Serving		Exchanges
Calories	224	3 vegetable
Carbohydrate	31 grams	1 starch
Cholesterol	12 milligrams	2 meat
Dietary Fiber	5 grams	
Fat	< 1 gram	
Protein	23 grams	
Sodium	407 milligrams	

Shopping List: 24 ounces frozen green beans, 1 red bell pepper, 1 green bell pepper, celery, 3 red potatoes, 3/4 pint cherry tomatoes, 2 (7-ounce) cans fat-free tuna, sliced black olives, 1 red onion, green onions, dried basil, 6 ounces fat-free red wine vinaigrette salad dressing

CHICKEN CORDON BLEU

AVERAGE - DO AHEAD - FREEZE

FRENCH

ingredients: 6 fat-free chicken breasts (about 1 1/2 lb.)
6 slices fat-free ham
6 slices fat-free Swiss cheese
1/2 cup flour
1/4 tsp. pepper
1/2 cup egg substitute
3/4 cup fat-free bread crumbs
1/4 cup fat-free Parmesan cheese

directions: Wrap chicken breasts tightly in plastic wrap; pound on flat surface until breasts are thin. Place 1 slice of ham on each chicken breast; top with 1 slice of cheese. Fold in sides of chicken and roll up; secure with wooden toothpick. Combine flour and pepper in a shallow baking dish and mix well. Pour egg substitute into shallow dish and beat lightly. Combine bread crumbs and Parmesan cheese in a shallow dish and mix well. Lightly spray large nonstick skillet with nonfat cooking spray and heat over medium heat.

To prepare chicken: roll in flour mixture, dip in egg substitute and roll to coat well in bread crumb mixture. Place chicken rolls, seam side down, in skillet and cook, turning occasionally, 25-30 minutes, until chicken is no longer pink and is cooked through. Remove toothpicks before serving.

Serves: 6

	Exchanges	
Calories	282	5 meat
Carbohydrate	21 grams	1 1/3 starch
Cholesterol	66 milligrams	
Dietary Fiber	1 gram	
Fat	< 1 gram	
Protein	40 grams	
Sodium	898 milligrams	

Shopping List: fat-free chicken breasts, 6 ounces fat-free ham slices, 6 ounces fat-free Swiss cheese slices, 4 ounces egg substitute, fat-free bread crumbs, 1 ounce fat-free Parmesan cheese, flour, pepper

CHICKEN DIVAN

AVERAGE - DO AHEAD

ingredients:

1 1/2 lb. fat-free chicken tenders
1 tbsp. onion powder
1/8 tsp. pepper
16 oz. frozen broccoli cuts, thawed and drained
8 oz. low-fat cream of chicken soup
12 oz. evaporated skim milk
1/2 cup fat-free plain yogurt
1/2 cup fat-free sour cream
1 tbsp. curry powder
1 1/2 cups fat-free finely-shredded Cheddar cheese

directions:

Lightly spray large nonstick skillet with nonfat cooking spray and heat over medium-high heat.
Add chicken tenders; sprinkle with onion powder and pepper. Stir-fry chicken 3 to 5 minutes, until no longer pink. Remove from skillet and set aside.
Combine soup, milk, yogurt, sour cream and curry powder in medium bowl; mix until blended smooth.
Preheat oven to 350 degrees. Lightly spray 10-inch baking dish with nonfat cooking spray.
Place chicken in baking dish. Top with thawed broccoli; cover with soup mixture and sprinkle with cheese.
Bake in preheated oven 30-35 minutes, until cheese is lightly browned and casserole is cooked through.

Serves: 6

Nutrition per Serving		Exchanges
Calories	271	2 vegetable
Carbohydrate	20 grams	4 meat
Cholesterol	59 milligrams	1 milk
Dietary Fiber	3 grams	
Fat	< 1 gram	
Protein	44 grams	
Sodium	764 milligrams	

Shopping List: 1 1/2 pounds fat-free chicken tenders, 16 ounces frozen broccoli cuts, 8 ounces low-fat cream of chicken soup, 12 ounces evaporated skim milk, 4 ounces fat-free plain yogurt, 4 ounces fat-free sour cream, 6 ounces fat-free finely shredded Cheddar cheese, curry powder, onion powder, pepper

COQUILLES SAINT-JAQUES PROVENCAL
(BAKED SCALLOPS)
EASY - DO AHEAD

ingredients: 2 1/4 lb. fat-free frozen scallops, uncooked
1 1/2 tbsp. minced garlic
1 1/2 cups chopped tomatoes, drained
1/4 cup dry white wine
2 tbsp. fat-free chicken broth
1 1/2 tsp. dried parsley
1 1/2 tsp. dried basil
1/8 tsp. pepper
3/4 cup fat-free bread crumbs
1 tsp. garlic powder

directions: Preheat oven to 450 degrees. Lightly spray 10-inch baking dish with nonfat cooking spray.
Combine scallops, garlic, tomatoes, wine, chicken broth, parsley, basil and pepper in baking dish and mix until scallops are coated.
Combine bread crumbs and garlic powder in a small cup and mix well. Sprinkle bread crumbs over scallops; lightly spray with nonfat cooking spray.
Bake in preheated oven 10-15 minutes, until scallops are opaque and top is lightly browned.

Serves: 6

Nutrition per Serving		Exchanges
Calories	197	4 vegetable
Carbohydrate	28 grams	1/2 starch
Cholesterol	20 milligrams	1 1/2 meat
Dietary Fiber	1 gram	
Fat	< 1 gram	
Protein	9 grams	
Sodium	1265 milligrams	

Shopping List: 2 1/4 pounds fat-free frozen scallops (uncooked), 16-ounce can chopped tomatoes, 2 ounces dry white wine, fat-free chicken broth, fat-free bread crumbs, dried parsley, dried basil, minced garlic, pepper, garlic powder

DIJON GRILLED CHICKEN
EASY - DO AHEAD

ingredients: 1 1/2 lb. fat-free chicken breasts
3 tbsp. chopped green onions
1 1/2 tsp. Dijon mustard
1/2 tsp. cayenne pepper
1 tbsp. Worcestershire sauce
3/4 cup fat-free chicken broth
1 1/2 tsp. parsley

directions: Preheat broiler on high heat. Line baking sheet
with foil and lightly spray with nonfat cooking
spray.
Arrange chicken breasts in a single layer on baking
sheet.
Combine green onions, mustard, cayenne,
Worcestershire sauce, chicken broth and parsley
in a medium bowl and mix until blended.
Gradually pour sauce over chicken; turn chicken
to coat on all sides. Pour remaining sauce over
chicken and broil 6-8 minutes, until chicken is no
longer pink and is lightly browned.

Serves: 6

Nutrition per Serving		Exchanges
Calories	117	3 meat
Carbohydrate	3 grams	
Cholesterol	71 milligrams	
Dietary Fiber	< 1 gram	
Fat	< 1 gram	
Protein	24 grams	
Sodium	452 milligrams	

Shopping List: 1 1/2 pounds fat-free chicken breasts, green onions, 6
ounces fat-free chicken broth, Dijon mustard,
Worcestershire sauce, cayenne pepper, parsley

QUICHE LORRAINE
AVERAGE - DO AHEAD - FREEZE

ingredients: 1 1/2 cups fat-free cooked rice
1 cup egg substitute, divided
1/2 tsp. onion powder
1/8 tsp. white pepper
1 cup chopped onions
1 cup fat-free Swiss cheese, shredded
8 slices fat-free turkey bacon, cooked and
    crumbled
1 tbsp. flour
1 cup skim milk

directions: Lightly spray 9-inch pie pan with nonfat cooking
spray. Preheat oven to 400 degrees.
Combine rice, 1/4 cup egg substitute, onion powder and pepper in a medium bowl and mix well.
Press into pie pan and bake in preheated oven 15
minutes. Remove from oven; sprinkle onions,
cheese and bacon on crust.
In a small bowl, combine flour, remaining egg
substitute, and milk, and mix until completely
blended. Pour into crust.
Increase oven temperature to 425 degrees. Bake 10
minutes; reduce heat to 350 degrees and bake an
additional 25 to 30 minutes, until cooked through.

Serves: 6

Nutrition per Serving		Exchanges
Calories	175	1 2/3 starch
Carbohydrate	24 grams	1 meat
Cholesterol	21 milligrams	
Dietary Fiber	< 1 gram	
Fat	<1 gram	
Protein	13 grams	
Sodium	397 milligrams	

Shopping List: fat-free rice (white or brown), 8 ounces egg substitute,
packaged chopped onions (fresh or frozen), 4 ounces
fat-free Swiss cheese, fat-free turkey bacon, 8 ounces
skim milk, onion powder, white pepper, flour

SPINACH AND BROCCOLI QUICHE

EASY - DO AHEAD - FREEZE

ingredients:
1 cup skim milk
1/2 cup egg substitute
2 large egg whites
1 cup frozen chopped broccoli, thawed and drained
1 cup frozen chopped spinach, thawed and drained
1/2 cup frozen pepper strips, thawed and drained
3/4 cup fat-free Swiss cheese, shredded
3 green onions, thinly sliced
2 tsp. dried dill
1/4 tsp. garlic powder
1/4 tsp. pepper
1/4 cup fat-free Parmesan cheese

directions:
Preheat oven to 375 degrees. Lightly spray 9-inch pie plate with nonfat cooking spray.
Combine all the ingredients except Parmesan cheese in a large bowl and mix well.
Add mixture to pie plate and sprinkle generously with Parmesan cheese.
Bake in preheated oven 30-35 minutes, until knife inserted in the center comes out clean. Quiche should be lightly browned on top.

Serves: 4

Nutrition per Serving		Exchange
Calories	123	1/3 milk
Carbohydrate	13 grams	2 vegetable
Cholesterol	1 milligram	1 1/2 meat
Dietary Fiber	3 grams	
Fat	< 1 gram	
Protein	15 grams	
Sodium	368 milligrams	

Shopping List: 8 ounces skim milk, 4 ounces egg substitute, eggs, 10 ounces frozen chopped broccoli, 10 ounces frozen chopped spinach, 10-ounce package frozen pepper stir-fry, 3 ounces fat-free Swiss cheese, 1 ounce fat-free Parmesan cheese, green onions, dried dill, garlic powder, pepper

TAPENADE STUFFED TOMATOES

EASY - DO AHEAD

FRENCH

ingredients:
3 large tomatoes, halved
1 1/2 tsp. garlic powder
18 oz. fat-free tuna, drained
3 anchovies, drained and rinsed
1/3 cup lemon juice
1 1/2 tbsp. Dijon mustard
1/4 tsp. pepper
1 tsp. dried parsley

directions:
Cut tomatoes in half; scoop out inside, leaving 1/2-inch shell.
Combine tuna, garlic powder, anchovies, lemon juice, mustard and pepper in a food processor or blender and process until smooth.
Stir in parsley.
Spoon tuna mixture into tomato shells; arrange on platters, on leaf lettuce. Refrigerate or serve immediately.

Serves: 6

Nutrition per Serving		Exchanges
Calories	134	3 meat
Carbohydrate	6 grams	1 vegetable
Cholesterol	14 milligrams	
Dietary Fiber	1 gram	
Fat	< 1 gram	
Protein	25 grams	
Sodium	384 milligrams	

Shopping List: 3 large tomatoes, 3 (6 ounce) cans fat-free tuna, anchovies, lemon juice, Dijon mustard, garlic powder, pepper, dried parsley

108

FONDUE DE TOMATOES
(TOMATO SAUCE)
EASY - DO AHEAD

ingredients:	2 tbsp. fat-free chicken broth
	2 tsp. minced garlic
	3 lb. fresh tomatoes, chopped
	1 tsp. onion powder
	1 tsp. dried basil
	1 tsp. dried parsley

directions: Lightly spray large nonstick skillet with nonfat cooking spray.

Add chicken broth and heat over medium-high heat. Add garlic and cook, stirring frequently, 1-2 minutes, until golden.

Add tomatoes soften. Add basil and parsley and mix well.

Serve over cooked pasta, baked potatoes, vegetables, chicken or fish.

Serves: 6

Nutrition per Serving

Calories	51	
Carbohydrate	11 grams	
Cholesterol	0 milligrams	
Dietary Fiber	3 grams	
Fat	< 1 gram	
Protein	2 grams	
Sodium	37 milligrams	

Exchanges
2 vegetable

Shopping List: 3 pounds fresh tomatoes, fat-free chicken broth, minced garlic, onion powder, dried parsley, dried basil

HONEY DIJON ASPARAGUS
EASY - DO AHEAD

ingredients:
2 lb. asparagus
1/4 cup honey
2 tbsp. Dijon mustard
1/4 cup red wine vinegar
2 tbsp. finely-minced onions
6 roma tomatoes, sliced thin (optional)

directions:
Trim, blanch, and chill asparagus; arrange on serving platter.
Blend honey, mustard, vinegar and onions and mix well; pour over asparagus.
Garnish with sliced roma tomatoes, if desired.

Serves: 6

Nutrition per Serving		Exchanges
Calories	82	3 1/2 vegetable
Carbohydrate	19 grams	
Cholesterol	0 milligrams	
Dietary Fiber	1 gram	
Fat	< 1 gram	
Protein	2 grams	
Sodium	79 milligrams	

Shopping List: 2 pounds fresh asparagus, onion, 6 roma tomatoes (optional), honey, Dijon mustard, red wine vinegar

POTATOES AU GRATIN

AVERAGE - DO AHEAD - FREEZE

ingredients:
2 1/4 lb. new potatoes, sliced 1/4-inch thick
1 large onion, sliced thin
2 tsp. low-fat margarine
2 tsp. Butter Buds, reconstituted
1 1/2 tbsp. flour
1 1/2 tbsp. dried parsley, divided
3/4 tsp. dried rosemary
1 1/2 tsp. garlic powder
1/4 tsp. pepper
2 1/4 cups skim milk
4 oz. fat-free shredded Swiss cheese
3 tbsp. fat-free Parmesan cheese (optional)

directions:
Preheat oven to 375 degrees. Lightly spray 10-inch baking dish with nonfat cooking spray. Arrange 1/2 the potato slices and 1/2 onion slices in baking dish; top with remaining potatoes and onions. Melt margarine in a small saucepan over medium heat; stir in Butter Buds and blend well. Add flour, 2 teaspoons parsley, rosemary, garlic powder and pepper, and mix well. Gradually add milk, stirring constantly, until mixture becomes thick and smooth. Pour sauce over top, cover with foil and bake in preheated oven 25-30 minutes. Remove from oven, stir again, and sprinkle with Swiss cheese. Bake, uncovered, 10-15 minutes, until cheese is melted and lightly browned. Sprinkle with Parmesan cheese, if desired.

Serves: 6

Nutrition per Serving		Exchanges
Calories	250	2 3/4 starch
Carbohydrate	48 grams	1/2 milk
Cholesterol	2 milligrams	
Dietary Fiber	5 grams	
Fat	< 1 gram	
Protein	11 grams	
Sodium	252 milligrams	

Shopping List:
2 1/4 pounds new potatoes, 18 ounces skim milk, 1 large onion, 4 ounces fat-free Swiss cheese, fat-free Parmesan cheese, low-fat margarine, Butter Buds, flour, dried parsley, dried rosemary, garlic powder, pepper

POTATOES CINDERELLA

EASY - DO AHEAD

FRENCH

ingredients:
6 medium baking potatoes
3/4 cup fat-free sour cream
3 tsp. fat-free Parmesan cheese
3 tbsp. fat-free shredded Swiss cheese
3 tbsp. chopped green onions
1/4 tsp. pepper
1 1/4 tsp. paprika

directions:
Preheat oven to 450 degrees. Pierce potatoes several times with a fork. Bake in preheated oven 1 hour, until tender. Remove from oven and let cool 15-20 minutes.

Combine sour cream, Parmesan cheese, Swiss cheese, onions and pepper in a medium bowl and mix well. Line baking sheet with foil and lightly spray with nonfat cooking spray. Cut potatoes in half, scoop out pulp, leaving 1/4-inch shell. Add potato pulp to sour cream mixture and blend until smooth and creamy. Spoon potato mixture back into shells and arrange on baking sheet; sprinkle with paprika. Reduce oven temperature to 400 degrees. Bake 15-20 minutes, until lightly browned and heated through.

Serves: 6

Nutrition per Serving		Exchanges
Calories	176	2 1/4 starch
Carbohydrate	37 grams	
Cholesterol	0 milligrams	
Dietary Fiber	4 grams	
Fat	< 1 gram	
Protein	6 grams	
Sodium	56 milligrams	

Shopping List:
6 medium baking potatoes, 6 ounces fat-free sour cream, fat-free Parmesan cheese, fat-free Swiss cheese, green onions, pepper, paprika

SAUTÉED ZUCCHINI AND CARROTS

EASY

ingredients: 2 tbsp. fat-free chicken broth
12 oz. shredded carrots
3 medium zucchini, shredded
1 1/2 tsp. minced garlic
1 1/2 tsp. dried basil

directions: Lightly spray large nonstick skillet with nonfat cooking spray.
Add chicken broth to skillet and heat over medium-high heat.
Add carrots, zucchini and garlic to skillet and cook, stirring constantly, 3-5 minutes, until tender.
Stir in basil and serve.

Serves: 6

Nutrition per Serving		Exchanges
Calories	36	1 1/2 vegetable
Carbohydrate	8 grams	
Cholesterol	0 milligrams	
Dietary Fiber	3 grams	
Fat	< 1 gram	
Protein	1 gram	
Sodium	38 milligrams	

Shopping List: 12-ounce package shredded carrots, 3 medium zucchini, minced garlic, dried basil, fat-free chicken broth

TRUFFADE
(FRENCH MASHED POTATOES)
EASY - DO AHEAD

ingredients: 4 large baking potatoes, peeled and cut into
1-inch pieces
16 oz. frozen chopped spinach, cooked and
drained
1 tsp. garlic powder
1 cup fat-free shredded Swiss cheese
2 tbsp. fat-free Parmesan cheese

directions: Place potatoes in large saucepan and cover with
water; bring to a boil over high heat.
Reduce heat to medium and cook 10-15 minutes,
until potatoes are tender. Drain well.
Place potatoes in medium bowl; mash with potato
masher or fork.
Add spinach, garlic powder, Swiss and Parmesan
cheese, and mix until blended.
Serve immediately, or reheat in microwave before
serving.

Serves: 6

Nutrition per Serving		Exchanges
Calories	133	1 1/2 vegetable
Carbohydrate	24 grams	1 starch
Cholesterol	0 milligrams	1/2 meat
Dietary Fiber	3 grams	
Fat	< 1 gram	
Protein	8 grams	
Sodium	232 milligrams	

Shopping List: 4 large baking potatoes, 16 ounces frozen chopped
spinach, 4 ounces fat-free Swiss cheese, fat-free Parmesan
cheese, garlic powder

114

CHOCOLATE-ALMOND FONDUE WITH STRAWBERRIES

EASY - DO AHEAD

ingredients:
1 1/2 cups skim milk
1/2 cup unsweetened cocoa powder
1 cup sugar
1 tbsp. cornstarch
1 1/2 tsp. almond extract
1 pint strawberries, washed and hulled

directions:
Lightly spray medium saucepan with nonfat cooking spray.
Combine all ingredients except strawberries in pan.
Cook over low heat, stirring frequently, until sauce thickens.
Transfer to fondue pot and keep warm.
Serve with fresh strawberries.

Serves: 8

Nutrition per Serving		Exchanges
Calories	134	2 fruit
Carbohydrate	33 grams	1/4 milk
Cholesterol	1 milligram	
Dietary Fiber	1 gram	
Fat	< 1 gram	
Protein	3 grams	
Sodium	28 milligrams	

Shopping List: 12 ounces skim milk, unsweetened cocoa powder, 1 pint strawberries, sugar, cornstarch, almond extract

CHOCOLATE CHEESE CREPES

AVERAGE - DO AHEAD

FRENCH

ingredients:
1 3/4 cups flour
1/4 cup unsweetened cocoa powder
2 tbsp. egg substitute
2 large egg whites
1/4 tsp. vanilla
3/8 cup sugar, divided
2 1/4 cups fat-free ricotta cheese
2 cups fat-free cottage cheese
1/3 cup fat-free peach melba yogurt
8 oz. raspberry-flavored peach slices
1/2 cup fat-free chocolate-raspberry sauce*

directions: Combine flour, cocoa, egg substitute, egg whites, vanilla and 1/4 cup sugar in a food processor or blender, and process until blended smooth.
Pour batter into large bowl and let stand at room temperature 30 minutes. Line baking sheet with foil and lightly spray with nonfat cooking spray. Lightly spray 10-inch nonstick skillet or crepe pan with nonfat cooking spray and heat over medium heat. Pour 1/4 cup batter into skillet and cover bottom of skillet; pour any excess batter back into the bowl. Cook crepe 1 minute, until bottom is lightly browned and top of crepe is dry. Invert crepe onto baking sheet. Repeat cooking process with remaining batter. Combine ricotta cheese, cottage cheese, yogurt and peach slices in a food processor or blender; pulse several times until mixture is blended and smooth. Spoon peach filling down center of crepe; roll crepe up and serve with fat-free chocolate-raspberry sauce.

Serves: 8

Nutrition per Serving		Exchanges
Calories	270	1 milk
Carbohydrate	53 grams	1 1/2 starch
Cholesterol	13 milligrams	1 fruit
Dietary Fiber	1 gram	
Fat	< 1 gram	
Protein	17 grams	
Sodium	216 milligrams	

Shopping List: 18 ounces fat-free ricotta cheese, 16 ounces fat-free cottage cheese, 3 ounces fat-free raspberry-peach yogurt (peach melba yogurt), 8 ounces raspberry-peach slices, flour, unsweetened cocoa powder, egg substitute, large eggs, vanilla, sugar, fat-free chocolate-raspberry sauce* (or substitute fat-free chocolate syrup)

CINNAMON 'N SPICE APPLE-RAISIN CREPES

AVERAGE - DO AHEAD - FREEZE

ingredients:
1 (28 oz.) can Cinnamon 'n Spice apples
1/4 cup raisins
1 cup flour
1 1/2 cups skim milk
1/2 cup egg substitute
1 tsp. cinnamon

directions:
Combine apples and raisins in a medium bowl and mix well; set aside. Combine flour, skim milk, egg substitute and cinnamon in a food processor or blender and process until smooth. Pour batter into medium bowl, cover and refrigerate 30-45 minutes. Remove batter from refrigerator and mix lightly. Lightly spray nonstick crepe pan (or small non-stick skillet) with nonfat cooking spray and heat over medium heat. Pour 3-4 tablespoons batter into pan; turn pan to cover bottom with batter. Pour any excess batter back into bowl. Cook crepe 1 minute, until bottom is lightly browned and crepe is cooked through.
Line baking sheet with foil and lightly spray with nonfat cooking spray; invert crepe onto foil. Spoon apple filling down the center of each crepe; roll crepe up. Repeat with remaining batter and filling. Keep cooked crepes warm, until finished with batter.

Serves: 6

Nutrition per Serving		Exchanges
Calories	214	2 2/3 fruit
Carbohydrate	47 grams	1/2 milk
Cholesterol	1 milligram	
Dietary Fiber	4 grams	
Fat	< 1 gram	
Protein	6 grams	
Sodium	63 milligrams	

Shopping List: 28 ounce can Cinnamon 'n Spice apples, raisins, flour, 12 ounces skim milk, 4 ounces egg substitute, cinnamon

FROZEN RASPBERRY CREAM

EASY - DO AHEAD - FREEZE

ingredients: 2 cups frozen raspberries
1 cup fat-free vanilla yogurt
1 cup fat-free raspberry yogurt
1 tbsp. sugar

directions: Place 1 cup raspberries in bowl of food processor; purée raspberries.
Add yogurt to food processor bowl and process until blended smooth.
Combine remaining raspberries and sugar in a medium bowl and toss until raspberries are coated.
Add puréed mixture and mix well.
Spoon mixture into 10-inch freezer-safe dish and freeze 6-8 hours, or overnight, until solid. Remove from freezer and let stand 15 minutes.
Cut mixture into cubes; place cubes in food processor or blender and process until smooth. Serve immediately.

Serves: 6

Nutrition per Serving		Exchanges
Calories	58	1 fruit
Carbohydrate	11 grams	
Cholesterol	2 milligrams	
Dietary Fiber	2 grams	
Fat	< 1 gram	
Protein	3 grams	
Sodium	47 milligrams	

Shopping List: 16 ounces frozen raspberries, 8 ounces fat-free vanilla yogurt, 8 ounces fat-free raspberry yogurt, sugar

FRUIT BRULÉE

AVERAGE

ingredients:
1/2 cup seedless grapes
1/2 cup sliced strawberries
1/2 cup raspberries
1/2 cup sliced peaches
1 cup fat-free sour cream
1 tsp. vanilla
1 cup light brown sugar
Cracked ice

directions:
Fill bottom of 9-inch ovenproof baking dish or glass pie pan with fruit.
Combine sour cream and vanilla and mix until blended; cover fruit with sour cream mixture.
Cover and refrigerate several hours, until thoroughly chilled.
Preheat broiler on high heat.
Sprinkle brown sugar over sour cream mixture until completely covered.
Place baking dish over a pan of equal size that has been filled with cracked ice.
Put the stacked pans under the broiler and cook, watching carefully, until the sugar caramelizes.
Serve immediately.

Serves: 4

Nutrition per Serving		Exchange
Calories	278	4 1/2 fruit
Carbohydrate	65 grams	
Cholesterol	0 milligrams	
Dietary Fiber	2 grams	
Fat	< 1 gram	
Protein	4 grams	
Sodium	57 milligrams	

Shopping List: Green seedless grapes*, strawberries*, raspberries*, peaches*, 8 ounces fat-free sour cream, 1/2 pound light brown sugar, vanilla
*or fruit of choice

STRAWBERRY TART

AVERAGE - DO AHEAD

FRENCH

ingredients:
1 1/4 cups flour
1/2 cup + 2 tbsp. sugar, divided
1 tsp. grated lemon zest
1/2 tsp. salt
1/4 cup skim milk
1/4 cup Lighter Bake
2 pints strawberries, rinsed and hulled
3 tbsp. cornstarch
1/2 cup water
1 tbsp. fresh lemon juice
Powdered sugar

directions: Preheat oven to 400 degrees. Combine flour, 2 tablespoons sugar, lemon zest and salt with a fork until well blended. Whisk milk and Lighter Bake together; gradually add to flour mixture, stirring with a fork until dough forms a ball. Add more milk, if dough is too dry. Form dough into disc shape and divide into 8 equal-size wedges. Roll each wedge between 2 sheets of waxed paper into circles large enough to fit 3-inch tart pans. Press dough into pans and trim edges. Place a 4-inch square of waxed paper in each tart pan and weight down with a layer of dried beans or rice. Bake 10 minutes; remove waxed paper and beans. Bake until golden brown, about 5-6 minutes. Cool completely. Remove pastry shells from pans. Reserve 24 berries for the top of tarts. Thinly slice remaining berries. Combine 1/2 cup sugar and cornstarch in small saucepan and mix until blended. Stir in water and half of the berry slices; cook, stirring frequently and mashing berries, until mixture boils and becomes thick and shiny. Remove from heat and add remaining sliced berries and lemon juice. Cool at room temperature. One hour before serving, spoon cooled berry mixture into pastry shells; smooth top and refrigerate. Before serving, slice reserved berries and arrange, cut-side down, on top of tart. Sprinkle with powdered sugar.

Serves: 8

Nutrition per Serving		Exchanges
Calories	182	1 starch
Carbohydrate	43 grams	1 3/4 fruit
Cholesterol	0 milligrams	
Dietary Fiber	2 grams	
Fat	< 1 gram	
Protein	3 grams	
Sodium	141 milligrams	

Shopping List: 2 pints strawberries, skim milk, Lighter Bake, flour, sugar, lemon juice, lemon zest, salt, cornstarch, powdered sugar

HOT MULLED CRANBERRY DRINK

EASY - DO AHEAD

ingredients: 1 1/2 cups cranberry-apple drink
1 cup cranberry-raspberry juice
1/2 cup orange juice
1/2 tsp. cinnamon
1/2 ground cloves
1 tsp. orange rind, cut in strips

directions: Combine all the ingredients in a medium saucepan and bring to a boil over medium heat. Reduce
heat to low and simmer 15-20 minutes. Serve in
warm mugs.

Serves: 4

Nutrition per Serving		Exchanges
Calories	106	1 2/3 fruit
Carbohydrate	26 grams	
Cholesterol	0 milligrams	
Dietary Fiber	< 1 gram	
Fat	< 1 gram	
Protein	< 1 gram	
Sodium	7 milligrams	

Shopping List: 12 ounces cranberry-apple juice, 8 ounces cranberry-
raspberry juice, 4 ounces orange juice, cinnamon, ground
cloves, orange rind

GERMAN

GERMAN

Influenced by centuries of traditions, foreign immigrants, geography, climate and history, German cooking is usually classified as "hearty" but not "heart healthy!" High sodium sauerkraut, fat-laden gravies, butter-filled pastries, soft pretzels and German beer are just a few foods characteristic of German culture. Germans have a love affair with food - holiday celebrations are food celebrations.

•*Fasching season* (January) is celebrated throughout the cities and towns of Southern Germany. It is a time to indulge in gastronomical pleasures with carnivals, street fairs, parades and masked balls.

•*Winzerfests* are wine festivals celebrated throughout the wine-growing regions of Germany. These celebrations usually include a feast of sausages, bread, and local wines.

•*Oktoberfest* is a two-week celebration (mid-September) with the focus on beer, food, costumes, and carnival rides. It began over 185 years ago (October 12, 1810) as an outdoor wedding reception for the Crown Prince Ludwig. The people of Munich had so much fun, they decided to repeat the celebration each year.

•*Plum Harvests, Onion Fairs, Asparagus Festivals and Apple Days* are just a few of the traditional German celebrations.

Enjoy the traditions of Germany without all the fat by selecting the right ingredients and using the proper cooking methods.

Popular German Ingredients (you can enjoy without all the guilt) include: asparagus, cabbage, mushrooms, beets, beans, cucumbers, onions, leeks, radishes, potatoes, poultry, fish, shellfish, pickles, mustards, sauerkraut, cheese (stick with low-fat or fat-free) and fresh fruit.

Traditional German foods on the lighter side include low-fat sausage, turkey bacon and fat-free smoked ham.

Common herbs and spices used in German cooking include: paprika, caraway seed, garlic, thyme, bay leaf, marjoram, nutmeg and anise seeds.

GERMAN TURKEY MEATBALLS

AVERAGE - DO AHEAD

ingredients:

8 oz. yolk-free noodles, cooked and drained
1 lb. fat-free ground turkey
1/4 cup egg substitute
3/4 cup fat-free bread crumbs
1 3/4 cups fat-free broth, divided
2 tsp. onion flakes
1/8 tsp. pepper
1/3 cup brown sugar
1/4 cup raisins
2 1/2 tsp. lemon juice

directions:

Cook noodles according to package directions; drain well and keep warm.

Combine turkey, egg substitute, bread crumbs, 1/4 cup beef broth, onion flakes and pepper in a medium bowl; mix well.

Shape turkey mixture into 1 1/2-inch balls. Cover and refrigerate 1-2 hours.

Pour remaining beef broth into large skillet and bring to a boil over high heat. Add brown sugar, raisins and lemon juice; mix until sugar is dissolved. Add meatballs to skillet and mix lightly with sauce; reduce heat to low, cover and simmer 20-25 minutes, until turkey is cooked through and no longer pink. Serve over cooked noodles.

Serves: 6

Nutrition per Serving		Exchanges
Calories	297	3 starch
Carbohydrate	48 grams	2 meat
Cholesterol	34 milligrams	
Dietary Fiber	3 grams	
Fat	< 1 gram	
Protein	24 grams	
Sodium	489 milligrams	

Shopping List: 8-ounce package yolk-free noodles, 1 pound fat-free ground turkey, 2 ounces egg substitute, fat-free bread crumbs, 15 ounces fat-free beef broth, brown sugar, raisins, lemon juice, onion flakes, pepper

LIPTAUER CHEESE SPREAD

EASY - DO AHEAD

ingredients: 6 oz. fat-free cream cheese, softened
1/4 cup fat-free margarine
1 tsp. paprika
1 tsp. capers
2 anchovies, chopped
1 green onion, chopped
1/2 tsp. caraway seed
1/4 tsp. salt
1/2 tsp. pepper

directions: Combine cream cheese and margarine; blend until smooth.
Add remaining ingredients and mix well. Pack into a serving dish, cover and refrigerate overnight.
Serve with your favorite crackers.

Serves: 4

Nutrition per Serving
Calories   43
Carbohydrate   3 grams
Cholesterol   0 milligrams
Dietary Fiber   < 1 gram
Fat   < 1 gram
Protein   6 grams
Sodium   500 milligrams

Exchanges
1/2 milk

Shopping List: 6 ounces fat-free cream cheese, fat-free margarine, paprika, capers, anchovies, green onion, caraway seed, salt, pepper

GERMAN

SAUERKRAUT BALLS

AVERAGE - DO AHEAD

ingredients:
2 tbsp. fat-free margarine
1 onion, chopped
1 cup fat-free ham, finely chopped
1 garlic clove, crushed
2 1/2 cups + 6 tbsp. flour, divided
2 cups sauerkraut
1 tbsp. parsley
1/2 cup fat-free chicken broth
1/4 cup fat-free egg substitute
2 cups skim milk
4 cups fat-free dry bread crumbs

directions:
Lightly spray large nonstick skillet with nonfat cooking spray; add margarine and heat over medium-low heat until melted. Add onion and cook, stirring frequently, until soft. Add ham and garlic; cook, stirring frequently, 1 minute. Stir in 6 tablespoons flour and cook over medium heat for 3 minutes. Add sauerkraut, parsley and chicken broth and cook 3 minutes until mixture becomes thick. Spread mixture onto platter and refrigerate for at least 3 hours. In a bowl, whisk together egg substitute, milk and remaining flour. Shape sauerkraut mixture into balls, dip into egg mixture and roll in bread crumbs. Lightly spray nonstick skillet with cooking spray and heat over medium-high heat. Add sauerkraut balls and cook until golden brown.

Serves: 6

Nutrition per Serving		Exchanges
Calories	102	1/2 milk
Carbohydrate	74 grams	2 1/2 starch
Cholesterol	15 grams	1 meat
Dietary Fiber	5 grams	5 vegetable
Fat	< 1 gram	
Protein	20 grams	
Sodium	1361 milligrams	

Shopping List: 1 onion, garlic clove, 16 ounces sauerkraut, fat-free ham, 4 ounces fat-free chicken broth, egg substitute, 1 pint skim milk, flour, fat-free bread crumbs, parsley, fat-free margarine

GERMAN

BAVARIAN BARLEY SOUP
(GERSTENSUPPE)
EASY - DO AHEAD

ingredients:
3/4 cup barley
2 cups shredded cabbage
1 cup sliced carrots
1 cup sliced celery
1/2 cup chopped onion
1 garlic clove, crushed
1 bay leaf
4 cups fat-free chicken broth
1 cup water
2 (14 1/2 oz.) cans stewed tomatoes
2 tbsp. mustard
1 cup fat-free croutons

directions:
Combine all ingredients, except mustard and croutons, in a large saucepan and bring to a boil over high heat; reduce heat to low. Cover and simmer 1 hour, until barley and vegetables are tender. Stir in mustard. Garnish each bowl with croutons before serving.

Serves: 6

Nutrition per Serving
Calories   178
Carbohydrate   40 grams
Cholesterol   0 milligrams
Dietary Fiber   7 grams
Fat   < 1 gram
Protein   5 grams
Sodium   1089 milligrams

Exchanges
1 starch
4 vegetable

Shopping List: barley, 8-ounce package shredded cabbage, carrots, celery, onion, garlic clove, 32 ounces fat-free chicken broth, 2 (14 1/2-ounce) cans stewed tomatoes, mustard, fat-free croutons, bay leaf

GERMAN POTATO SOUP
(KARTOFFELSUPPE)
EASY - DO AHEAD

GERMAN

ingredients: 1 onion, chopped
10 cups + 2 tbsp. fat-free chicken broth
4 cups peeled and chopped potatoes
1 cup thin yolk-free noodles

directions: Pour 2 tablespoons chicken broth into a large soup pot and heat over medium-high heat.
Add onion and sauté until onion is soft. Add remaining chicken broth and potatoes; bring to a boil over high heat.
Reduce heat to low and cook until potatoes are tender.
Add noodles and cook over medium heat until tender.

Serves: 8

Nutrition per Serving		Exchanges
Calories	108	1 1/3 starch
Carbohydrate	23 grams	
Cholesterol	5 milligrams	
Dietary Fiber	2 grams	
Fat	< 1 gram	
Protein	2 grams	
Sodium	1131 milligrams	

Shopping List: 6 (16-ounce) cans fat-free chicken broth, 4 large potatoes, 8-ounce package thin yolk-free noodles, 1 onion

HEARTY GERMAN SOUR CREAM SOUP

AVERAGE - DO AHEAD

ingredients:
4 cups + 3 tbsp. fat-free chicken broth
3/4 cup chopped cabbage
1/2 cup chopped onion
1/2 cup chopped celery
1/2 cup chopped carrots
3/4 cup chopped potatoes
3/4 cup sliced zucchini
4 cups chopped tomatoes
1/4 cup barley
1/4 cup rice
1/4 cup flour
2 cups warm water
1/2 cup vinegar
1 garlic clove, crushed
1 tsp. caraway seed
1 tsp. salt
2 tsp. Worcestershire sauce
1/4 tsp. thyme
1 cup fat-free sour cream

directions:
Pour 3 tablespoons chicken broth into large skillet; heat over medium-high heat. Add cabbage, onion, celery, carrots, potatoes and zucchini; cook until vegetables are softened. Reduce heat to low and simmer 20 minutes. Add tomatoes, remaining chicken broth, barley and rice. Simmer over low heat 2 hours. Combine flour and warm water in a small bowl and mix until blended; gradually add to soup and mix well. Add vinegar, garlic, caraway seed, salt, Worcestershire sauce and thyme to soup; cook over low heat 15 minutes. When ready to serve, garnish each bowl with sour cream.

Serves: 6

Nutrition per Serving		Exchanges
Calories	176	1 starch
Carbohydrate	36 grams	4 vegetable
Cholesterol	0 milligrams	
Dietary Fiber	4 grams	
Fat	< 1 gram	
Protein	7 grams	
Sodium	1275 milligrams	

Shopping List: cabbage, onion, celery, carrots, zucchini, 1 large potato, 4 tomatoes, garlic, 3 (16-ounce) cans fat-free chicken broth, barley, rice, flour, vinegar, Worcestershire sauce, 8 ounces fat-free sour cream, caraway seed, salt, thyme

ASPARAGUS SALAD WITH LEMON GARLIC DRESSING

EASY - DO AHEAD

ingredients:
3 tbsp. fat-free sour cream
1 1/2 tbsp. fat-free plain yogurt
1 tsp. minced garlic
1/8 tsp. lemon juice
24 whole asparagus spears, cleaned
Romaine lettuce leaves
Lemon slices (optional)

directions:
Combine sour cream, yogurt, garlic and lemon juice in a small bowl and mix until well blended. Cover and refrigerate 3-4 hours or overnight. Lightly spray large nonstick skillet with nonfat cooking spray and heat over medium-high heat. Add asparagus; pour enough water over asparagus to cover. Bring to a boil over high heat and cook until tender-crisp (about 5 minutes). Drain asparagus and rinse with cold water.
Arrange asparagus on platter; cover and refrigerate several hours or overnight. Pour dressing over asparagus and toss lightly.
Place several lettuce leaves on each plate; arrange 6 asparagus spears on each plate and serve. Garnish with lemon slices, if desired.

Serves: 4

Nutrition per Serving

Calories	36	
Carbohydrate	6 grams	
Cholesterol	0 milligrams	
Dietary Fiber	1 gram	
Fat	< 1 gram	
Protein	4 grams	
Sodium	17 milligrams	

Exchanges
1 1/2 vegetables

Shopping List: fat-free sour cream, fat-free plain yogurt, minced garlic, lemon juice, fresh asparagus spears, romaine lettuce, lemon (optional)

CUCUMBER SALAD
(GURKENSALAT)
EASY - DO AHEAD

ingredients:
3 large cucumbers, peeled and sliced
1 1/2 tsp. salt
1 1/2 cups fat-free sour cream
1/4 tsp. white pepper
1/4 cup white wine vinegar
1 tbsp. chopped green onions

directions:
Combine cucumbers and salt in a large bowl and mix well; cover and refrigerate 1 hour. Drain the juice from cucumbers and discard.
Combine sour cream, pepper, vinegar and green onions in a medium bowl and mix well.
Add cucumbers and toss until coated. Cover and refrigerate several hours before serving.

Serves: 6

Nutrition per Serving

Calories	60
Carbohydrate	9 grams
Cholesterol	0 milligrams
Dietary Fiber	2 grams
Fat	< 1 gram
Protein	5 grams
Sodium	526 milligrams

Exchanges
2 vegetable

Shopping List: 3 large cucumbers, 12 ounces fat-free sour cream, white wine vinegar, green onions, salt, white pepper

GERMAN POTATO SALAD
(KARTOFFELSALAT)
AVERAGE - DO AHEAD

ingredients:
1 1/2 lb. red potatoes, scrubbed
1/3 cup fat-free chicken broth
2 tsp. onion powder
1/3 cup cider vinegar
2 tbsp. sugar
1 bay leaf
3/4 tsp. marjoram
1/4 tsp. pepper
3/4 cup chopped celery
3 tbsp. bacon bits

directions:
Place potatoes in a large pan and cover with water; bring to a boil over high heat. Reduce heat to medium and cook, uncovered, 15-20 minutes, until potatoes are tender. Place potatoes in colander and drain well. Cool to room temperature; slice potatoes and place in a large bowl.

Combine chicken broth, onion powder, vinegar, sugar, bay leaf, marjoram, pepper and chopped celery in a medium saucepan; bring to a boil over high heat. Cook, stirring constantly, 1-2 minutes, until mixture is heated through. Remove bay leaf and discard. Sprinkle bacon bits over potatoes and toss lightly; spoon hot salad dressing over top; toss and serve.

Great served hot or at room temperature.

Serves: 6

Nutrition per Serving		Exchanges
Calories	140	1 3/4 starch
Carbohydrate	31 grams	
Cholesterol	0 milligrams	
Dietary Fiber	3 grams	
Fat	< 1 gram	
Protein	4 grams	
Sodium	145 milligrams	

Shopping List: 1 1/2 pounds red potatoes, fat-free chicken broth, celery, cider vinegar, sugar, bay leaf, marjoram, pepper, bacon bits, onion powder

RADISH SALAD
(RETTICHSALAT)
EASY - DO AHEAD

ingredients: 1 lb. radishes, thinly sliced
3 tbsp. sliced green onions
1/2 cup fat-free sour cream
1/4 tsp. white pepper
1/4 tsp. dill weed
1 1/2 cups cherry tomatoes (whole)
Lettuce leaves, chilled

directions: Combine radishes, green onions, sour cream, pepper and dill in a medium bowl and toss until mixed.
Cover and refrigerate several hours before serving.
Serve on chilled lettuce leaves with whole tomatoes.

Serves: 6

<u>**Nutrition per Serving**</u>

		<u>Exchanges</u>
Calories	38	1 1/2 vegetable
Carbohydrate	7 grams	
Cholesterol	0 milligrams	
Dietary Fiber	2 grams	
Fat	< 1 gram	
Protein	2 grams	
Sodium	129 milligrams	

Shopping List: 1 pound radishes (red or white), green onions, 4 ounces fat-free sour cream, 1 pint cherry tomatoes, lettuce leaves, white pepper, dill weed

GERMAN

BAKED CHICKEN WITH VEGETABLES

(GEBACKENES HÄNCHEN MIT GEMÜSE)
AVERAGE - DO AHEAD

GERMAN

ingredients:
3/4 cup fat-free chicken broth, divided
2 medium onions, thinly sliced
2 medium green bell peppers, thinly sliced lengthwise
1 1/2 lb. fat-free chicken breasts
1 tsp. garlic powder
1/4 tsp. ground sweet paprika
2 tomato wedges, cut into wedges
3/4 cup fat-free Swiss cheese, shredded

directions:
Lightly spray large nonstick skillet with nonfat cooking spray; add 2 tablespoons chicken broth to skillet and heat over medium-high heat.
Add onions and cook over medium heat, about 8-10 minutes, until tender. Add bell peppers and cook 5-7 minutes, until peppers are soft. Remove vegetables from skillet and set aside. Respray skillet with cooking spray; add 2 tablespoons chicken broth and heat over medium-high heat. Add chicken to skillet; sprinkle with garlic powder and paprika and cook over medium heat 5-6 minutes on each side, until lightly browned.
Preheat oven to 350 degrees. Lightly spray square baking dish with nonfat cooking spray; arrange chicken in dish. Combine remaining broth with juices in skillet and pour over chicken. Arrange onions, peppers and tomato wedges on top of chicken; sprinkle with cheese. Cover dish tightly with foil and bake in preheated oven 20-25 minutes. Remove foil and bake 5-10 minutes, until cheese is completely melted and lightly browned. Serve over cooked noodles, if desired.

Serves: 4

Nutrition per Serving		Exchanges
Calories	345	2 vegetable
Carbohydrate	11 grams	5 1/2 meat
Cholesterol	84 milligrams	
Dietary Fiber	2 grams	
Fat	< 1 gram	
Protein	44 grams	
Sodium	578 milligrams	

Shopping List:
1 1/2 pounds fat-free chicken breasts, 6 ounces fat-free chicken broth, 2 onions, 2 green bell peppers, 2 tomatoes, 3 ounces fat-free Swiss cheese, garlic powder, paprika

PAPRIKA CHICKEN
(HÄHNCHEN)
EASY - DO AHEAD

ingredients;   1 tbsp. fat-free margarine
                 1 1/2 lb. fat-free chicken breasts
                 10 3/4 oz. can reduced-fat cream of mushroom
                     soup
                 1 tbsp. paprika
                 1/8 tsp. cayenne pepper
                 3/4 cup fat-free sour cream
                 1 cup yolk-free noodles, cooked and drained

directions: Melt margarine in a large nonstick skillet over
                 medium heat; add chicken breasts and cook until
                 browned, about 10 minutes.
                 Remove chicken from skillet and drain well. Add
                 soup, paprika and cayenne pepper to skillet and
                 bring to a boil over high heat.
                 Return chicken to skillet, cover and cook over low
                 heat 5 minutes, until chicken is tender.
                 Stir in sour cream and heat through. Serve over
                 cooked noodles.

                 Serves: 6

Nutrition per Serving		Exchanges
Calories	166	3 meat
Carbohydrate	13 grams	2/3 starch
Cholesterol	42 milligrams	
Dietary Fiber	1 gram	
Fat	< 1 gram	
Protein	24 grams	
Sodium	367 milligrams	

Shopping List: 1 1/2 pounds fat-free chicken breasts, 10 3/4-ounce can
                 reduced-fat cream of mushroom soup, 6 ounces fat-free
                 sour cream, 8-ounce package yolk-free noodles, fat-free
                 margarine, paprika, cayenne pepper

SAUSAGE AND SIMMERED CABBAGE
(WURST UND WEISSKOHL)
EASY

ingredients:
1 tbsp. cornstarch
1 1/2 tbsp. cold water
21 oz. fat-free smoked sausage, cut into 1/2-inch slices
8 cups shredded cabbage mix
3/4 cup chopped onions
1 1/4 cups fat-free chicken broth
3 tbsp. white wine vinegar
1 tbsp. spicy brown mustard
1 1/2 tsp. sugar
3/4 tsp. caraway seed
1/4 tsp. pepper

directions: Combine cornstarch and water in a small cup and mix until cornstarch is completely dissolved. Lightly spray large nonstick skillet with nonfat cooking spray and heat over medium-high heat. Add sausage slices to skillet and cook until browned and cooked through. Remove sausage from skillet and set aside. Remove skillet from heat and respray with cooking spray. Add cabbage mix, onion, chicken broth, vinegar, mustard, sugar, caraway seed and pepper to skillet and bring to a boil over high heat. Reduce heat to low, cover and simmer 5-6 minutes, until cabbage is tender-crisp. Add cornstarch mixture to skillet and cook 2-3 minutes, until mixture becomes thick and bubbly. Add sausage to skillet and cook 1-2 minutes, stirring frequently, until heated through.

Serves: 6

Nutrition per Serving		Exchanges
Calories	115	3 vegetable
Carbohydrate	14 grams	1 1/2 meat
Cholesterol	40 milligrams	
Dietary Fiber	3 grams	
Fat	< 1 gram	
Protein	18 grams	
Sodium	1103 milligrams	

Shopping List: 21 ounces fat-free smoked sausage, 16-ounce package shredded cabbage mix, 8-ounce package chopped onions, 10 3/4-ounce can fat-free chicken broth, white wine vinegar, spicy brown mustard, sugar, cornstarch, caraway seed, pepper

TOMATO-CHICKEN BAKE
(GEBACKENES HÄHNCHEN MIT TOMATEN)
EASY - DO AHEAD

---

ingredients:
1/4 cup fat-free margarine
2 lb. fat-free chicken breasts
1 onion, chopped
3 garlic cloves, crushed
1/2 cup sliced mushrooms
3 tomatoes, chopped
1/2 cup chopped parsley
1 tsp. rosemary
1/4 tsp. pepper
6 ounces spaghetti, cooked and drained

directions:
Preheat oven to 350 degrees. Lightly spray 9x13-inch baking dish with nonfat cooking spray.
Melt margarine in large nonstick skillet over medium heat. Add chicken and cook until well browned on all sides. Transfer chicken to baking dish; reserve 2 tablespoons drippings from skillet and set aside. Add onion, garlic and mushrooms to skillet; cook over medium-high heat until tender. Add tomatoes, parsley, rosemary and pepper; cover and cook over low heat 5 minutes. Spoon mixture over chicken, cover with foil and bake in preheated oven 35-40 minutes, until chicken is cooked through. Cook spaghetti according to package directions and drain well.
Serve chicken over spaghetti.

Serves: 6

GERMAN

Nutrition per Serving

		Exchanges
Calories	223	1/3 starch
Carbohydrate	15 grams	2 vegetable
Cholesterol	74 milligrams	4 meat
Dietary Fiber	2 grams	
Fat	< 1 gram	
Protein	38 grams	
Sodium	366 milligrams	

Shopping List: 2 pounds fat-free chicken breasts, 1 onion, garlic cloves, sliced mushrooms, 3 tomatoes, 6 ounces spaghetti, fat-free margarine, parsley, rosemary, pepper

CREAMED SPINACH

EASY - DO AHEAD

GERMAN

ingredients: 2 (10 oz.) packages frozen chopped spinach,
cooked and drained
1 tsp. fat-free chicken broth
3/4 cup chopped onion
1 1/2 tsp. minced garlic
1 tbsp. cornstarch
1 1/2 cups evaporated skim milk
1/8 tsp. pepper
1/8 tsp. ground cloves

directions: Lightly spray large nonstick skillet with nonfat
cooking spray; add chicken broth to skillet and
heat over medium-high heat.
Add onion and garlic to skillet and cook, stirring
frequently, until soft.
Gradually stir in cornstarch, milk, pepper and
cloves.
Cook over medium heat, stirring constantly, until
mixture bubbles and becomes thick.
Stir in spinach and cook until heated through.

Serves: 6

Nutrition per Serving		Exchanges
Calories	90	1/2 milk
Carbohydrate	15 grams	2 vegetable
Cholesterol	3 milligrams	
Dietary Fiber	2 grams	
Fat	< 1 gram	
Protein	8 grams	
Sodium	158 milligrams	

Shopping List: 2 (10-ounce) packages frozen chopped spinach, 12-ounce
can evaporated skim milk, fat-free chicken broth, pack-
aged chopped onion (or 1 small onion), minced garlic,
cornstarch, pepper, ground cloves

DUMPLINGS
(SPAETZLE)
AVERAGE - DO AHEAD

ingredients:
1 cup flour
1 tsp. onion powder
1/8 tsp. pepper
1/8 tsp. salt
2 tbsp. egg substitute
1/3 cup skim milk

directions:
Fill a Dutch oven 3/4 full of water and bring to a boil over high heat. Combine flour, onion powder, pepper and salt in a medium bowl and mix well. Combine egg substitute and milk in a small bowl and mix until blended.

Gradually add egg mixture to flour mixture and mix until blended. Hold a colander with large holes over the boiling water.

Pour batter into the colander and carefully press batter (with back of spoon) through the holes until batter falls into boiling water.

Cook 5 minutes, stirring occasionally.

Remove from heat and drain well.

Great accompaniment to any German meal.

Serves: 4

GERMAN

Nutrition per Serving		Exchanges
Calories	124	1 1/2 starch
Carbohydrate	25 grams	
Cholesterol	1 milligram	
Dietary Fiber	1 gram	
Fat	< 1 gram	
Protein	4 grams	
Sodium	80 milligrams	

Shopping List: flour, skim milk, egg substitute, pepper, salt, onion powder

GERMAN RED CABBAGE
(ROTKOHLSALAT)
EASY

ingredients:

16 oz. shredded red cabbage
1 cup water
3/4 cup chopped red onion
1 cup chopped red apple
1/4 cup white wine vinegar
2 tbsp. brown sugar
4 slices fat-free turkey bacon, cooked and crumbled

directions:

Combine shredded cabbage, water, onion and apples in a medium saucepan; bring to a boil over high heat and cook 15 minutes.
Drain mixture in colander and transfer to serving bowl.
Add vinegar, brown sugar and bacon.
Toss until well mixed and serve immediately.

Serves: 4

Nutrition per Serving

Calories	104
Carbohydrate	22 grams
Cholesterol	15 milligrams
Dietary Fiber	4 grams
Fat	< 1 gram
Protein	5 grams
Sodium	154 milligrams

Exchanges
4 vegetable

Shopping List:

16-ounce package shredded red cabbage, 4-ounce package chopped onions, 1 red apple, 2 ounces white wine vinegar, brown sugar, fat-free turkey bacon

HOT SAUERKRAUT
(HEISSER SAUERKRAUT)
EASY - DO AHEAD

ingredients:
1 cup chopped onions
27 oz. can sauerkraut
1/2 tsp. celery seeds
1/8 cup cooking wine
1/8 cup water
1/2 tsp. chicken bouillon granules
2 tbsp. brown sugar
1/2 cup shredded apple

directions:
Lightly spray large pot with nonfat cooking spray and heat over medium heat.

Add onions and cook, stirring frequently, until onions are browned.

Add remaining ingredients and mix well; bring to a boil over high heat.

Reduce heat to medium-high and continue cooking until most of the liquid is absorbed.

Serves: 4

Nutrition per Serving		Exchanges
Calories	92	4 vegetable
Carbohydrate	21 grams	
Cholesterol	0 milligrams	
Dietary Fiber	6 grams	
Fat	< 1 gram	
Protein	2 grams	
Sodium	1306 milligrams	

Shopping List: 8-ounce package chopped onions, 27-ounce can sauerkraut, cooking wine, fat-free chicken bouillon granules, 1 small apple, brown sugar, celery seeds

POTATO PANCAKES
(KARTOFFELNPUFFER)
EASY - DO AHEAD - FREEZE

GERMAN

ingredients:
3 cups shredded potatoes
3 large egg whites
3/4 cup egg substitute
2 1/4 tbsp. flour
1 1/2 tbsp. onion powder
1/4 tsp. ground pepper
1 1/2 cups lite applesauce (optional)

directions:
Combine shredded potatoes with egg whites and egg substitute in a large bowl and mix well.
Add flour, onion powder and pepper; mix well.
Cover and refrigerate 30-45 minutes.
Preheat oven to 300 degrees.
Line baking sheet with foil and lightly spray with cooking spray. Lightly spray nonstick skillet with nonfat cooking spray and heat over medium-high heat. Form potato mixture into 1/4-inch-thick patties. Add patties to skillet (about 3 at a time) and cook 5-6 minutes.
Carefully flip patties and cook until both sides are browned and crisp. Remove patties and place on baking sheet. Keep warm in oven while cooking remaining patties.
Serve with applesauce, if desired.

Serves: 6

Nutrition per Serving		Exchanges
Calories	122	1 starch
Carbohydrate	25 grams	2/3 fruit
Cholesterol	0 milligrams	
Dietary Fiber	2 grams	
Fat	< 1 gram	
Protein	6 grams	
Sodium	72 milligrams	

Shopping List: frozen or refrigerated packaged shredded potatoes, large eggs, 6 ounces egg substitute, flour, onion powder, pepper, 12 ounces lite applesauce (optional)

SWEET AND SOUR RED CABBAGE

(SÜSS-SAURER ROTKOHL)
EASY

ingredients:
2 med. apples, sliced 1/4-inch thick
3/4 cup + 1 1/2 tbsp. unsweetened apple juice, divided
3 tbsp. brown sugar
6 cups shredded red cabbage
3 tbsp. cider vinegar

directions:
Lightly spray large nonstick skillet with nonfat cooking spray. Pour 1 1/2 tablespoons apple juice into skillet and heat over medium-high heat.
Add apple to skillet and cook, stirring constantly, 2-3 minutes.
Sprinkle apples with sugar and cook until sugar is dissolved. Add cabbage, vinegar and remaining apple juice.
Bring to a boil over medium-high heat. Reduce heat to medium, cover and cook 5-6 minutes.
Increase heat to medium-high, uncover, and cook, stirring frequently, 5-6 minutes, until most of liquid has evaporated. Serve warm.

Serves: 6

Nutrition per Serving		Exchanges
Calories	82	1 fruit
Carbohydrate	21 grams	1 vegetable
Cholesterol	0 milligrams	
Dietary Fiber	2 grams	
Fat	< 1 gram	
Protein	1 gram	
Sodium	28 milligrams	

Shopping List: 2 medium apples, 2 (8-ounce) packages shredded red cabbage, cider vinegar, apple juice, brown sugar

ANISE KUCHEN

AVERAGE - DO AHEAD

ingredients:
1 package yeast
1/2 cup + 2 tbsp. warm skim milk, divided
3 cups flour
2 tbsp. fat-free margarine
1/4 cup sugar
2 tsp. grated lemon peel
2 tsp. grated orange peel
1/2 tsp. salt
1/4 tsp. nutmeg
1 1/2 tbsp. anise seeds
1/2 cup egg substitute
2 tbsp. water

directions:
Lightly spray large loaf pan with nonfat cooking spray.
Dissolve yeast in warm milk in a small bowl. Combine remaining ingredients in a large bowl and mix well; add yeast mixture and knead to form soft dough. Lightly spray bowl with nonfat cooking spray; place dough in bowl and turn to coat.
Cover bowl and let dough rise until doubled, about 1 1/2 hours. Punch dough down and place in loaf pan. Let rise 1 hour, until doubled.
Preheat oven to 350 degrees. Bake 20-25 minutes, until top is lightly browned.

Serves: 8

Nutrition per Serving

Calories	214	
Carbohydrate	44 grams	
Cholesterol	< 1 milligram	
Dietary Fiber	2 grams	
Fat	< 1 gram	
Protein	7 grams	
Sodium	187 milligrams	

Exchanges
2 2/3 starch

Shopping List: 1 package yeast, skim milk, flour, egg substitute, fat-free margarine, sugar, lemon peel, orange peel, salt, nutmeg, anise seeds

GERMAN

CHERRY COMPOTE
(KIRSCHKOMPOTT)
EASY - DO AHEAD

ingredients: 3 cups frozen sour (pitted) cherries
4 cups water
1/2 cup sugar
1 whole cinnamon stick
3 whole cloves

directions: Combine all ingredients in a large saucepan and bring to a boil over medium heat.
Reduce heat to medium-low; cook 25-30 minutes.
Remove cinnamon stick and cloves from saucepan.
Spoon cherries into one-third of a medium glass and spoon compote juice over cherries.
Serve hot, or refrigerate several hours before serving.

Serves: 6

GERMAN

Nutrition per Serving		Exchanges
Calories	96	1 2/3 fruit
Carbohydrate	25 grams	
Cholesterol	0 milligrams	
Dietary Fiber	1 gram	
Fat	< 1 gram	
Protein	1 gram	
Sodium	1 milligrams	

Shopping List: 2 (10-ounce) packages frozen sour (pitted) cherries, sugar, cinnamon stick, whole cloves

GERMAN APPLE PANCAKES

AVERAGE

ingredients: 5 tbsp. reconstituted Butter Buds, divided
5 tbsp. granulated sugar, divided
4 apples, peeled, cored and sliced
1 cup flour
1/2 tsp. salt
1 cup egg substitute
1 1/2 cups skim milk
1/2 tsp. vanilla
1/4 cup powdered sugar
1 tsp. cinnamon

directions: Pour 2 tablespoons Butter Buds into a large nonstick skillet; add 3 tablespoons granulated sugar and cook, stirring constantly, until sugar is dissolved and lightly browned. Add apples and cook until browned, but not mushy. Transfer apples to a small bowl.

In a separate bowl, combine flour, remaining granulated sugar and salt; mix well. Stir in egg substitute, milk and vanilla; beat until batter is smooth. Pour remaining Butter Buds into skillet as needed; pour batter into skillet; tilt pan to spread batter evenly. Flip pancake when bottom is lightly browned. Place apples on one side of pancake and fold in half. Arrange pancake on serving platter, spoon loose apples over top. Sprinkle with powdered sugar and cinnamon; cut into 4 equal pieces.

Serves: 4

Nutrition per Serving		Exchanges
Calories	342	1 starch
Carbohydrate	72 grams	1 milk
Cholesterol	2 milligrams	3 fruit
Dietary fiber	4 grams	
Fat	< 1 gram	
Protein	12 grams	
Sodium	508 milligrams	

Shopping List: 4 apples, 8 ounces egg substitute, 12 ounces skim milk, fat-free margarine, flour, sugar, powdered sugar, vanilla, cinnamon, salt

GERMAN CHERRIES
(KIRSCH)
EASY - DO AHEAD

ingredients:
1 1/2 oz. dried cherries
2 tbsp. rum
1 lb. dried apricots, chopped fine
1 tbsp. grated lemon peel
2 tbsp. honey
1/2 cup sugar

directions:
Combine cherries and rum in a small saucepan and cook over low heat, stirring gently.
Remove from heat, cover and set aside for 15 minutes.
Combine chopped apricots, lemon peel and honey in a medium bowl and mix well.
Shape mixture into 1-inch balls, inserting plump dried cherries into the center of each.
Roll in sugar and place on wire rack to dry.

Yields: 24

Nutrition per Serving		Exchanges
Calories	73	1 1/3 fruit
Carbohydrate	19 grams	
Cholesterol	0 milligrams	
Dietary Fiber	2 grams	
Fat	< 1 gram	
Protein	1 gram	
Sodium	2 milligrams	

Shopping List: 1 1/2 ounces dried cherries, 1 pound dried apricots, rum, honey, lemon peel, sugar

GERMAN APPLE CAKE
(APFELKUCHEN)
AVERAGE - DO AHEAD - FREEZE

ingredients:
1/2 cup egg substitute
3 tbsp. Smucker's Baking Healthy
1 cup flour
1 tsp. baking powder
3/4 cup + 1 3/4 tbsp. sugar, divided
1/4 cup brown sugar
4 1/2 cups cinnamon-spice apple slices
1 tsp. cinnamon

directions:
Preheat oven to 350 degrees. Lightly spray 9-inch springform pan with nonfat cooking spray.
Combine egg substitute, Baking Healthy, flour, baking powder, 3/4 cup sugar and brown sugar in a medium bowl and mix until completely blended.
Press into springform pan with 3/4-inch edge.
Combine remaining sugar and cinnamon in a small bowl and mix well.
Arrange apples on top of dough and sprinkle with 1 tablespoon cinnamon-sugar mixture. Bake in a preheated oven 45-60 minutes, until knife inserted in center comes out clean.
Immediately sprinkle top of cake with remaining cinnamon-sugar mixture.
Cut and serve.

Serves: 8

Nutrition per Serving

		Exchanges
Calories	220	1 starch
Carbohydrate	53 grams	2 1/3 fruit
Cholesterol	0 milligrams	
Dietary Fiber	2 grams	
Fat	< 1 gram	
Protein	3 grams	
Sodium	66 milligrams	

Shopping List: 4 ounces egg substitute, Smucker's Baking Healthy, 2 (28 ounce) cans cinnamon-spice apple slices, sugar, brown sugar, flour, baking powder, cinnamon

HONEY COOKIES
(HONIGPLATZCHEN)
AVERAGE - DO AHEAD - FREEZE

ingredients:
1 cup honey
3/4 cup brown sugar
1 cup fat-free granola, finely ground
2 tbsp. lemon peel
2 tsp. lemon juice
3 cups flour
1 tsp. baking soda
1/2 tsp. nutmeg
1/4 tsp. cinnamon
1/4 tsp. ground cloves
1/2 tsp. allspice
2 tbsp. egg substitute
Sugar
6 oz. packet fat-free icing glaze (Cakemate)

directions: Pour honey into medium saucepan and bring to a boil over medium heat. Remove saucepan from heat; stir in brown sugar, granola, lemon peel and lemon juice; mix well and cool 10-15 minutes. Combine flour, baking soda, nutmeg, cinnamon, cloves and allspice in a large bowl and mix well. Stir in egg substitute and honey mixture. Using your hands, blend ingredients until a soft, sticky dough forms. Lightly spray plastic wrap with nonfat cooking spray; place dough on wrap, cover tightly and refrigerate overnight. Preheat oven to 375 degrees. Line baking sheets with foil and lightly spray with cooking spray. Form dough into 1-inch balls and arrange on cookie sheets. Using glass dipped in sugar, flatten cookies. Bake 10-12 minutes, until cookies are lightly browned. Cool completely; drizzle with vanilla glaze. Let cookies stand until glaze is dried, before serving.

Serves: 48

Nutrition per Serving		Exchanges
Calories	81	1 starch
Carbohydrate	19 grams	
Cholesterol	0 milligrams	
Dietary Fiber	< 1 gram	
Fat	< 1 gram	
Protein	1 gram	
Sodium	21 milligrams	

Shopping List: 8 ounces honey, brown sugar, sugar, fat-free granola, flour, egg substitute, lemon peel, lemon juice, baking soda, nutmeg, cinnamon, ground cloves, allspice, fat-free vanilla glaze (Cakemate)

SPICE COOKIES
(PFEFFERNUSSEKUCHLEIN)
EASY - DO AHEAD - FREEZE

ingredients:
1 cup egg substitute
1 cup sugar
1/4 cup brown sugar
3 1/2 cups flour
1 tsp. baking powder
1 1/2 tsp. cinnamon
1/4 tsp. ground cloves
1/2 cup candied orange peel, finely chopped

directions:
Preheat oven to 350 degrees.
Line baking sheets with foil and lightly spray with nonfat cooking spray.
Combine all the ingredients in a large bowl and Mix until a stiff dough forms; if necessary, add extra flour, 2 tablespoons at a time, until dough is stiff.
Roll dough into 1-inch balls and flatten on cookie sheet. Bake 10-15 minutes, until lightly browned.

Serves: 48

Nutrition per Serving

		Exchanges
Calories	55	3/4 starch
Carbohydrate	12 grams	
Cholesterol	0 milligrams	
Dietary Fiber	0 grams	
Fat	< 1 gram	
Protein	1 gram	
Sodium	14 milligrams	

Shopping List: 8 ounces egg substitute, sugar, brown sugar, flour, baking powder, cinnamon, ground cloves, candied orange peel (or other citrus peel).

GERMAN

HOT APPLE CIDER
(HEISSER APFELWEIN)
EASY

ingredients: 6 cups apple cider
6 whole cinnamon sticks
6 whole cloves
1/4 lemon, thinly sliced
Sugar, to taste

directions: Combine cider, cinnamon sticks, cloves and lemon
in a medium saucepan; bring to boil over medium
heat.
Add sugar to taste; reduce heat to medium-low
and simmer, uncovered, 10-15 minutes.
Remove cinnamon sticks, cloves and lemon before
pouring into glasses.
Serve immediately.

Serves: 6

GERMAN

Nutrition per Serving

		Exchanges
Calories	116	2 fruit
Carbohydrate	29 grams	
Cholesterol	0 milligrams	
Dietary Fiber	< 1 gram	
Protein	< 1 gram	
Sodium	7 milligrams	

Shopping List: 1 1/2 quarts apple cider, cinnamon sticks, whole cloves,
lemon, sugar

GREEK

GREEK

Influenced by history and the culture of neighboring countries, Greek food is simple, yet unique; pragmatic, yet versatile. Greek cuisine distinguishes itself from others with distinctive ingredients and the country's philosophy on sharing meals with friends and family. Mealtimes are generally informal, yet social, as most meals are served family style (everything put on the table at once). Greeks have a zest for life and a love for simple, well-seasoned foods that has developed along with the customs and traditions of the Greek people.

Common Herbs and Spices used in Greek cuisine: oregano, thyme, rosemary, basil, flat-leaf parsley, bay leaf, mint, garlic, dill and cinnamon

Common Fruits and Vegetables: tomatoes, eggplant, zucchini, carrots, onions, grapes, apricots, peaches, cherries, melons, figs, oranges and apples.

Greek food terminology:
- *bourekakia* - fila puffs made with various fillings
- *dolmades* - grapevine leaves stuffed with rice or meat
- *feta* - class white goat cheese of Greece (look for low-fat varieties or substitute dry cottage cheese, farmer's cheese or fat-free ricotta cheese)
- *gouvetsi* - Greek word for casserole or food baked in the oven
- *garides* - shrimp
- *glykismata* - desserts
- *kafes* - coffee
- *kalamata* - Greek olive
- *kourabiedes* - butter cookies topped with powdered sugar
- *mezethes* - small appetizers
- *moussaka* - layered casserole usually made with eggplant and chopped meat
- *orzo* - tiny seed-shaped pasta about the same size as rice
- *patatosalata* - potato salad
- *phyllo* - strudel dough made of flour and water
- *pilafi* - rice boiled in broth and flavored with onion and spices
- *pasri* - fish
- *rigani* - oregano
- *rizogalo* - creamy rice pudding topped with cinnamon
- *skordalia* - garlic sauce
- *souvlakia* - skewered food
- *tahini* - crushed sesame seed paste (very high fat content)
- *tsatziki* - cucumber yogurt dip

CHILI MINTED MEATBALLS

AVERAGE - DO AHEAD - FREEZE

ingredients:
1/4 cup bulgur, uncooked
3/8 cup boiling water
1/2 lb. fat-free Morningstar Farms beef crumbles
1 1/2 tsp. onion powder
1 tsp. dried parsley
1/4 tsp. dried mint leaves
1/8 tsp. pepper
1/3 cup chili sauce
1/2 cup mint apple jelly

directions:
Preheat oven to 375 degrees.

Lightly spray 10x15x1-inch jellyroll pan with non-fat cooking spray.

Place bulgur in medium bowl and cover with boiling water; let stand 15 minutes; drain bulgur. Add beef crumbles, onion powder, parsley, mint and pepper to bulgur; mix until blended. Shape mixture into meatballs and place on prepared pan. Bake in preheated oven 15-20 minutes, until lightly browned and cooked through.

In a medium saucepan, combine chili sauce and mint jelly. Cook over medium heat until mixture comes to a boil, stirring frequently. Reduce heat to medium; add meatballs to sauce and cook over medium heat 6-8 minutes, until heated through.

Serves: 4

GREEK

Nutrition per Serving

Calories	267
Carbohydrate	54 grams
Cholesterol	0 milligrams
Dietary Fiber	4 grams
Fat	< 1 gram
Protein	12 grams
Sodium	553 milligrams

Exchanges
3 1/3 starch

Shopping List: bulgur, 1/2 pound fat-free Morningstar Farms beef crumbles, onion powder, dried parsley, mint leaves, pepper, 3 ounces chili sauce, 4 ounces mint apple jelly

FETA RED PEPPER DIP

EASY - DO AHEAD

ingredients: 1 cup fat-free cream cheese, softened
7 ounces roasted red peppers, drained
1/2 tsp. dried rosemary
3 tbsp. reduced-fat feta cheese
1/8 tsp. cayenne pepper

directions: Combine all ingredients in a food processor or blender and process until smooth. Cover and refrigerate 2-3 hours before serving.
Great dip with fresh cut-up vegetables, fat-free pita chips or fat-free crackers.

Serves: 6

GREEK

Nutrition per Serving		Exchanges
Calories	46	1/2 milk
Carbohydrate	5 grams	
Cholesterol	1 milligram	
Dietary Fiber	< 1 gram	
Fat	< 1 gram	
Protein	6 grams	
Sodium	285 milligrams	

Shopping List: 8 ounces fat-free cream cheese, 7 ounces roasted red peppers, dried rosemary, reduced-fat feta cheese, cayenne pepper

SPANAKOPITA

DIFFICULT - DO AHEAD - FREEZE

ingredients:
2 cups fat-free cream cheese, softened
1/2 cup fat-free cottage cheese
1/4 cup fat-free ricotta cheese
3 tbsp. flour
1 cup chopped green onions
1 1/4 tbsp. dried parsley
1 tsp. dried dill weed
1/2 tsp. pepper
16 oz. frozen chopped spinach, thawed and
drained
5 sheets phyllo dough
3 tbsp. Butter Buds, reconstituted

directions:
Preheat oven to 375 degrees. Lightly spray a 9-10-inch pan with nonfat cooking spray.
Combine cream cheese, cottage cheese, ricotta cheese, flour, green onions, parsley, dill and pepper in a large bowl; mix until blended smooth. Fold in spinach and mix well; set aside. Unfold phyllo dough; cover it with a damp towel. Place 1 sheet of dough in prepared pan and brush lightly with Butter Buds. Layer remaining phyllo sheets in a crisscross pattern so sheets hang over sides of pan. Spoon cheese mixture into pan; fold sheets to cover completely. Brush with remaining Butter Buds. Bake in preheated oven 15-20 minutes, until lightly browned. Cut spanakopita and serve.

Serves: 8

Nutrition per Serving		Exchanges
Calories	123	1 1/2 meat
Carbohydrate	17 grams	1 starch
Cholesterol	2 milligrams	
Dietary Fiber	1 gram	
Fat	< 1 gram	
Protein	13 grams	
Sodium	534 milligrams	

Shopping List: 16 ounces fat-free cream cheese, 16-ounce package frozen chopped spinach, 4 ounces fat-free cottage cheese, 2 ounces fat-free ricotta cheese, green onions, flour, dried parsley, dried dill, pepper, Butter Buds, phyllo dough

STUFFED CUCUMBER SLICES

AVERAGE - DO AHEAD

ingredients:
3 large cucumbers
1 1/2 tbsp. reduced-fat feta cheese
1/2 cup fat-free ricotta cheese
1/4 cup fat-free cream cheese
2 tbsp. fat-free mayonnaise
2 tsp. dried parsley
2 tsp. dried dill weed
1 1/2 tbsp. chopped green olives

directions:
Peel cucumbers and cut in half lengthwise; scoop out cucumber seeds and pulp, leaving 1/2-inch shell.

Combine feta, ricotta, cream cheese and mayonnaise in a food processor or blender and process until smooth. Spoon mixture into bowl; add remaining ingredients and mix until blended. Spoon mixture into half the cucumber shells; place remaining shells on top of halves. Cover and refrigerate several hours.

Just before serving, slice cucumbers into 3/4-inch slices.

Serves: 6

GREEK

Nutrition per Serving		Exchanges
Calories	51	1 vegetable
Carbohydrate	7 grams	1/3 milk
Cholesterol	4 milligrams	
Dietary Fiber	2 grams	
Fat	< 1 gram	
Protein	5 grams	
Sodium	172 milligrams	

Shopping List: 3 large cucumbers, reduced-fat feta cheese, 2 ounces fat-free ricotta cheese, 1-ounce fat-free cream cheese, dried parsley, dried dill, green olives, 1 ounce fat-free mayonnaise

LEMON-FLAVORED GREEK SOUP

EASY - DO AHEAD

GREEK

ingredients:
4 cups fat-free chicken broth
4 cups fat-free vegetable broth
1 1/2 tbsp. cornstarch
1/3 cup fat-free rice (raw)
6 tbsp. lemon juice
1 cup egg substitute

directions:
Combine 3/4 cup chicken broth and 3/4 cup vegetable broth in a small bowl. Add cornstarch and mix until cornstarch is dissolved. Pour mixture into large soup pot. Add remaining chicken and vegetable broth; bring to a boil over high heat. Add rice to broth; reduce to low, cover and cook until rice is tender. Remove soup from heat.
Combine egg substitute and lemon juice in a medium bowl and mix until blended. Gradually add 2 cups hot broth to egg mixture and mix until blended. Pour into pot and mix well. Cook over low heat, stirring constantly, until soup becomes thick.

Serves: 6

Nutrition per Serving

		Exchanges
Calories	65	3/4 starch
Carbohydrate	12 grams	
Cholesterol	0 milligrams	
Dietary Fiber	0 grams	
Fat	< 1 gram	
Protein	4 grams	
Sodium	888 milligrams	

Shopping List: 32 ounces fat-free chicken broth, 32 ounces fat-free vegetable broth, fat-free rice, 8 ounces egg substitute, lemon juice, cornstarch

SOUPA AVGOLEMONO

EASY - DO AHEAD

---

ingredients: 8 cups fat-free chicken broth
1/2 cup rice
1/2 cup egg substitute
Juice from 2 lemons
1/2 tsp. salt

directions: Bring chicken broth to a boil in a large saucepan.
Gradually add rice, stirring constantly until broth
comes to a boil again. Reduce heat to low, cover
and simmer until rice is tender, about 12-14 minutes. Remove from heat and keep warm.
Beat egg substitute for about 2 minutes; continue
beating while gradually adding lemon juice. Slowly
add some of the hot broth to egg mixture and mix
until blended. Stir mixture into soup and cook
over low heat, without boiling, until the soup
thickens. Stir in salt.

Serves: 8

Nutrition per Serving		Exchanges
Calories	58	2/3 starch
Carbohydrate	12 grams	
Cholesterol	0 milligrams	
Dietary Fiber	< 1 gram	
Fat	< 1 gram	
Protein	2 grams	
Sodium	829 milligrams	

Shopping List: 64 ounces fat-free chicken broth, fat-free rice, egg substitute, 2 lemons, salt

GREEK PASTA SALAD

EASY - DO AHEAD

ingredients: 8 oz. fat-free pasta, cooked and drained
1/2 lb. fat-free chicken tenders, cooked and cubed
1/2 cup chopped celery
1 cup chopped red bell pepper
2 tbsp. chopped black olives
2 tbsp. reduced-fat feta cheese
3 tbsp. chopped green onions
1 cup *Greek Salad Dressing* (see recipe)

directions: Prepare pasta according to package directions; drain well. Place pasta in a large mixing bowl. Add chicken, celery, bell pepper, olives, feta cheese and green onions; mix well. Pour salad dressing over top and mix until all ingredients are well coated. Serve hot or cold.

Serves: 8

Nutrition per Serving		Exchanges
Calories	131	1/2 vegetable
Carbohydrate	21 grams	1 starch
Cholesterol	18 milligrams	1 meat
Dietary Fiber	1 gram	
Fat	< 1 gram	
Protein	9 grams	
Sodium	231 milligrams	

Shopping List: 8 ounces fat-free pasta (rotini, rotelle, or shells), 1/2 pound fat-free chicken tenders, celery, 1 red bell pepper, chopped black olives, reduced-fat feta cheese, green onions, *Greek Salad Dressing*

GREEK VEGETABLE SALAD
EASY - DO AHEAD

ingredients: 4 cups romaine lettuce, torn in bite-size pieces
2 cups iceberg lettuce, torn in bite-size pieces
1 small red onion, sliced thin
1 cup frozen pepper strips, thawed and drained
1 cup cherry tomatoes, cut in half
1 small cucumber, sliced thin
3 anchovies, chopped
3/4 tsp. dried dill weed
2 tbsp. reduced-fat feta cheese
3/4 cup fat-free salad dressing*

directions: Combine lettuce, onion, peppers, tomatoes, cucumber and anchovies in a large mixing bowl and toss to mix. Sprinkle dill and feta cheese over top and toss lightly. Pour salad dressing over top and mix well. Cover and refrigerate 1-2 hours before serving.

Serves: 6

Nutrition per Serving		Exchanges
Calories	49	2 vegetable
Carbohydrate	8 grams	
Cholesterol	3 milligrams	
Dietary Fiber	2 grams	
Fat	< 1 gram	
Protein	2 grams	
Sodium	413 milligrams	

Shopping List: romaine lettuce**, iceberg lettuce**, 1 red onion, 16-ounce package frozen pepper strips, 1/2 pint cherry tomatoes, 1 small cucumber, dried dill weed, reduced-fat feta cheese, fat-free salad dressing*, anchovies

*fat-free vinaigrette, Parmesan-onion, or *Greek Salad Dressing*
**for quick preparation, purchase packaged salad mix

MEDITERRANEAN PASTA SALAD

EASY - DO AHEAD

ingredients: 6 oz. rotini or spiral twist pasta, cooked and
drained
1 medium carrot, sliced thin
1 small zucchini, sliced thin
1 small yellow squash, sliced thin
2 tbsp. chopped olives
1 tbsp. reduced-fat feta cheese
2 tbsp. fat-free Parmesan cheese
1/2 tsp. crushed red pepper
1 cup fat-free Italian Parmesan salad dressing*

directions: Combine all ingredients except salad dressing in a
large bowl and mix well. Pour dressing over top
and toss until ingredients are well coated. Cover
and refrigerate at least 1 hour before serving.

Serves: 6

Nutrition per Serving		Exchanges
Calories	128	2 vegetable
Carbohydrate	25 grams	1 starch
Cholesterol	2 milligrams	
Dietary Fiber	1 gram	
Fat	< 1 gram	
Protein	5 grams	
Sodium	227 milligrams	

Shopping List: 6 ounces pasta (rotini, spiral, twist, or pasta of choice), 1
carrot, 1 zucchini, 1 yellow squash, 4-ounce can chopped
olives, reduced-fat feta cheese, fat-free Parmesan cheese,
8 ounces fat-free Italian salad dressing (*dressing of
choice), crushed red pepper

GREEK SALAD DRESSING

EASY - DO AHEAD

ingredients: 2 medium cucumbers
1 1/2 cups fat-free plain yogurt
3/4 cup chopped fresh mint
1/2 cup lemon juice
2 tbsp. sugar
1/4 tsp. garlic powder
1/8 tsp. black pepper

directions: Combine all ingredients in a food processor or blender and process until smooth. Cover and refrigerate several hours before serving. Store in sealed container up to one week. Great served with *Greek Pasta Salad* or mixture of greens, tomatoes, cucumbers, scallions, and a sprinkling of feta cheese.

Serves: 8

Nutrition per Serving

		Exchanges
Calories	51	2 vegetable
Carbohydrate	10 grams	
Cholesterol	1 milligram	
Dietary Fiber	1 gram	
Fat	< 1 gram	
Protein	3 grams	
Sodium	37 milligrams	

Shopping List: 2 medium cucumbers, 12 ounces fat-free plain yogurt, fresh mint, 4 ounces lemon juice, sugar, garlic powder, black pepper

GREEK SPINACH FRITTATA

AVERAGE

ingredients:
1 1/2 cups egg substitute
4 large egg whites
1/2 cup skim milk
1/2 tsp. garlic powder
1/4 tsp. pepper
2 tbsp. reduced-fat feta cheese, crumbled
1 cup chopped red onion
1 cup chopped red bell pepper
10 ounces frozen spinach leaves, thawed and drained
14 1/2 oz. diced tomatoes with roasted garlic

directions:
Combine egg substitute, egg whites, milk, garlic powder and pepper in a food processor or blender and process until blended smooth. Pour mixture into bowl and fold in cheese. Lightly spray large nonstick skillet with nonfat cooking spray and heat over medium-high heat. Add onion and bell pepper to skillet and cook, stirring frequently, until vegetables are tender. Add spinach to skillet and cook 1 minute until hot. Reduce heat to medium-low; pour egg mixture into skillet and cook, without stirring, until edges are set. Lift skillet and turn so eggs can flow to the bottom. Cover pan and cook 4 to 5 minutes, until eggs are cooked through. Spoon tomatoes into small saucepan. Cook over medium-high heat until heated through. Serve with eggs.

Serves: 6

Nutrition per Serving

		Exchanges
Calories	87	2 vegetable
Carbohydrate	11 grams	1 meat
Cholesterol	1 milligram	
Dietary Fiber	2 grams	
Fat	< 1 gram	
Protein	11 grams	
Sodium	356 milligrams	

Shopping List: 12 ounces egg substitute, large eggs, 4 ounces skim milk, 10 ounces frozen spinach leaves, 1 red onion, 1 red bell pepper, 14 1/2-ounce can diced tomatoes with roasted garlic, reduced-fat feta cheese, garlic powder, pepper

GRILLED LEMON CHICKEN TENDERS WITH ORZO AND SPINACH

AVERAGE

ingredients: 1 1/2 lb. fat-free chicken tenders
1 tbsp. lemon pepper
Butter Buds (dry)
1/4 fresh lemon juice
1 lb. cooked orzo
1/2 cup fat-free chicken broth
1 lb. fresh chopped spinach

directions: Preheat grill with medium-high heat.
Sprinkle chicken tenders with lemon pepper and
Butter Buds. Cook 1 1/2-2 minutes per side, brushing with lemon juice.
Pour chicken broth into large skillet and heat over
medium-high heat; add spinach and cook until
soft. Stir in orzo and mix lightly. Divide orzo
mixture among 6 plates and top with chicken.

Serves: 6

Nutrition per Serving		Exchanges
Calories	235	3 vegetable
Carbohydrate	32 grams	2 meat
Cholesterol	34 milligrams	1 starch
Dietary Fiber	3 grams	
Fat	< 1 gram	
Protein	25 grams	
Sodium	257 milligrams	

Shopping List: 1 1/2 pounds fat-free chicken tenders, 1/2 pound orzo
(yields 1 pound cooked), fat-free chicken broth, 1 pound
fresh chopped spinach, lemon juice, Butter Buds, lemon
pepper

LEMONY CHICKEN VEGETABLE KABOBS
EASY - DO AHEAD

ingredients: 12 ounces fat-free chicken tenders, cut in chunks
12 whole cherry tomatoes
1 medium red bell pepper, cut in 1-inch pieces
1 medium green bell pepper, cut in 1-inch pieces
1 medium onion, cut in 1-inch pieces
1/2 tsp. lemon pepper
1 tsp. dried parsley
2 tbsp. lemon juice
1/2 tsp. dried thyme
4 slices lemon, cut into 1/4-inch slices

directions: Combine all ingredients, except lemon slices, in a medium bowl and toss until well mixed. Refrigerate 15 minutes; drain and discard marinade.
Preheat broiler on high heat. Lightly spray broiler pan or foil with nonfat cooking spray. Thread lemon slice, chicken, tomato, red pepper, green pepper, onion, and another lemon slice on metal skewers. Arrange skewers on broiler pan and broil 6-8 minutes, turning once or twice, until chicken is cooked through and vegetables are golden.
Kabobs can be microwaved on wooden skewers; cook on High 7-8 minutes, turning once.

Serves: 6

Nutrition per Serving		**Exchanges**
Calories	84	1 vegetable
Carbohydrate	8 grams	2 meat
Cholesterol	35 milligrams	
Dietary Fiber	2 grams	
Fat	< 1 gram	
Protein	13 grams	
Sodium	144 milligrams	

Shopping List: 12 ounces fat-free chicken tenders, cherry tomatoes, 1 red bell pepper, 1 green bell pepper, 1 onion, dried parsley, lemon pepper, dried thyme, 1 ounce lemon juice, 1 lemon

PASTA WITH CHICKEN AND CHEESE

AVERAGE - DO AHEAD

ingredients:
1 1/2 cups orzo, cooked and drained
1 1/2 tbsp. fat-free chicken broth
1 1/2 lb. fat-free chicken tenders, cubed
1 1/2 tbsp. onion powder
1 tsp. garlic powder
2 cups fat-free pasta sauce
1 1/2 tsp. dried oregano
3/4 tsp. cumin
1/4 tsp. cinnamon
1 small yellow squash, sliced
1 small zucchini, sliced
1 1/2 tbsp. reduced-fat feta cheese, crumbled

directions: Cook orzo according to package directions; drain and keep warm. Lightly spray large nonstick skillet with nonfat cooking spray. Pour chicken broth into skillet and heat over medium-high heat. Season chicken with onion and garlic powder. Add chicken to skillet and cook, stirring constantly, 3-4 minutes, until chicken is no longer pink. Remove chicken from skillet and set aside. Combine pasta sauce, oregano, cumin, cinnamon, squash and zucchini in skillet; bring to a boil over high heat. Reduce heat to low, cover and simmer 5-6 minutes, until vegetables are tender. Add chicken to skillet; mix well and cook until heated through. Serve over cooked orzo and sprinkle with feta cheese.

Serves: 6

Nutrition per Serving		Exchanges
Calories	267	3 vegetable
Carbohydrate	30 grams	1 starch
Cholesterol	57 milligrams	3 meat
Dietary Fiber	2 grams	
Fat	< 1 gram	
Protein	33 grams	
Sodium	483 milligrams	

Shopping List: 1 1/2 pounds fat-free chicken tenders, orzo, fat-free chicken broth, 16 ounces fat-free pasta sauce, reduced-fat feta cheese, 1 small yellow squash, 1 small zucchini, onion powder, garlic powder, dried oregano, cumin, cinnamon

TURKEY POCKETS
EASY - DO AHEAD

ingredients: 1 lb. fat-free ground turkey
1 cup chopped onion, divided
1 garlic clove, chopped
1 tbsp. dried parsley
1 tbsp. dried oregano
8 fat-free pita pockets
1 cup chopped tomatoes
1 cup sliced cucumber
2 ounces reduced-fat feta cheese

directions: Lightly spray large nonstick skillet with nonfat cooking spray and heat over medium-high heat. Add turkey, 1/2 cup onions and garlic to skillet; cook until turkey is lightly browned, about 5-6 minutes. Stir in parsley and oregano; cook 1-2 minutes. Trim 1/2-inch off the top of pita pockets. Spoon turkey mixture into pockets and top with remaining onion, tomato, cucumber and feta cheese.

Serves: 8

GREEK

Nutrition per Serving		Exchanges
Calories	174	1 meat
Carbohydrate	27 grams	2 vegetable
Cholesterol	20 milligrams	1 starch
Dietary Fiber	1 gram	
Fat	< 1 gram	
Protein	13 grams	
Sodium	893 milligrams	

Shopping List: 1 pound fat-free ground turkey, 1 onion, garlic, fat-free pita pockets, 1 tomato, 1 cucumber, reduced-fat feta cheese, dried parsley, oregano

COLORFUL COUSCOUS

EASY

ingredients: 2 cups fat-free chicken broth
1 1/2 cups papaya nectar
2 cups couscous
1 tbsp. chopped green onions
1/2 tsp. allspice
1/2 tsp. ginger
1/4 tsp. crushed red pepper
2 tbsp. lime juice
1 1/2 cups corn kernels, drained
1 1/2 cups fat-free black beans, rinsed and drained
1/4 cup chopped green chilies
Fresh cilantro sprigs

directions: Combine chicken broth and nectar in a large saucepan; bring to a boil over high heat. Remove from heat and stir in all ingredients except cilantro sprigs. Cover and let stand 10 minutes. Fluff with a fork before serving, and garnish with cilantro sprigs.

Serves: 6

Nutrition per Serving		Exchanges
Calories	362	4 starch
Carbohydrate	76 grams	2/3 fruit
Cholesterol	0 milligrams	
Dietary Fiber	13 grams	
Fat	< 1 gram	
Protein	13 grams	
Sodium	229 milligrams	

Shopping List: couscous, 16 ounces fat-free chicken broth, 12 ounces papaya nectar, 14-ounce can corn kernels, 14-ounce can black beans, 4-ounce can chopped green chilies, green onion, lime juice, allspice, ginger, crushed red pepper, fresh cilantro sprigs

GREEK-STYLE ORZO

EASY

ingredients: 28 oz. can crushed tomatoes
1 1/2 tsp. onion powder
1/2 tsp. garlic powder
1 tsp. dried oregano
1/2 tsp. dried sage
1/2 tsp. pepper
1/4 tsp. red pepper flakes
1 tsp. capers
1 cup cooked orzo
2 tsp. reduced-fat feta cheese

directions: Lightly spray large nonstick skillet with nonfat cooking spray and heat over medium heat. Add crushed tomatoes, onion powder, garlic powder, oregano, sage, pepper, pepper flakes and capers to skillet and cook, stirring frequently, 12-15 minutes, until most of liquid from tomatoes is evaporated. Cook orzo according to package directions; drain and add to skillet. Stir in cheese and cook 1-2 minutes, until cheese begins to melt.

Serves: 4

Nutrition per Serving		Exchanges
Calories	83	2 vegetable
Carbohydrate	17 grams	1/2 starch
Cholesterol	1 milligram	
Dietary Fiber	3 grams	
Fat	< 1 gram	
Protein	3 grams	
Sodium	213 milligrams	

Shopping List: 28-ounce can crushed tomatoes, orzo, reduced-fat feta cheese, capers, onion powder, garlic powder, dried oregano, dried sage, pepper, red pepper flakes

GREEK

FRIED EGGPLANT

EASY - DO AHEAD

ingredients: 1 lb. eggplant, pared and cut into strips
1/2 cup egg substitute
1 1/2 cups fat-free bread crumbs
1 tsp. garlic powder

directions: Pare eggplant and cut into strips.
Combine bread crumbs and garlic powder in a shallow dish.
Lightly spray large nonstick skillet with nonfat cooking spray and heat over medium-high heat.
Dip eggplant in egg substitute and roll in bread crumbs until coated. Cook over medium-high heat, turning frequently, until browned and crisp.

Serves: 6

GREEK

Nutrition per Serving		Exchanges
Calories	49	2 vegetable
Carbohydrate	10 grams	
Cholesterol	0 milligrams	
Dietary Fiber	< 1 gram	
Fat	< 1 gram	
Protein	2 grams	
Sodium	60 milligrams	

Shopping List: 1 pound eggplant, 4 ounces egg substitute, fat-free bread crumbs, garlic powder

LEMON SKILLET RICE

EASY - DO AHEAD

ingredients: 2 tbsp. fat-free margarine
1 cup fat-free rice
2 cups water
1 tsp. lemon juice

directions: Melt margarine in nonstick skillet over medium heat; add rice and cook, stirring frequently, about 2 minutes. Add water and lemon juice; cover and cook over low heat 15 minutes.

Serves: 4

Nutrition per Serving		Exchanges
Calories	172	2 1/4 starch
Carbohydrate	37 grams	
Cholesterol	0 milligrams	
Dietary Fiber	< 1 gram	
Fat	< 1 gram	
Protein	3 grams	
Sodium	47 milligrams	

Shopping List: fat-free rice, fat-free margarine, lemon juice

PEPPERS WITH FETA RICE

AVERAGE - DO AHEAD

ingredients:
6 medium red bell peppers
3 cups fat-free cooked rice
2 tbsp. reduced-fat feta cheese, crumbled
1 tbsp. chopped green olives
3/4 cup chopped green onions
1/3 cup fat-free chicken broth
3/4 tsp. cumin
1/4 tsp. saffron
1/8 tsp. pepper

directions:
Remove stems, seeds and membranes from peppers.
Fill a large saucepan 3/4-full with water and bring to a boil over high heat. Drop peppers into water and cook 2 minutes, until tender; remove and rinse with cold water.
Preheat oven to 400 degrees.
Lightly spray large 6-cup muffin tin with nonfat cooking spray. Place 1 pepper in each cup.
Combine remaining ingredients in a medium bowl and mix until blended. Fill peppers with rice mixture. Bake in preheated oven 10-15 minutes. Turn broiler on high heat. Broil peppers 3-4 minutes, until browned.

Serves: 6

Nutrition per Serving

Calories	124	
Carbohydrate	28 grams	
Cholesterol	1 milligram	
Dietary Fiber	1 gram	
Fat	< 1 gram	
Protein	3 grams	
Sodium	65 milligrams	

Exchanges
2 vegetable
1 starch

Shopping List: 6 medium red bell peppers, fat-free rice, reduced-fat feta cheese, green olives, green onions, fat-free chicken broth, cumin, saffron, pepper

SPINACH PIE
AVERAGE - DO AHEAD - FREEZE

ingredients:
10 oz. fat-free frozen bread dough, thawed
3/4 cup fat-free cottage cheese
1/2 cup fat-free ricotta cheese
2 tbsp. reduced-fat feta cheese, crumbled
2 tsp. onion powder
3/4 tsp. garlic powder
1/2 tsp. dried basil
3/4 cup evaporated skim milk
4 large egg whites
1/2 cup egg substitute
2 (10 oz.) pkg. frozen chopped spinach, thawed
and drained

directions:
Preheat oven to 350 degrees. Lightly spray a 9-inch pie plate with nonfat cooking spray.
Roll dough on lightly-floured surface until flattened to 12-inch circle. Press the dough into pie plate and trim edges. Combine cottage cheese, ricotta cheese, feta cheese, onion powder, garlic powder and basil in a food processor or blender and process just until smooth. Add milk, egg whites and egg substitute to cheese mixture and pulse several times until blended. Pour mixture into large bowl; fold in spinach and mix well. Spoon filling into pie plate and bake in preheated oven 45 minutes to 1 hour, until knife inserted in the center comes out clean and crust is lightly browned. Let pie stand at room temperature for 10-15 minutes before serving.

Serves: 6

Nutrition per Serving		Exchanges
Calories	229	1 vegetable
Carbohydrate	38 grams	1 milk
Cholesterol	6 milligrams	1 1/2 starch
Dietary Fiber	4 grams	
Fat	< 1 gram	
Protein	18 grams	
Sodium	472 milligrams	

Shopping List:
10-ounce package fat-free frozen bread dough, 2 (10-ounce) packages frozen chopped spinach, 6 ounces fat-free cottage cheese, 4 ounces fat-free ricotta cheese, reduced-fat feta cheese, 6 ounces evaporated skim milk, large eggs, 4 ounces egg substitute, onion powder, garlic powder, dried basil

GINGERED FIGS

EASY - DO AHEAD

ingredients: 20 figs
      3 cups cold water
      1 tbsp. molasses
      2 tsp. ginger
      1/2 cup sugar

directions: Combine figs and water in a medium saucepan
      and bring to a boil over high heat. Reduce heat to
      low, cover and cook 20 minutes. Carefully stir in
      remaining ingredients and simmer over low heat
      15 minutes, until figs are plump and tender.

      Serves: 6

GREEK

Nutrition per Serving		Exchanges
Calories	194	3 1/3 fruit
Carbohydrate	51 grams	
Cholesterol	0 milligrams	
Dietary Fiber	11 grams	
Fat	< 1 gram	
Protein	1 gram	
Sodium	2 milligrams	

Shopping List: 20 figs, molasses, sugar, ginger

PINEAPPLE AND FIG TARTS

AVERAGE - DO AHEAD

ingredients:
4 oz. figs, finely chopped
8 1/4 oz. can pineapple chunks in juice
1/2 cup water
1/2 tsp. grated orange peel
4 large sheets phyllo dough
3 tbsp. fat-free margarine, melted
2 tsp. sugar

directions:
Combine figs, pineapple (with juice), water and orange peel in a large saucepan; bring to a boil over high heat. Reduce heat to low and simmer 5-10 minutes, until thickened.

Separate phyllo sheets; brush each sheet with margarine and sprinkle with sugar. Cut into 3-inch squares.

Preheat oven to 350 degrees.

Lightly spray muffin tin with nonfat cooking spray. Arrange phyllo sheets in cups (overlapping as needed), to completely cover bottom and sides of cups. Divide fruit mixture and spoon into phyllo cups. Bake in preheated oven, 12-15 minutes, until golden brown. Cool completely before removing from pan.

Serves: 4

Nutrition per Serving		Exchanges
Calories	80	1 1/3 fruit
Carbohydrate	17 grams	
Cholesterol	0 milligrams	
Dietary Fiber	2 grams	
Fat	< 1 gram	
Protein	1 gram	
Sodium	107 milligrams	

Shopping List:
4 ounces figs, 8 1/4-ounce can pineapple chunks in juice, phyllo dough, orange peel, fat-free margarine, sugar

GREEK TEA

EASY

---

ingredients: 6 tsp. dried mint leaves
6 cups water

directions: Pour water into large saucepan. Add dried mint; bring to a boil over high heat. Strain mint and serve.

Serves: 6

<u>**Nutrition per Serving**</u>
Calories	2
Carbohydrate	< 1 gram
Cholesterol	0 milligrams
Dietary Fiber	0 grams
Fat	< 1 gram
Protein	< 1 gram
Sodium	5 milligrams

<u>**Exchanges**</u>
Free

GREEK

Shopping List: dried mint leaves

INDIAN

INDIAN

Indian cooking stimulates the senses with the aroma of spices, herbs, onions, garlic and chilies used to enhance the flavor of traditional fare. The **7 Golden Rules for** (delicious and healthy) **Indian cuisine** define the art of Indian cooking.

1. Use whole grains and flours whenever possible. Balance the menu by serving a refined grain dish with a hearty entrée.
2. Limit the use of oil and other cooking fats by substituting fat-free broth, juice or wine.
3. Use fresh, seasonal produce whenever possible.
4. Get to know your **Indian spices** (garam masala, cumin, cinnamon, cloves, chili powder, cayenne pepper, black pepper, saffron, tamarind, nutmeg, ace, fennel, anise, pomegrante seeds, mango powder, cardamom, turmeric, fresh ginger, yogurt and mustard seeds) and **herbs** (scallions, green garlic, curry leaves, cilantro, ginger, and fresh chilies). Use spices and herbs to enhance (not mask) the flavor of Indian cuisine. Leave the salt and pepper shakers off the table and spice it up the Indian way!
5. Sweets for treats? Sweets, representing prosperity and good fortune, are generally reserved for Indian holidays and guests.
6. For authentic Indian fare, include a bread (or rice), vegetable, **dal** (peas, bean and lentils) and **chutney** served on the traditional **thali** (round metal plate with small **katories**, cups or bowls). The ritual of eating together is a sacred tradition in Indian households and at least one meal each day is shared with the entire family.
7. Always serve your Indian meal with water!

Most popular Indian ingredients include:
*   *Basmati Rice* — authentic, long-grain Indian rice served plain (boiled, steamed or fried), or with vegetables and fruits. Rice is a staple food in India and is included in at least one meal each day. Offering rice during religious holidays is a symbol of prosperity.
*   *Buttermilk* and *Yogurt* — select low-fat and fat-free varieties for making sauces and thickening curries.
*   *Cardamom (ilaichi)* — the #1 spice in Indian cuisine.
*   *Cayenne (mirchi)* — the main heating ingredient in Indian food, cayenne is obtained from dry, hot chilies, so use with care!

- *Chutney* — fresh relishes made from fruits, vegetables and herbs. Essential parts of any Indian meal, a few teaspoons of chutney are placed at the edge of the plate to complement the meal.
- *Cinnamon (taj)* — used in stick form, whole or ground.
- *Dal* — includes peas, beans and lentils, dal may be cooked whole, puréed or ground (used in unleavened breads, crackers and spice mixtures). Dal-based dishes contribute a significant amount of protein to the traditional Indian meal.
- *Flatbread* — unleavened bread (resembles thick tortillas)
- *Garam Masala* — a sweet spice mix made from cardamom, cinnamon and cloves that is roasted and then ground into powder or granules.
- *Masala* — spice mixture.
- *Nimu* or *Limnu* — lemon or lime fruits are served as fresh spices with every Indian meal.
- *Nuts* — commonly used in Indian cooking but not recommended for low-fat cooking. Nuts are densely packed with calories and fat; substitute low-fat crunchy cereals or nut flavorings.
- *Pulau* — Indian version of pilaf
- *Rai* — black or brown mustard seeds essential for authentic Indian cooking.
- *Raita*
- *Sultana* — golden raisins used in Indian cooking.
- *Tamarind (imli)* — the pulp of the tamarind fruit is used in chutneys, sauces and marinades.
- *Whole Grains* — millet, bulgur, rye, kasha (buckwheat), quinoa
- Most common *Vegetables* — cabbage (red or green), eggplant, cauliflower, green beans, carrots, peas, mustard greens, okra, spinach, squash, potatoes, tomatoes and bell peppers.

Equip your kitchen for Indian cooking:
- **spice grinder** or mortar and pestle for crushing seeds, herbs and dry spices
- **kadhai** — any shallow pot similar to a wok or frying pan
- **tava** — roasting pan
- **velan** — rolling pin
- **patli** — bread rolling board
- **jara** — slotted spoon

CURRY CHICKPEA (CHANA DAL) DIP

EASY - DO AHEAD

ingredients:
3/4 cup canned chickpeas (*chana dal*), drained
1/2 cup fat-free ricotta cheese
1/4 cup fat-free yogurt
1/4 cup fat-free sour cream
3/4 tsp. garlic (*lasan*) powder
1 tsp. onion powder
2 tsp. curry powder
1/4 tsp. Worcestershire sauce
1/2 tsp. sugar
1/4 tsp. cayenne pepper (*mirchi*)
3/4 cup frozen chopped spinach, thawed and drained

directions:
Combine all ingredients except spinach in a food processor or blender, and process until smooth. Spoon mixture into medium bowl; fold in spinach and mix well.
Cover and refrigerate several hours before serving.
Serve with fresh cut-up vegetables, pita crisps or fat-free crackers.

Serves: 6

INDIAN

Nutrition per Serving

Calories	56
Carbohydrate	9 grams
Cholesterol	< 1 gram
Dietary Fiber	2 grams
Fat	< 1 gram
Protein	4 grams
Sodium	165 milligrams

Exchanges
2 vegetable

Shopping List: 8-ounce can chickpeas, 4 ounces fat-free ricotta cheese, 2 ounces fat-free yogurt, 2 ounces fat-free sour cream, 10 ounces frozen chopped spinach, garlic powder, onion powder, curry powder, Worcestershire sauce, sugar, cayenne pepper

PITA CHIP SNACKS
(FARASAN)
EASY - DO AHEAD

ingredients: 6 whole fat-free pita breads, split through center
3/4 cup fat-free Italian salad dressing
1 tbsp. garlic (*lasan*) powder
3/4 cup fat-free Parmesan cheese (optional)

directions: Preheat oven to 350 degrees.
Line baking sheets with foil and lightly spray with nonfat cooking spray. Combine salad dressing and garlic powder in a sealed container and shake until blended.
Cut pita breads in half through the center (keeping circles whole); generously brush pita circles with salad dressing.
Cut pitas into 4-6 wedges and arrange in a single layer on baking sheets. Sprinkle with Parmesan cheese, if desired.
Bake in preheated oven 12-15 minutes, until golden brown and crisp.
Serve with *Curry Chickpea Dip*.

Serves: 6

Nutrition per Serving

Calories	160	
Carbohydrate	30 grams	
Cholesterol	0 milligrams	
Dietary Fiber	1 gram	
Fat	< 1 gram	
Protein	8 grams	
Sodium	425 milligrams	

Exchanges
2 starch

Shopping List: Fat-free pita breads (or pockets), 6 ounces fat-free Italian salad dressing, 3 ounces fat-free Parmesan cheese (optional), garlic powder

INDIAN

GINGER BROCCOLI SOUP
EASY - DO AHEAD

ingredients: 3 3/4 cups + 1 tbsp. fat-free chicken broth, divided
1 medium onion, finely sliced
3 3/4 cups fat-free chicken broth
2 1/2 cups water
1-inch piece of ginger, grated
1/2 tsp. cayenne pepper
Juice of 1 lemon
3/4 lb. fresh broccoli, cut into bite-size pieces

directions: Pour 1 tablespoon chicken broth into saucepan and heat over medium-high heat; add onion and cook, stirring frequently, until onions begin to brown.
In a separate saucepan, combine remaining chicken broth, water and ginger; cook over medium-high heat, but do not boil.
Add cooked onions, cayenne pepper, lemon juice and broccoli.
Cook over medium heat, stirring occasionally, 7 minutes, until broccoli is tender-crisp. Serve immediately.

Serves: 4

Nutritional per Serving

		Exchanges
Calories	51	2 vegetable
Carbohydrate	10 grams	1 starch
Cholesterol	0 milligrams	
Dietary Fiber	1 gram	
Fat	< 1 gram	
Protein	3 grams	
Sodium	722 milligrams	

Shopping List: 1 onion, 3/4 pound fresh broccoli, 1 lemon, 32 ounces fat-free chicken broth, ginger, cayenne pepper

INDIAN

INDIAN GAZPACHO

EASY - DO AHEAD

ingredients:
6 large tomatoes, blanched, skinned and chopped
1 large red onion, chopped
1 large green or red bell pepper, chopped
2 bunches radishes, chopped
3 large carrots, chopped
3 large celery ribs, chopped
2 medium cucumbers, unpeeled and chopped
2 hot green chilies, seeded and chopped
6 large garlic cloves, peeled and chopped
1/2 cup tomato paste
6 1/4 cups fat-free chicken broth
1 2/4 cups dry red wine
Salt

directions:
Combine all ingredients in a large bowl and mix well.

Process mixture in food processor or blender in several batches, blending until no chunks remain, but soup is still thick. Add salt to taste; refrigerate several hours before serving.

Serves: 6

Nutrition per Serving

Calories	162	
Carbohydrate	26 grams	
Cholesterol	0 milligrams	
Dietary Fiber	7 grams	
Fat	< 1 gram	
Protein	4 grams	
Sodium	1133 milligrams	

Exchanges
6 vegetable

Shopping List:
6 large tomatoes, 1 large red onion, 1 green or red bell pepper, 2 bunches radishes, 3 large carrots, 3 large celery ribs, 3 medium cucumbers, 2 hot green chilies, 6 large garlic cloves, tomato paste, 4 (16-ounce) cans fat-free chicken broth, red wine, salt

INDIAN

INDIAN-STYLE CHICKEN SOUP

EASY - DO AHEAD -FREEZE

ingredients: 1 1/2 lb. fat-free chicken tenders, cut into
1-inch pieces
1 tbsp. minced garlic
1 tbsp. minced ginger
1/4 tsp. ground turmeric
1 cup chopped onions
3/4 cup chopped celery
3/4 cup chopped carrots
2 whole cloves
2 cinnamon sticks
3/4 tsp. pepper
3 cups fat-free chicken broth
3 cups water

directions: Combine all ingredients in a large soup pot or
Dutch oven and bring to a boil over high heat.
Reduce heat to medium-low, cover and cook 45-60
minutes. Discard cinnamon sticks and cloves before serving.

Serves: 6

INDIAN

Nutrition per Serving		Exchanges
Calories	128	1 vegetable
Carbohydrate	6 grams	3 meat
Cholesterol	71 milligrams	
Dietary Fiber	1 gram	
Fat	< 1 gram	
Protein	24 grams	
Sodium	518 milligrams	

Shopping List: 1 1/2 pounds fat-free chicken tenders, 24 ounces fat-free
chicken broth, chopped onions, celery, 2 carrots, minced
garlic, minced ginger, ground turmeric, whole cloves,
cinnamon sticks, pepper

RED LENTIL (MASOOR DAL) SOUP

EASY - DO AHEAD - FREEZE

ingredients:
1 1/4 cups red lentils (*masoor dal*)
Cold water (to soak lentils)
3 cups + 1 tbsp. fat-free chicken broth, divided*
1 cup chopped onions (*kanda*)
3/4 cup chopped celery
28 oz. can crushed tomatoes
1 cup diced carrots
3/4 tsp. garlic (*lasan*) powder
1/4 tsp. ground turmeric (*haldi*)
1 tsp. sugar
1/2 tsp. pepper (*kala mirch*)
3 cups water

directions: Wash lentils in cold water and drain well. Lightly spray large saucepan with nonfat cooking spray; pour 1 tablespoon chicken broth into pan and heat over medium-high heat. Add onions and celery and cook, stirring frequently, 1-2 minutes, until soft. Add tomatoes, carrots, garlic, turmeric, sugar and pepper and mix well. Cook over medium-high heat, stirring frequently, 4-5 minutes, until carrots soften. Pour remaining chicken broth, water and lentils into pan; bring to a boil over high heat. Reduce heat to low, cover, and simmer 40-45 minutes until lentils are soft. Mix lightly before serving.

*substitute fat-free vegetable broth, if desired.

Serves: 6

Nutrition per Serving		Exchanges
Calories	165	1 starch
Carbohydrate	31 grams	3 vegetable
Cholesterol	0 milligrams	
Dietary Fiber	7 grams	
Fat	< 1 gram	
Protein	11 grams	
Sodium	765 milligrams	

Shopping List: red lentils, 26 ounces fat-free or vegetable broth, 1 large onion, celery, 28-ounce can crushed tomatoes, 2 small carrots, garlic powder, ground turmeric, sugar, pepper

SPICY PUMPKIN SOUP

EASY - DO AHEAD

ingredients: 3 cups canned pumpkin
1 tbsp. onion powder
1 1/2 tbsp. ground coriander (*dhania*), divided
3/4 tsp. ground cumin (*jeera*)
3/4 tsp. turmeric (*haldi*)
1/4 cup brown sugar
1/4 cup tomato paste
1/4 tsp. pepper (*kala mirch*)
4 1/2 cups water

directions: Combine all ingredients in a large soup pot and
mix well; bring to a boil over high heat.
Reduce heat to low, cover and simmer 45-60 minutes.

Serves: 6

Nutrition per Serving		Exchanges
Calories	92	1 1/2 fruit
Carbohydrate	22 grams	
Cholesterol	0 milligrams	
Dietary Fiber	3 grams	
Fat	< 1 gram	
Protein	2 grams	
Sodium	18 milligrams	

Shopping List: 24 ounces canned mashed pumpkin, 2 ounces tomato
paste, onion powder, coriander, ground cumin, turmeric, brown sugar, pepper

SPINACH AND LENTIL (MASOOR DAL) SOUP

EASY - DO AHEAD

ingredients:
1 1/2 cups red lentils (*masoor dal*)
8 cups water
1 tbsp. onion powder
2 tsp. garlic (*lasan*) powder
20 oz. frozen chopped spinach, thawed and drained
2 tbsp. dried parsley
1/4 tsp. pepper (*kala mirch*)
1/8 tsp. crushed red pepper
1/4 cup lemon (*nimu*) juice

directions:
Combine lentils, water, onion powder and garlic powder in a large soup pot and bring to a boil over high heat.
Reduce heat to medium-low, cover and simmer 45-60 minutes.
Add spinach, parsley, pepper and red pepper and mix well; cook over medium heat 10-15 minutes.
Add lemon juice just before serving.

Serves: 6

INDIAN

Nutrition per Serving		Exchanges
Calories	152	1 starch
Carbohydrate	28 grams	3 vegetable
Cholesterol	0 milligrams	
Dietary Fiber	7 grams	
Fat	< 1 gram	
Protein	12 grams	
Sodium	85 milligrams	

Shopping List:
Red lentils, 20 ounces frozen chopped spinach, onion powder, garlic powder, dried parsley, pepper, crushed red pepper, 2 ounces lemon juice

CURRIED CHICKEN POTATO SALAD
(BATATA KACHUMBER)
AVERAGE - DO AHEAD

---

ingredients:
2 cups red potatoes (*batata*),quartered
1 large red pepper, quartered
1 large red onion (*kanda*), quartered
1 tsp. onion powder
1/2 tsp. garlic powder
1/2 cup fat-free yogurt
1/2 cup fat-free sour cream
2 tbsp. fat-free mayonnaise
2 tbsp. rice vinegar
2 tbsp. peach preserves
1 1/4 tsp. curry powder
3 cups fat-free chicken tenders, cooked and cubed
8 cups lettuce leaves, washed and torn

directions: Preheat oven to 400 degrees. Lightly spray baking sheet with nonfat cooking spray. Arrange potatoes, red pepper and onions in a single layer. Lightly spray vegetables with nonfat cooking spray and sprinkle with onion and garlic powders. Bake in preheated oven 30-40 minutes, until vegetables are tender and lightly browned. Combine yogurt, sour cream, mayonnaise, vinegar, preserves and curry powder in blender or food processor and process until blended smooth and creamy. Combine potatoes, chicken, pepper, onion and lettuce in a large bowl and toss until mixed. Pour yogurt dressing over salad and mix lightly until coated. Serve immediately.

Serves: 6

	Exchanges	
Calories	223	1 starch
Carbohydrate	23 grams	2 vegetable
Cholesterol	55 milligrams	3 meat
Dietary Fiber	2 grams	
Fat	< 1 gram	
Protein	31 grams	
Sodium	294 milligrams	

Shopping List: 1 1/2 pounds fat-free chicken tenders, 1 pound red potatoes, 1 red onion, 1 red pepper, 2 pounds lettuce (or prepackaged lettuce leaves equivalent to 8 cups), 4 ounces fat-free yogurt, 4 ounces fat-free sour cream, fat-free mayonnaise, rice vinegar, peach preserves, onion powder, garlic powder, curry powder

INDIAN

189

CURRY CHICKEN SALAD
(KACHUMBER)
EASY - DO AHEAD

INDIAN

ingredients:
1 1/2 lb. fat-free chicken tenders
1 tbsp. onion powder
3/4 tsp. pepper (*kala mirch*), divided
1/4 cup fat-free mayonnaise
3/4 cup fat-free yogurt
2 tsp. curry powder
1 1/2 cups pineapple tidbits in juice, drained
1 cup frozen pepper strips, thawed and drained
3/4 cup raisins
3/4 cup green seedless grapes
2 1/4 cups fat-free cooked rice ·

directions: Preheat oven to 350 degrees. Line baking sheet(s) with foil and lightly spray with nonfat cooking spray. Arrange chicken tenders on baking sheet; sprinkle with onion powder and 1/2 teaspoon pepper. Bake in preheated oven 5-6 minutes, turn chicken over and cook 3-4 minutes, until no longer pink and cooked through. Remove from oven and set aside; cut into bite-size pieces when cooled. Combine mayonnaise, yogurt, curry powder and 1/4 teaspoon pepper in a food processor or blender and process until smooth. Spoon salad dressing into large bowl; add pineapple and mix well. Add peppers, raisins, grapes, rice and cooked chicken to dressing and toss until well coated. Cover and refrigerate several hours before serving.

Serves: 6

Nutrition per Serving		Exchanges
Calories	319	1 starch
Carbohydrate	50 grams	2 vegetable
Cholesterol	56 milligrams	1 2/3 fruit
Dietary Fiber	2 grams	3 meat
Fat	< 1 gram	
Protein	31 grams	
Sodium	319 milligrams	

Shopping List: 1 1/2 pounds fat-free chicken tenders, 2 ounces fat-free mayonnaise, 6 ounces fat-free yogurt, 15 ounces pineapple tidbits in juice, 12 ounces frozen pepper strips, raisins, green seedless grapes, fat-free rice, onion powder, pepper, curry powder

INDIAN SALAD WITH CITRUS DRESSING

EASY - DO AHEAD

ingredients:
1 large onion, cut into round slices
2 cups tomatoes with green chilies, drained
1/2 cup cucumber, cut into thin rounds
1 cup carrots, cut into thin rounds
1 cup radishes, thinly sliced
1 cup frozen pepper strips, thawed and drained
1/2 cup chopped cilantro
1/8 tsp. ground cumin
3 cups mixed salad greens, washed and cut
1/2 cup lemon juice

directions:
Combine all ingredients except lemon juice in a large bowl and mix well.
Sprinkle with lemon juice and toss until mixed.
Refrigerate several hours before serving.

Serves: 4

INDIAN

Nutrition per Serving

		Exchanges
Calories	88	3 1/2 vegetable
Carbohydrate	20 grams	
Cholesterol	0 milligrams	
Dietary Fiber	5 grams	
Fat	< 1 gram	
Protein	3 grams	
Sodium	219 milligrams	

Shopping List: 2 packages mixed salad greens, 1 large onion, 15-ounce can tomatoes with green chilies, 1 cucumber, 2 carrots, radishes, 10-ounce package frozen pepper strips, fresh cilantro, ground cumin, lemon juice

TOMATO AND ONION SALAD

(KACHUMBER)
EASY - DO AHEAD

---

ingredients: 1 1/2 cups diced tomatoes, drained
1 1/2 cups onions, cut into round slices
1 tbsp. chopped green chilies
1/8 tsp. ground cumin
1/4 cup chopped cilantro
2 tbsp. white wine vinegar

directions: Combine all ingredients in a medium bowl and mix well.
Toss and serve.

Serves: 4

Nutrition per Serving		Exchanges
Calories	218	2 vegetable
Carbohydrate	10 grams	
Cholesterol	0 milligrams	
Dietary Fiber	2 grams	
Fat	< 1 gram	
Protein	2 grams	
Sodium	176 milligrams	

Shopping List: 14 1/2-ounce can diced tomatoes, 2 medium onions, 4-ounce can chopped green chilies, chili powder, ground cumin, cilantro, white wine vinegar

APRICOT CHICKEN AND COUSCOUS

AVERAGE

ingredients:
4 cups cooked couscous
1 lb. fat-free chicken tenders
1 tbsp. onion (*kada*) powder
1 1/2 tsp. garlic (*lasan*) powder
1 1/2 tbsp. curry powder
1 tbsp. fat-free chicken broth
3 tbsp. cornstarch
1 cup fat-free sour cream
1 cup fat-free yogurt
1/3 cup apricot preserves
1/2 cup golden raisins
1/2 cup water

directions:
Cook couscous according to package directions; cover and keep warm. Generously season chicken tenders with onion powder, garlic powder and curry. Lightly spray large nonstick skillet with nonfat cooking spray; pour chicken broth into skillet and heat over medium heat. Add chicken to skillet and cook 4-6 minutes, stirring frequently, until no longer pink. Combine cornstarch, sour cream and yogurt in a small bowl and blend until smooth. Gradually add apricot preserves, raisins and water to chicken; mix well. Stir sour cream mixture into skillet and cook, stirring constantly, until thick and bubbly. Cook 2-3 minutes until heated through. Serve over couscous.

Serves: 6

Nutrition per Serving

		Exchanges
Calories	366	2 starch
Carbohydrate	61 grams	2 fruit
Cholesterol	38 milligrams	2 1/2 meat
Dietary Fiber	7 grams	3 meat
Fat	< 1 gram	
Protein	28 grams	
Sodium	223 milligrams	

Shopping List: Couscous, 1 pound fat-free chicken tenders, apricot preserves, golden raisins, 8 ounces fat-free sour cream, 8 ounces fat-free yogurt, cornstarch, onion powder, garlic powder, curry powder, fat-free chicken broth

BULGUR CEREAL WITH DRIED FRUIT
EASY - DO AHEAD

INDIAN

ingredients:
1 1/2 cups bulgur
Cold water (to rinse bulgur)
1 1/2 cups water
1 1/2 cups peach nectar
1/4 cup dried peaches, chopped
1/4 cup dried apricots, chopped
1 tbsp. oat bran
2 tsp. honey
3/4 tsp. cinnamon
1 tsp. brown sugar
1 1/2 cups skim milk

directions: Place bulgur in colander and rinse with cold water; drain well and transfer to a medium bowl. Add water, peach nectar, peaches, apricots, oat bran, honey, cinnamon and brown sugar and mix well. Cover and seal tightly; refrigerate overnight. Place mixture into medium saucepan and bring to a boil over medium-high heat (or cook on High in microwave 8-10 minutes until heated through). Use 3/4 cup cereal per serving and top with 1/4 cup milk. Store cereal in refrigerator 2-3 days.

Serves: 6

Nutrition per Serving		Exchanges
Calories	217	2 starch
Carbohydrate	49 grams	1 fruit
Cholesterol	1 milligrams	3 meat
Dietary Fiber	9 grams	
Fat	< 1 gram	
Protein	7 grams	
Sodium	43 milligrams	

Shopping List: bulgur, 12 ounces skim milk, 12 ounces peach nectar, dried peaches, dried apricots, oat bran, honey, brown sugar, cinnamon

CURRY VEGETABLES AND BEANS

EASY - DO AHEAD

ingredients:
1/2 cup fat-free sour cream
1/4 cup fat-free yogurt
1 tsp. garlic (*lasan*) powder
1 1/2 cups + 1 1/2 tbsp. fat-free chicken broth, divided
1 large onion (*kada*), cut in 1-inch pieces
10 ounces frozen green beans, thawed and drained
32 oz. frozen cauliflower florets, thawed and drained
1 tsp. curry powder
1 tbsp. dried basil
14 1/2 oz. diced tomatoes with roasted garlic
1 1/2 cups kidney beans
6 cups fat-free cooked rice or couscous

directions: Combine sour cream, yogurt and garlic powder in a small bowl and mix until ingredients are blended. Cover and refrigerate 30 minutes. Lightly spray Dutch oven with nonfat cooking spray; pour 1 1/2 tablespoons chicken broth into pan and heat over medium-high heat. Add onions to pan and cook 3-4 minutes until softened; add green beans and cauliflower and cook 2-3 minutes, until vegetables are tender-crisp. Sprinkle curry powder over vegetables and mix well. Reduce heat to medium; stir in remaining chicken broth, basil and tomatoes. Cook, stirring frequently, 15-20 minutes; stir in beans and cook 5 minutes until heated through. Serve over cooked rice or couscous with sour cream sauce.

Serves: 6

Nutrition per Serving		Exchanges
Calories	344	2 starch
Carbohydrate	74 grams	8 vegetable
Cholesterol	< 1 gram	
Dietary Fiber	7 grams	
Fat	< 1 gram	
Protein	14 grams	
Sodium	775 milligrams	

Shopping List: 14 ounces fat-free chicken broth, 10 ounces frozen green beans, 32 ounces frozen cauliflower florets, 1 large onion, 14 1/2-ounce can diced tomatoes with roasted garlic, fat-free kidney beans, 4 ounces fat-free sour cream, 2 ounces fat-free yogurt, garlic powder, dried basil, curry powder, rice or couscous

HOT COUSCOUS CEREAL

EASY - DO AHEAD

ingredients: 3/4 cup couscous
3/8 cup orange juice
1 1/8 cups water
3 tbsp. Grape-Nuts
1 1/2 tbsp. brown sugar
1 1/2 tbsp. frozen apple juice concentrate
1/4 tsp. cinnamon (*taj*)

directions: Combine all ingredients in a medium microwave-safe bowl and cover with plastic wrap. Pierce wrap to release steam. Microwave on High heat 3-4 minutes; rotate bowl and microwave 2-3 minutes, until couscous is tender. Let stand 1 minute before serving. Sprinkle with brown sugar or cinnamon-sugar just before serving, if desired.

Serves: 6

INDIAN

Nutrition per Serving

Calories	126	
Carbohydrate	27 grams	
Cholesterol	0 milligrams	
Dietary Fiber	4 grams	
Fat	< 1 gram	
Protein	3 grams	
Sodium	29 milligrams	

Exchanges
1 starch
2/3 fruit

Shopping List: couscous, 3 ounces orange juice, Grape-Nuts, brown sugar, frozen apple juice concentrate, cinnamon

INDIAN CHICKEN AND POTATOES

(BASTATA)
EASY - DO AHEAD

ingredients:
1/2 cup fat-free yogurt
1/4 cup fat-free sour cream
1 1/2 tbsp. lemon (*nimu*) juice
1 1/2 tsp. curry powder
3/4 tsp. ground cumin (*jeera*)
1/4 tsp. crushed red pepper
1/2 tsp. pepper (*kala mirch*)
1 1/2 lb. fat-free chicken breasts
3 large baking potatoes (*batata*), cut in 1-inch pieces
2 medium sweet potatoes (*batata*), cut in 1-inch pieces
1 tbsp. garlic (*lasan*) powder
16 oz. frozen carrot slices
1 large onion (*kada*), cut in 1-inch pieces
3 tbsp. fat-free chicken broth
2 tbsp. fresh coriander (*dhania*), chopped

directions:
Combine yogurt, sour cream, lemon juice, curry powder, cumin, red pepper, and pepper in a large bowl and mix until blended smooth. Add chicken breasts and turn to coat well. Cover and refrigerate 3-4 hours or overnight. Preheat oven to 400 degrees. Lightly spray 9x13-inch baking dish with nonfat cooking spray. Arrange potatoes, carrots, and onions in baking dish. Sprinkle with garlic powder. Pour chicken broth over vegetables and bake in preheated oven 10-15 minutes. Reduce oven temperature to 350 degrees. Add chicken and marinade to vegetables and mix well. Cover dish with foil and bake 25-30 minutes, until chicken is no longer pink and is cooked through. Sprinkle chicken with coriander just before serving.

Serves: 6

Nutrition per Serving		Exchanges
Calories	295	2 starch
Carbohydrate	40 grams	1 1/2 vegetable
Cholesterol	56 milligrams	3 meat
Dietary Fiber	6 grams	
Fat	< 1 gram	
Protein	32 grams	
Sodium	324 milligrams	

Shopping List:
1 1/2 pounds fat-free chicken breasts, 4 ounces fat-free yogurt, 2 ounces fat-free sour cream, 3 large baking potatoes, 2 medium sweet potatoes, 16-ounce package frozen carrot slices, 1 large onion, lemon juice, fat-free chicken broth, curry powder, ground cumin, crushed red pepper, pepper, garlic powder, fresh coriander

INDIAN FALAFEL BURGERS
EASY - DO AHEAD

directions:
1/2 cup fat-free ricotta cheese
1/3 cup egg substitute
1 tbsp. dried parsley
1 1/2 tsp. ground cumin
1 1/2 tsp. coriander
1 1/2 tsp. garlic powder
1 1/2 tsp. chili powder
15 oz. can garbanzo beans
3/4 cup fat-free bread crumbs

directions: Combine ricotta cheese, egg substitute, parsley, cumin, coriander, garlic powder and chili powder in a food processor or blender and process until blended. Add garbanzo beans and process until smooth. Transfer to medium mixing bowl and stir in bread crumbs. Form mixture into patties and place on platter; cover with plastic wrap and refrigerate 30-45 minutes. Lightly spray large non-stick skillet with nonfat cooking spray and heat over medium-high heat. Place patties in skillet and cook 5-6 minutes per side, until golden brown and cooked throughout.

Serves: 6

Nutrition per Serving

		Exchanges
Calories	115	1 starch
Carbohydrate	19 grams	1 meat
Cholesterol	3 milligrams	
Dietary Fiber	1 gram	
Fat	< 1 gram	
Protein	8 grams	
Sodium	276 milligrams	

Shopping List: 15 ounces canned garbanzo beans, 4 ounces fat-free ricotta cheese, egg substitute, fat-free bread crumbs, dried parsley, ground cumin, coriander, garlic powder, chili powder

INDIAN TURKEY KABOBS
(SEEKH KABAB)
EASY - DO AHEAD - FREEZE

ingredients:
1 lb. fat-free ground turkey
1/2 cup flour
1 1/2 tsp. garlic powder
3/4 tsp. ground ginger
1 tbsp. onion powder
1/4 cup chopped cilantro
2 tsp. ground coriander
2 tsp. ground cumin
1/4 tsp. ground turmeric
2 tbsp. lemon juice

directions:
Preheat broiler on high heat. Line baking sheet with foil and lightly spray with nonfat cooking spray. Soak wooden skewers in water and dry. Combine all ingredients in a medium bowl and mix well. Form mixture into 1-inch balls; thread onto skewers and arrange on baking sheet. Broil kabobs 8-10 minutes, turning frequently, until cooked through. Serve with chutney or raita.

Serves: 6

Nutrition per Serving		Exchanges
Calories	119	2/3 starch
Carbohydrate	13 grams	2 meat
Cholesterol	27 milligrams	
Dietary Fiber	< 1 gram	
Fat	< 1 gram	
Protein	12 grams	
Sodium	840 milligrams	

Shopping List: 1 pound fat-free ground turkey, flour, garlic powder, onion powder, ground ginger, chopped cilantro, ground coriander, ground cumin, ground turmeric, lemon juice

INDIAN

MORACCAN STEW

AVERAGE - DO AHEAD - FREEZE

ingredients: 2 1/2 cups + 1 tbsp. fat-free chicken broth, divided
1 cup chopped onion
2 cups butternut squash, peeled and cubed
3 medium carrots, sliced 1/4-inch thick
1/2 cup garbanzo beans
1 cup white kidney beans
14 1/2 oz. can stewed tomatoes
1/2 cup raisins
1/2 tsp. cinnamon
1/4 tsp. crushed red pepper
1 cup couscous

directions: Lightly spray large Dutch oven or soup pot with nonfat cooking spray; add 1 tablespoon chicken broth and heat over medium-high heat. Add onions, squash and carrots to pot and cook, stirring frequently, about 8-10 minutes until lightly browned. Add garbanzo beans, kidney beans, tomatoes, raisins, cinnamon, red pepper and remaining chicken broth to pot. Bring to a boil over high heat. Reduce heat to low, cover and simmer 25-30 minutes, until vegetables are tender. Prepare couscous according to package directions, substituting chicken broth for water. Serve stew over couscous.

Serves: 6

Nutrition per Serving		Exchanges
Calories	281	3 vegetable
Carbohydrate	61 grams	2 fruit
Cholesterol	0 milligrams	1 starch
Dietary Fiber	12 grams	
Fat	< 1 gram	
Protein	10 grams	
Sodium	708 milligrams	

Shopping List: 2 (15-ounce) cans fat-free chicken broth, 8-ounce package chopped onions, 1 medium butternut squash, 3 carrots, garbanzo beans, 15-ounce can white kidney beans, 14 1/2 ounces stewed tomatoes, raisins, cinnamon, crushed red pepper, couscous

SPICY CHICKEN WITH COUSCOUS

AVERAGE

ingredients:
1 tsp. garlic powder
1 1/4 tsp. ground cumin
1 tsp. paprika
3/4 tsp. ground ginger
3/4 tsp. ground allspice
1/4 tsp. pepper
1 1/2 lb. fat-free chicken tenders, cubed
1 1/4 cups couscous
2 cups fat-free chicken broth, divided
1 1/2 cups chopped tomatoes, drained
1/3 cup chopped red onion
3 tbsp. fresh cilantro, chopped
1 tbsp. fresh mint, chopped

directions:
Combine garlic powder, cumin, paprika, ginger, allspice and pepper in a large plastic, sealed bag and shake until completely blended. Add chicken to bag and toss until coated. Set aside. Cook couscous according to package directions, substituting equal portion of chicken broth for water. Stir in tomatoes, onions, cilantro and mint. Lightly spray large nonstick skillet with nonfat cooking spray. Add remaining chicken broth to skillet and heat over medium-high heat. Add chicken and cook, stirring frequently, about 5-6 minutes, until cooked through. Place couscous on large serving platter and top with chicken.

Serves: 8

INDIAN

Nutrition per Serving		Exchanges
Calories	205	2 vegetable
Carbohydrate	27 grams	2 meat
Cholesterol	53 milligrams	1 starch
Dietary Fiber	5 grams	
Fat	< 1 gram	
Protein	22 grams	
Sodium	456 milligrams	

Shopping List:
1 1/2 pounds fat-free chicken tenders, 15-ounce can fat-free chicken broth, 14 1/2-ounce can chopped tomatoes, 1 small red onion, fresh cilantro, fresh mint, garlic powder, ground cumin, paprika, ground ginger, ground allspice, pepper, couscous

CUCUMBER RAITA

EASY - DO AHEAD

ingredients:
1 cup fat-free sour cream
1 cup fat-free plain yogurt
1/4 cup cilantro
1 tbsp. chopped green chilies
1 tsp. minced garlic
1/8 tsp. pepper
2 cups finely-chopped cucumber
1/4 tsp. ground cumin
1/2 tsp. paprika

directions:
Combine sour cream and yogurt in a medium bowl and mix until completely blended. Combine cilantro, green chilies, garlic and pepper in a food processor or blender and process until smooth. Stir into sour cream mixture. Add cucumber and cumin and mix well. Sprinkle with paprika just before serving.

Serve: 6

Nutrition per Serving

Calories	55	
Carbohydrate	7 grams	
Cholesterol	1 milligram	
Dietary Fiber	< 1 gram	
Fat	< 1 gram	
Protein	5 grams	
Sodium	74 milligrams	

Exchanges
1 vegetable
1/3 milk

Shopping List: 8 ounces fat-free yogurt, 8 ounces fat-free sour cream, 1 large cucumber, chopped green chilies, cilantro, pepper, ground cumin, paprika, minced garlic

INDIAN

CURRIED VEGETABLES WITH LENTILS

AVERAGE - DO AHEAD

ingredients:
2 cups + 2 tbsp. fat-free chicken broth
1 large onion, sliced
1/2 cup sliced carrots
1/2 cup sliced celery
3/4 tsp. garlic powder
1 tbsp. curry powder
1 tsp. ground cumin
1/4 tsp. turmeric
1/4 tsp. ground cardamom
3/4 tsp. ground ginger
1 cup dry lentils
1 medium sweet potato, peeled and diced
1 cup frozen peas, thawed and drained
1 cup frozen green beans, thawed and drained
1 cup fat-free plain yogurt

INDIAN

directions:
Lightly spray Dutch oven or large nonstick skillet with nonfat cooking spray. Add 2 tablespoons chicken broth and heat over medium-high heat. Sauté onion, carrots and celery in broth until tender. Add garlic powder, curry, cumin, turmeric, cardamom and ginger and cook 1 minute until blended. Add remaining broth, lentils and sweet potato to pot; bring to a boil over high heat. Reduce heat to medium, cover, and cook 20-25 minutes, until lentils are tender. Add peas and beans to pot and cook 3-5 minutes over medium-high heat. Remove pot from heat and gradually stir in yogurt.

Serves: 6

Nutrition per Serving		Exchanges
Calories	127	2 vegetable
Carbohydrate	23 grams	1 starch
Cholesterol	1 milligram	
Dietary Fiber	3 grams	
Fat	< 1 gram	
Protein	9 grams	
Sodium	440 milligrams	

Shopping List: 24 ounces fat-free chicken broth, 1 large onion, 2 small carrots, celery, 1 sweet potato, 10-ounce package frozen peas, 10-ounce package frozen cut green beans, 8 ounces fat-free plain yogurt, dry lentils, garlic powder, curry, cumin, turmeric, cardamom, ginger

MINT CHUTNEY
(FUDINA CHUTNEY)
EASY - DO AHEAD

ingredients:
1/2 cup mint leaves, washed and drained
1/2 cup fresh cilantro
2 tbsp. chopped green chilies
3/4 tsp. sugar
4 tbsp. lemon juice

directions:
Combine all ingredients in food processor or blender and process until smooth.
Pour into small bowl, cover and refrigerate until ready to serve.
Serve with kabobs or curry dishes.

Serves: 4

Nutrition per Serving		Exchanges
Calories	19	Free
Carbohydrate	5 grams	
Cholesterol	0 milligrams	
Dietary Fiber	1 gram	
Fat	< 1 gram	
Protein	< 1 gram	
Sodium	56 milligrams	

Shopping List: mint leaves, cilantro, chopped green chilies, sugar, lemon juice

SPINACH RAITA
EASY - DO AHEAD

ingredients: 16 oz. frozen chopped spinach, thawed and drained
1 cup fat-free yogurt
1 cup fat-free sour cream
1/4 tsp. pepper
1/2 tsp. ground cumin

directions: Drain spinach in colander and press to remove all excess water. Combine yogurt and sour cream in a medium bowl and mix until blended. Add spinach, pepper and cumin to yogurt and mix until completely blended. Serve as a salad or side dish.

Serves: 6

Nutrition per Serving		Exchanges
Calories	70	2 vegetable
Carbohydrate	10 grams	1/2 meat
Cholesterol	1 milligram	
Dietary Fiber	2 grams	
Fat	< 1 gram	
Protein	7 grams	
Sodium	121 milligrams	

Shopping List: 16-ounce package frozen chopped spinach, 8 ounces fat-free plain yogurt, 8 ounces fat-free sour cream, pepper, cumin

INDIAN

TABBOULEH

EASY - DO AHEAD

ingredients:
3/4 cup bulgur
1 3/4 cup boiling water
1/3 cup chopped green onions (*kada*)
3 tbsp. chopped mint leaves (*phodino*)
1 1/2 cups chopped tomatoes, drained
3/4 cup chopped parsley
1/4 cup fat-free Italian salad dressing
6 large lettuce leaves
1/4 tsp. pepper (*kala mirch*)

directions:
Place bulgur in a medium bowl; pour water over bulgur and mix lightly. Cover bowl and let stand 30-35 minutes until liquid is absorbed. Drain any remaining water from bowl. Add green onions, mint, tomatoes, and parsley and mix well. Gradually pour dressing over bulgur mixture and mix lightly. Use lettuce leaves to scoop tabouleh from bowl and serve.

Serves: 6

Nutrition per Serving		Exchanges
Calories	82	1/2 starch
Carbohydrate	18 grams	2 vegetable
Cholesterol	0 milligrams	
Dietary Fiber	5 grams	
Fat	< 1 gram	
Protein	3 grams	
Sodium	54 milligrams	

Shopping List: bulgur, green onions, fresh mint leaves, 2 medium tomatoes, fresh parsley, 2 ounces fat-free Italian salad dressing, lettuce leaves, pepper

INDIAN

VEGETABLE MEDLEY WITH COUSCOUS
EASY - DO AHEAD

ingredients:
1 1/2 cups + 2 tbsp. vegetable broth, divided
1 1/2 cups water
1 cup raw couscous
1 large onion (*kada*), sliced
2 tsp. minced garlic (*lasan*)
28 oz. diced tomatoes, with roasted garlic, undrained
2 large carrots, cut in chunks
3 large celery, cut in chunks
4 medium sweet potatoes (*batata*), peeled and
    cut in chunks
2 tsp. brown sugar
1 tsp. cinnamon (*taj*)
1/2 tsp. ground cumin (*jeers*)
1/4 tsp. ground turmeric (*haldi*)
1/2 tsp. pepper (*kala mirch*)
1 large zucchini, cut in chunks
1 large yellow squash, cut in chunks
1 1/2 cups broccoli florets
1 1/2 cups cauliflower florets
1 large red bell pepper, chopped
1/2 cup canned garbanzo beans, drained
1/2 cup golden raisins

directions:
Combine 1 1/2 cups vegetable broth and water in a medium saucepan and bring to a boil over high heat. Stir in couscous; cover. Remove from heat. Let stand 5-7 minutes until liquid is absorbed. Fluff with a fork just before serving. Keep warm. Lightly spray large Dutch oven with nonfat cooking spray. Add 2 tablespoons vegetable broth and heat over medium-high heat. Add onion and garlic; cook, stirring frequently, about 5 minutes until onion is soft. Add tomatoes, carrots, celery, sweet potatoes, brown sugar, cinnamon, cumin, turmeric and pepper and mix well. Reduce heat to low, cover. Simmer 15 minutes; add zucchini, squash, broccoli, cauliflower and red pepper. Cover and cook over low heat 15-20 minutes, until vegetables are tender. Add beans and raisins; mix well, cover and cook over low heat 15-20 minutes. Serve over cooked couscous.

Serves: 8

Nutrition per Serving		Exchanges
Calories	247	1 starch
Carbohydrate	56 grams	1 fruit
Cholesterol	0 milligrams	4 1/2 vegetable
Dietary Fiber	10 grams	
Fat	< 1 gram	
Protein	7 grams	
Sodium	429 milligrams	

Shopping List: 1 large onion, 28-ounce can diced tomatoes with roasted garlic, 2 large carrots, celery, 4 sweet potatoes, 1 large zucchini, 1 large yellow squash, broccoli florets, cauliflower florets, 1 red bell pepper, canned garbanzo beans, 14 ounces couscous, 12 ounces fat-free vegetable* (or chicken) broth, golden raisins, minced garlic, brown sugar, cinnamon, ground cumin, ground turmeric, pepper

YOGURT CHUTNEY

EASY - DO AHEAD

ingredients: 3/4 cup fat-free yogurt
1/4 cup fat-free sour cream
1/2 cup cilantro
2 tbsp. chopped green chilies
1 tsp. sugar
1/4 tsp. ground cumin
1/8 tsp. pepper

directions: Combine all ingredients in a food processor or blender and process until smooth.
Cover and refrigerate until ready to serve.
Great as a salad dressing or sauce.

Serves: 4

Nutrition per Serving		Exchanges
Calories	218	1/2 milk
Carbohydrate	6 grams	1 starch
Cholesterol	1 milligram	
Dietary Fiber	< 1 gram	
Fat	< 1 gram	
Protein	4 grams	
Sodium	96 milligrams	

Shopping List: 6 ounces fat-free plain yogurt, 2 ounces fat-free sour cream, cilantro, chopped green chilies, sugar, ground cumin, pepper

FRUIT KABOBS

EASY - DO AHEAD

ingredients: 1 cup diced cantaloupe
1 cup sliced strawberries
1 cup pineapple chunks
1 apple, diced
1 banana, sliced
2 tbsp. lemon juice

directions: Arrange fruit alternately on skewers.
Dip in lemon juice to prevent browning; cover and
refrigerate until ready to serve.

Serves: 6

Nutrition per Serving		Exchanges
Calories	62	1 fruit
Carbohydrate	16 grams	
Cholesterol	0 milligrams	
Dietary Fiber	2 grams	
Fat	< 1 gram	
Protein	1 gram	
Sodium	3 milligrams	

Shopping List: cantaloupe, strawberries, pineapple chunks, 1 apple, 1
banana, lemon juice

INDIAN

GINGERED BANANAS

EASY

ingredients: 3 bananas, peeled and sliced into quarters
1 tbsp. fat-free margarine
1 tbsp. grated ginger root
1 tbsp. dark brown sugar
1 tsp. lime juice

directions: Lightly spray large nonstick skillet with nonfat cooking spray; melt margarine in skillet over medium heat.
Add ginger root and cook, stirring frequently. Add bananas to skillet and sprinkle with brown sugar.
Cook until browned, about 2 minutes. Turn bananas and cook until the sauce begins to caramelize, about 2 minutes.
Remove from heat and carefully place bananas on serving platter.
Sprinkle lime juice in the skillet and mix with sauce.
Drizzle over bananas and serve.

Serves: 2

Nutrition per Serving		Exchanges
Calories	188	3 fruit
Carbohydrate	47 grams	
Cholesterol	0 milligrams	
Dietary Fiber	3 grams	
Fat	< 1 gram	
Protein	2 grams	
Sodium	49 milligrams	

Shopping List: 3 bananas, fat-free margarine, ginger root, dark brown sugar, lime juice

INDIAN PUDDING

EASY - DO AHEAD

ingredients:
4 cups hot skim milk
1/2 cup yellow cornmeal
1/2 cup maple syrup
1/4 cup light molasses
1/2 cup egg substitute
2 tbsp. fat-free margarine
1/3 cup brown sugar
1 tsp. salt
1/4 tsp. cinnamon
3/4 tsp. ginger
1/2 cup cold skim milk
Fat-free frozen yogurt or ice cream (optional)

directions:
Pour hot milk into top of double boiler and slowly add cornmeal, mixing well. Cook over boiling water, stirring occasionally, about 20 minutes. Preheat oven to 300 degrees. Lightly spray 2-quart baking dish with nonfat cooking spray. In a small bowl, combine syrup, molasses, egg substitute, margarine, brown sugar, salt, cinnamon and ginger; mix well; add mixture to cornmeal mixture and blend. Spoon into baking dish; pour cold milk over top (do not stir); bake in preheated oven 2 hours, until pudding is set. Be careful not to overcook. Remove from oven and let pudding stand at room temperature 30 minutes before serving. Top with frozen yogurt or ice cream, if desired.

INDIAN

Serves: 8

Nutrition per Serving		Exchanges
Calories	196	1/2 milk
Carbohydrate	43 grams	2 fruit
Cholesterol	2 milligrams	1/2 starch
Dietary Fiber	0 grams	
Fat	< 1 gram	
Protein	6 grams	
Sodium	405 milligrams	

Shopping List: yellow cornmeal, 1 1/2 quarts skim milk, maple syrup, light molasses, 4 ounces egg substitute, fat-free margarine, brown sugar, salt, cinnamon, ginger, fat-free frozen yogurt ice cream (optional)

MANGO KULFI
DIFFICULT - DO AHEAD

ingredients: 3 tbsp. water
                     1 tbsp. unflavored gelatin
                     4 ripe mangoes, pitted and peeled
                     1/2 cup sugar
                     1 tbsp. lemon juice
                     1 cup evaporated skim milk
                     1/2 cup fat-free plain yogurt

directions: Place water in a medium saucepan and sprinkle with gelatin. Let gelatin soak in water for 5 minutes; then, cook over low heat until gelatin dissolves.
Purée mangoes in food processor or blender until smooth; spoon into large bowl. Add sugar, lemon juice and dissolved gelatin to mangoes; stir until sugar is dissolved.
Fold in evaporated milk and yogurt until mixture is blended. Place bowl in freezer; freeze about 1 hour, until half of mixture is frozen. Remove from freezer and beat until smooth. Pack mixture into individual bowls or molds and return to freezer until half-frozen, but still creamy.

Serves: 6

Nutrition per Serving		Exchanges
Calories	199	1/2 milk
Carbohydrate	46 grams	2 2/3 fruit
Cholesterol	2 milligrams	
Dietary Fiber	3 grams	
Fat	< 1 gram	
Protein	6 grams	
Sodium	68 milligrams	

Shopping List: unflavored gelatin, 4 mangoes, 8 ounces evaporated skim milk, 4 ounces fat-free plain yogurt, sugar, lemon juice

RICE PUDDING A LA INDIA
EASY - DO AHEAD

---

ingredients

2 cups boiling water
1/2 tsp. salt
1/2 cup fat-free rice, uncooked
4 cups skim milk
1 tbsp. fat-free margarine
3 tbsp. sugar
2 tbsp. grated coconut
1/8 cup raisins

directions:

Preheat oven to 275 degrees. Lightly spray 8-inch baking dish with nonfat cooking spray.

Pour 2 cups water into medium saucepan and bring to a boil over high heat. Add salt and rice; cook, stirring, until water is evaporated and rice is almost dry.

Place rice in baking dish; add milk, margarine and sugar; mix well. Bake in preheated oven 3 hours, stirring occasionally.

Add coconut and raisins; cook 10 minutes until heated through. Serve hot or cold.

Serves: 6

Nutrition per Serving		Exchanges
Calories	152	1/2 fruit
Carbohydrate	29 grams	1/2 milk
Cholesterol	3 milligrams	1 starch
Dietary Fiber	< 1 gram	
Fat	< 1 gram	
Protein	7 grams	
Sodium	278 milligrams	

Shopping List: 1 quart skim milk, fat-free rice, fat-free margarine, sugar, grated coconut, raisins, salt

SPICED GRAPEFRUIT

EASY - DO AHEAD

ingredients
5 grapefruits
1/2 cup reserved grapefruit juice
2 cups sugar
1 cup vinegar
1 tsp. whole cloves
2 cinnamon sticks

directions:
Peel and section grapefruit, reserving 1/2 cup juice. Pack the grapefruit into a jar and set aside. Combine remaining ingredients in a small saucepan and bring to a boil over high heat. Reduce heat to low and cook, stirring constantly, 10 minutes; strain liquid.
Pour over the grapefruit sections, covering completely. Cover and cool.
Refrigerate overnight.

Serves: 4

INDIAN

Nutrition per Serving		Exchanges
Calories	466	8 fruit
Carbohydrate	126 grams	
Cholesterol	0 milligrams	
Dietary Fiber	4 grams	
Fat	< 1 gram	
Protein	2 grams	
Sodium	3 milligrams	

Shopping List: 5 grapefruits, sugar, vinegar, whole cloves, 2 cinnamon sticks

INDIAN PUDDING DESSERT
(FIRNI)
AVERAGE

ingredients: 1/4 cup yellow cornmeal
3 cups skim milk, divided
3/4 cup corn syrup
1/3 cup brown sugar
3 tbsp. Butter Buds, reconstituted
1/3 cup raisins
3/4 tsp. cinnamon (*taj*)
1/2 tsp. allspice
1/8 tsp. ground ginger

directions: Preheat oven to 325 degrees. Lightly spray 1 1/2-quart casserole with nonfat cooking spray. Combine cornmeal and 1 cup skim milk in a medium bowl; mix well and set aside. Pour 1 3/4 cups skim milk in medium saucepan; cook, stirring frequently, over medium heat, just until milk begins to bubble. Gradually add cornmeal mixture and cook 12-15 minutes, stirring frequently, until mixture thickens. Add corn syrup and brown sugar and mix well. Remove from heat and stir mixture until sugar is completely dissolved. Add Butter Buds, raisins, cinnamon, allspice and ginger; mix well. Pour mixture into casserole; pour remaining milk over the top and bake in preheated oven 1 to 1 1/2 hours, until knife inserted in center comes out clean. Serve immediately.

Serves: 6

Nutrition Per Serving

		Exchanges
Calories	262	1 starch
Carbohydrate	60 grams	3 fruit
Cholesterol	2 milligrams	
Dietary Fiber	1 gram	
Fat	< 1 gram	
Protein	5 grams	
Sodium	162 milligrams	

Shopping List: yellow cornmeal, 24 ounces skim milk, 6 ounces corn syrup, brown sugar, Butter Buds, raisins, cinnamon, allspice, ground ginger

ITALIAN

ITALIAN

Italians have an intense love affair with food, including everything from cheesy lasagna and fettuccine alfredo to almond biscotti and cheesecake...super-rich, high in fat, high in calories and totally irresistible. WRONG! Italian cooking with all the flair, all of the flavor but none of the fat, is possible in the world of healthy cooking. Simple substitutions, along with fat-free cooking methods, make Italian dishes simple to prepare and sumptuous to eat. Create everything from appetizers to desserts with all the fat-free products available on the market today. A little experimentation and improvisation will help you create low-fat Italian cooking dishes too good to resist.

The Best Substitutions You Can Make for Healthy Italian Cooking
- **FAT-FREE DAIRY PRODUCTS** including cheese, milk, sour cream and yogurt, provide healthy alternatives for healthy Italian cooking. Start slow - if the thought of "fat-free" products turns your taste buds off, start with partial substitutions. (Start with 3/4 regular or low-fat product and 1/4 fat-free; gradually decrease the regular products and increase the amount of fat-free. Season up and learn to love the new flavor without all the fat.)
  - **fat-free cottage cheese:** Great for dips, spreads, sauces or salad dressings, fat-free cottage cheese can be used in place of whole or low-fat varieties in your favorite recipes.

Watch the savings grow as you change
from whole to fat-free cottage cheese!

	Calories	Fat	Sodium
4% fat	232	10.10 gm	911 mg
2% fat	203	4.36 gm	918 mg
1% fat	164	2.30 gm	918 mg
0% fat	140	0 gm	600 mg

- **fat-free cream cheese:** Great in dips, spreads, white cream sauces and desserts. For best results:
  --cook fat-free cream cheese over low heat when melting
  --bring to room temperature before blending into batters.
  Savings per 1 ounce serving:
  30-70 calories; 5-10 grams of fat

- **fat-free Mozzarella cheese:** What's Italian cooking without some Mozzarella? For best results:

  --purchase finely shredded varieties

  --toss with a sprinkle of flour or cornstarch before melting in soups or sauces

  --if used for topping (i.e. pizza), add cheese during last 10 minutes of baking.

  Savings per 1 ounce serving:
  20-40 calories/ 4.5-7 grams of fat

- **fat-free Parmesan cheese:** Use fat-free Parmesan cheese for toppings and coatings, as well as in sauces, soups, salads and casseroles.

  Savings per 2 teaspoon serving:
  1.5 grams of fat

- **fat-free ricotta cheese:** Great in dips, pasta dishes, cheesecakes, casseroles and Italian omelets. For a creamy consistency, process ricotta cheese in a food processor or blender before blending with other ingredients.

  Savings per 1 cup serving:
  180-270 calories; 19-32 grams of fat

- **fat-free sour cream:** Use to flavor dips, salad dressings, casseroles and sauces. Fat-free sour cream can be used in place of regular sour cream or yogurt in most recipes.

  Savings per 1 cup serving:
  320 calories; 48 grams of fat

- **fat-free yogurt:** Substitute fat-free yogurt for regular yogurt, sour cream or buttermilk in most recipes. For best results: if adding yogurt to hot dishes, add 1 tablespoon flour or cornstarch to yogurt (at room temperature) and gradually mix into hot sauces without curdling.

  Savings per 1 cup serving:
  25-60 calories; 3-7 grams of fat

- **fat-free egg substitute** can be used in place of whole eggs in sauces, salad dressings, breads, baked goods and more. Be sure to select fat-free egg substitutes (Egg Beaters, NuLaid, Second Nature, or Better 'n Eggs). Don't use egg substitutes when the recipe calls for whipped egg whites - only egg whites will do!

  Savings per egg (1/4 cup egg substitute per egg):
  55-65 calories; 5 grams of fat; 210 milligrams of cholesterol

- **fat-free meat substitutes:** Can't imagine spaghetti and meat sauce without the meat? Substitute frozen Harvest Burger Beef crumbles (Green Giant) or fat-free ground turkey/chicken in place of beef, for sauce, meat balls and more. Fat-free chicken breasts or chicken tenders are excellent substitutes for higher fat varieties; they can be baked, broiled, or even sautéed in fat-free broth or white wine.

How can you be sure your fat-free Italian dishes won't be bland or boring? Work with a variety of herbs, spices and condiments to add the flair without the fat.

Commonly used Italian herbs and spices:
anise seeds, basil, bay leaves, capers, crushed red pepper, fennel, garlic, Italian parsley, Italian seasoning, oregano, rosemary, sage, shallots, thyme

Vegetables commonly used in Italian cooking:
artichokes, arugula, eggplant, escarole, fennel, leeks, mushrooms, tomatoes, radicchio

Pasta Trivia
- **1 cup uncooked** pasta equals **2 cups cooked** pasta
- **Cook pasta until firm** and slightly chewy; overcooking diminishes the nutrient content.
- **To avoid sticky pasta**--place cooked pasta in a warm colander (rather than cold, which causes "sticky pasta syndrome") and then into a warm dish.
- **To prevent pasta boil-over mess:** Spray the upper rim of the pot with nonfat cooking spray to prevent the water from boiling over.
- **Italians** consume an average of 60 pounds of pasta each year!

What's the difference?
- **cannelloni** - hollow tubes of pasta up to 2 inches long
- **ditalini** - small thimble-shaped pasta
- **farfalle** - bowtie-shaped pasta
- **fusilli** - corkscrew shaped pasta
- **macaroni** - cured pasta with a hollow center
- **orcchiette** - pasta shaped like ears
- **vermicelli** - Italian word for "worms" but better known as spaghetti
- **ziti** - very short tubular-shaped pasta

ITALIAN

Top It Off (pasta sauces)!

- **Alfredo** - usually made with fresh cream, garlic and Parmesan cheese (for low-fat variety, substitute evaporated skim milk for cream and fat-free Parmesan cheese for regular)
- **Clam Sauce** - combination of clam broth, tomatoes and crushed red pepper
- **Genovese** - thick meat sauce, flavored with garlic, tomato and herbs (for low-fat variety, substitute fat-free ground turkey or "beef crumbles" for ground beef)
- **Marinara** - tomato sauce flavored with garlic and herbs
- **Neopolitan** - tomato sauce blended with herbs, garlic, mushrooms and bell pepper
- **Pesto** - made from olive oil, fresh basil, garlic, pine nuts and fresh cream, the "real" stuff is a waist buster!

ITALIAN

BAY SHRIMP BRUSCHETTA

EASY - DO AHEAD

ingredients: 1/4 lb. bay shrimp, peeled,
                     deveined and cooked
                     1/2 lb. French baguette
                     4 oz. fat-free cream cheese
                     2 cloves garlic, minced
                     1 oz. sun-dried tomato, rehydrated in water
                     and chopped
                     6 large fresh basil leaves, finely chopped
                     Toasted cracked black pepper
                     Kosher salt

directions: Preheat oven to 350 degrees. Slice baguette into 12
                     1/2-inch-thick slices.
                     Lightly spray nonstick baking sheet with nonfat
                     cooking spray and arrange bread on sheet.
                     In a small bowl, combine cream cheese, minced
                     garlic, chopped sun-dried tomato and chopped
                     basil leaves.
                     Season with salt and pepper.
                     Spread this mixture evenly on toast slices and
                     garnish with bay shrimp.
                     Bake in oven for 10-15 minutes, or until toasted.

                     Serves: 12

Nutrition per Serving   **Exchanges**
Calories   70   1/2 meat
Carbohydrate   11 grams   1/3 starch
Cholesterol   15 milligrams   1 vegetable
Dietary Fiber   1 gram
Fat   < 1 gram
Protein   5 grams
Sodium   197 milligrams

Shopping List: 1/4 pound bay shrimp, 1/2 pound French baguette, 4
                     ounces fat-free cream cheese, 2-ounce package sun-
                     dried tomato (not oil-packed), 1 bag fresh basil, 1 head
                     fresh garlic, black peppercorns, kosher salt

ITALIAN

BRUSCHETTA

EASY

ingredients:

1 tbsp. crushed garlic, divided
2 cups chopped Italian plum tomatoes
2 tbsp. dried basil
2 tbsp. fat-free Italian salad dressing
1 lb. fat-free Italian bread loaf, cut in 12 slices

directions:

Combine 2 teaspoons garlic, tomatoes, basil and Italian dressing in a small bowl; let stand at room temperature while preparing bread.
Preheat broiler on high heat. Line baking sheet with foil; spread 1 teaspoon crushed garlic over bottom of baking pan.
Arrange bread slices in a single layer on baking sheet and lightly spray with cooking spray.
Broil 30-45 seconds, until lightly browned.
Remove from oven; immediately spread each piece with tomato mixture.
Serve immediately.

Serves: 6

Nutrition per Serving		Exchanges
Calories	194	2 starch
Carbohydrate	39 grams	1 1/2 vegetable
Cholesterol	0 milligrams	
Dietary Fiber	2 grams	
Fat	< 1 gram	
Protein	7 grams	
Sodium	455 milligrams	

Shopping List: 1 pound fat-free Italian bread, 2-4 Italian plum tomatoes, crushed garlic, dried basil, fat-free Italian salad dressing

CAPONATA
EASY - DO AHEAD

ingredients: 3/4 lb. eggplant, peeled and cut into 1/2-inch cubes
1/2 cup chopped onion
1/4 cup chopped celery
1 cup chopped tomatoes, drained
2 tbsp. red wine vinegar
1 1/2 tbsp. tomato paste
3/4 tsp. sugar
1/2 tsp. garlic powder
1/8 tsp. pepper
1/8 tsp. ground red pepper
1 tsp. dried parsley
2 tsp. dried basil
3/4 tsp. oregano
3/4 tsp. lemon juice

directions: Lightly spray large nonstick skillet with nonfat cooking spray and heat over medium-high heat. Add eggplant, onion and celery to skillet and cook 5-6 minutes, until vegetables are tender. Add tomatoes, vinegar, tomato paste, sugar, garlic powder, pepper and ground red pepper; mix well. Cover skillet and cook, stirring occasionally, over low heat, 5-6 minutes, until heated through. Remove skillet from heat; stir in parsley, basil, oregano and lemon juice; mix well. Spoon mixture into serving bowl; cover and refrigerate 1-2 hours. Let mixture stand at room temperature 20 minutes before serving. Great with fat-free pita chips.

Serves: 6

Nutrition per Serving		Exchanges
Calories	35	1 vegetable
Carbohydrate	8 grams	
Cholesterol	0 milligrams	
Dietary Fiber	1 gram	
Fat	< 1 gram	
Protein	1 gram	
Sodium	74 milligrams	

Shopping List: 3/4 pound eggplant, 1 small onion, celery, 1 large tomato, red wine vinegar, tomato paste, sugar, garlic powder, pepper, ground red pepper, dried parsley, dried basil, oregano, lemon juice

ITALIAN

ITALIAN BREAD

EASY - DO AHEAD - FREEZE

ingredients:
1 cup water
1/4 tsp. Italian seasoning
1/8 tsp. garlic powder
2 3/4 cups bread flour
2 1/4 tsp. active dry yeast

directions:
Combine all ingredients in a bread machine in the order recommended by the manufacturer, and bake according to manufacturer's directions.

Serves: 6 (2 slices per serving)

Nutrition per Serving		Exchanges
Calories	94	1 1/3 starch
Carbohydrate	20 grams	
Cholesterol	0 milligrams	
Dietary Fiber	1 gram	
Fat	< 1 gram	
Protein	3 grams	
Sodium	1 milligram	

Shopping List: bread flour, active dry yeast, Italian seasoning, garlic powder

ITALIAN

ITALIAN PITA CRISPS
EASY - DO AHEAD

ingredients:
3 whole fat-free pita breads
3/4 cup Butter Buds, reconstituted
1 1/2 tsp. garlic powder
2 tsp. Italian seasoning
3/4 cup fat-free Parmesan cheese

directions:
Preheat oven to 375 degrees.
Line baking sheet(s) with foil and lightly spray with nonfat cooking spray.
Using a sharp, serrated knife, slice pita pockets in half to separate into 2 separate rounds.
Arrange pitas on baking sheet(s) in a single layer. Combine Butter Buds, garlic powder and Italian seasoning in a small bowl and blend well. Brush pitas with Butter Bud mixture until completely coated (about 2 tablespoons per pita). Cut each pita round into 6 equal pieces; sprinkle with Parmesan cheese.
Bake pitas in preheated oven 5-6 minutes, until crisp and lightly browned.
Great with dips, or use whole for pizza crust.

Serves: 6

Nutrition per Serving

Calories	98	
Carbohydrate	16 grams	
Cholesterol	0 milligrams	
Dietary Fiber	< 1 gram	
Fat	< 1 gram	
Protein	6 grams	
Sodium	698 milligrams	

Exchanges
1 1/3 starch

Shopping List: fat-free pita pockets, 3 ounces fat-free Parmesan cheese, Butter Buds, garlic powder, Italian seasoning

PARMESAN BREADSTICKS
EASY - DO AHEAD

ingredients: 1 cup water
2 3/4 cups bread flour
2 1/4 tsp. active dry yeast
1 tsp. garlic powder
2 tbsp. fat-free Parmesan cheese

directions: Combine ingredients in a bread machine in the order recommended by the manufacturer, and process on the dough cycle.
Divide dough into 12 equal pieces. Roll each piece into an 8-inch rope.
Line baking sheet with foil and lightly spray with nonfat cooking spray.
Arrange breadsticks on the baking sheet. Cover with plastic wrap or towel and let rise in a warm place for 30 minutes, until doubled in size.
Preheat oven to 375 degrees.
Lightly spray breadsticks with nonfat cooking spray. Sprinkle with garlic powder and Parmesan cheese.
Bake in preheated oven 20-25 minutes, until golden brown.

Serves: 6 (2 breadsticks per serving)

Nutrition per Serving		Exchanges
Calories	97	1 1/3 starch
Carbohydrate	1 gram	
Cholesterol	0 milligrams	
Dietary Fiber	1 gram	
Fat	< 1 gram	
Protein	3 grams	
Sodium	8 milligrams	

Shopping List: bread flour, active dry yeast, garlic powder, fat-free Parmesan cheese

SPINACH ARTICHOKE DIP

EASY - DO AHEAD

ingredients: 10 oz. frozen chopped spinach, thawed and drained
14 oz. chopped artichoke hearts, drained
1/2 cup fat-free mayonnaise
1 tsp. crushed garlic
1/2 cup fat-free Parmesan cheese
2 tbsp. spicy brown mustard

directions: Preheat oven to 350 degrees.
Lightly spray 1-quart baking dish with nonfat cooking spray.
Combine spinach, artichokes, mayonnaise, crushed garlic, 1/3 cup Parmesan cheese and mustard in medium bowl, and mix until ingredients are blended.
Spread mixture in baking dish and top with remaining Parmesan cheese.
Bake in preheated oven 20-25 minutes, until top is browned and dip is heated through.
Serve immediately, with crackers, Italian bread or Parmesan pita chips.

Serves: 6

ITALIAN

Nutrition per Serving		Exchanges
Calories	85	3 vegetable
Carbohydrate	16 grams	
Cholesterol	0 milligrams	
Dietary Fiber	4 grams	
Fat	< 1 gram	
Protein	7 grams	
Sodium	372 milligrams	

Shopping List: 10-ounce package frozen chopped spinach, 14-ounce can artichoke hearts, 4 ounces fat-free mayonnaise, 2 ounces fat-free Parmesan cheese, spicy brown mustard, crushed garlic

SUN-DRIED TOMATO DIP

EASY - DO AHEAD

ingredients: 4 sun-dried tomatoes, cut in half
1/2 cup boiling water
1/2 cup fat-free ricotta cheese
1 1/2 cups fat-free cottage cheese
1 tbsp. dried basil
1 tsp. onion powder
1 tbsp. lemon juice
1/2 tsp. pepper

directions: Place tomatoes in a small bowl and cover with boiling water; let stand 5 minutes to soften. Drain and dry tomatoes.
Insert metal blade into food processor bowl; feed tomatoes through chute and pulse several times, just until finely chopped.
Remove tomatoes and set aside.
Combine ricotta and cottage cheese in bowl of food processor; process 10-15 seconds, until blended smooth.
Add tomatoes, basil, onion powder, lemon juice and pepper. Pulse several times, until blended smooth.
Refrigerate several hours before serving.
Serve with fresh vegetables or crusty Italian bread.

Serves: 6

Nutrition per Serving		Exchanges
Calories	99	1/4 milk
Carbohydrate	21 grams	3 vegetable
Cholesterol	3 milligrams	
Dietary Fiber	2 grams	
Fat	< 1 gram	
Protein	7 grams	
Sodium	100 milligrams	

Shopping List: sun-dried tomatoes (not packed in oil), 4 ounces fat-free ricotta cheese, 12 ounces fat-free cottage cheese, dried basil, onion powder, pepper, lemon juice

TOMATO-ONION SPREAD WITH ITALIAN BREAD CRISPS
EASY - DO AHEAD

ingredients: 1/4 cup sun-dried tomatoes, finely chopped
1/4 cup water
10 oz. fat-free cream cheese, softened
1 tsp. onion powder
1/3 cup chopped green onions
6 slices fat-free Italian bread
1 cup fat-free Parmesan cheese

directions: Combine tomatoes and water in a small saucepan and bring to a boil over high heat. Reduce heat to low, cover and simmer 2-3 minutes, until tomatoes have softened; drain well. Blend cream cheese and onion powder in food processor or blender and process until creamy and smooth. Spoon into medium bowl. Add tomatoes and green onions; mix until blended. Cover and refrigerate several hours or overnight. Preheat oven to 400 degrees. Line baking sheet with foil; cut bread slices into quarters and arrange on baking sheet. Lightly spray with nonfat cooking spray; sprinkle half the Parmesan cheese over the top. Bake in preheated oven 5-6 minutes; turn slices over. Lightly spray with nonfat cooking spray and sprinkle with remaining Parmesan cheese. Bake 3-4 minutes, until crisp and lightly browned. Serve tomato spread with Italian bread crisps.

Serves: 6

ITALIAN

Nutrition per Serving
Calories	148
Carbohydrate	27 grams
Cholesterol	0 milligrams
Dietary Fiber	1 gram
Fat	< 1 gram
Protein	10 grams
Sodium	459 milligrams

Exchanges
1 starch
2 1/2 vegetable

Shopping List: 1/2 pound fat-free Italian bread loaf, sun-dried tomatoes (not packed in oil), 10 ounces fat-free cream cheese, 1 bunch green onions, onion powder, 4 ounces fat-free Parmesan cheese

CHILLED FENNEL SOUP
AVERAGE - DO AHEAD

ingredients:　3 cups fat-free vegetable broth, divided
1 large fennel bulb, chopped
1 small onion, chopped
Juice of 1 lemon
Pinch of ground nutmeg
Cracked black peppercorns, toasted
1 cup fat-free sour cream
4 fennel sprigs for garnish

directions:　Pour 1/4 cup vegetable broth into large nonstick skillet.
Add fennel and onion; cook, stirring often, until vegetables are transparent.
In a blender or food processor, combine fennel and onion with remaining stock and purée.
Chill in refrigerator 30 minutes. Combine fennel mixture, lemon juice, nutmeg and toasted pepper in a large bowl. Whisk in sour cream.
Serve in chilled bowls and garnish with fennel sprigs.

Serves: 4

Nutrition per Serving

		Exchanges
Calories	61 grams	2 vegetable
Carbohydrate	9 grams	
Cholesterol	0 milligrams	
Dietary Fiber	1 gram	
Fat	< 1 gram	
Protein	5 grams	
Sodium	379 milligrams	

Shopping List:　1 large fennel bulb, 1 small white onion, 24 ounces fat-free vegetable broth, 8 ounces fat-free sour cream, cracked black peppercorns, lemon, ground nutmeg, fennel sprigs

ITALIAN BEAN SOUP

EASY - DO AHEAD - FREEZE

ingredients: 8 cups fat-free chicken broth
1 cup chopped carrots
1/4 cup chopped celery
1 cup frozen chopped onions, thawed and drained
2 tsp. garlic powder
1 1/2 cups canned white beans, drained
15 oz. Italian-style stewed tomatoes
1 1/2 tbsp. Italian seasoning
1/4 tsp. crushed red pepper
1 cup shell pasta, uncooked
3/4 cup fat-free Parmesan cheese (optional)

directions: Lightly spray Dutch oven with nonfat cooking spray. Pour 1 tablespoon chicken broth into pan and heat over medium-high heat. Add carrots, celery, onions and garlic powder to pan and cook 2-3 minutes, stirring frequently, until vegetables are tender. Add remaining broth, beans, tomatoes (undrained), seasoning and pepper to pan and mix well. Bring to a boil over high heat; reduce heat to low, cover and simmer, stirring occasionally, 30-45 minutes, until heated through. Carefully remove half the soup mixture and transfer to food processor or blender; process until blended smooth. Return to pan and mix well. Add pasta to soup; bring to a boil over high heat. Reduce heat to medium-low and simmer until pasta is cooked through but firm. Sprinkle with Parmesan cheese just before serving, if desired. Serve with crusty Italian bread.

Serves: 6

Nutrition per Serving		Exchanges
Calories	207	2 starch
Carbohydrate	39 grams	2 vegetable
Cholesterol	0 milligrams	
Dietary Fiber	4 grams	
Fat	< 1 gram	
Protein	12 grams	
Sodium	1299 milligrams	

Shopping List: 4 (16-ounce) cans fat-free chicken broth, 14 1/2-ounce can white beans, frozen chopped onions, 2 carrots, celery, 15-ounce can Italian-style stewed tomatoes, 8-ounce package shell pasta, Italian seasoning, crushed red pepper, fat-free Parmesan cheese, garlic powder

231

MINESTRONE SOUP

AVERAGE - DO AHEAD - FREEZE

ingredients:
8 cups fat-free beef broth
2 tsp. Italian seasoning
1 tbsp. onion flakes
1 tsp. garlic powder
8 oz. baby carrots
6 stalks celery, sliced
14 1/2 oz. Italian-style crushed tomatoes
12 oz. shredded cabbage
1 1/2 cups canned corn kernels, drained
2 small zucchini, sliced
15 oz. can fat-free kidney beans, drained
1 1/2 cups orzo, cooked and drained
1/2 cup fat-free Parmesan cheese

directions:
Combine broth, Italian seasoning, onion flakes and garlic powder in a large soup pot; add half the carrots and half the celery. Bring to a boil over high heat; reduce heat to low, cover and simmer 15-20 minutes, until vegetables are tender. Carefully remove vegetables from broth. Place 1 1/2 cups broth and vegetables in food processor or blender, and process until smooth. Return to soup pot and mix well. Add remaining carrots, celery and tomatoes (undrained) to pot; bring to a boil over high heat. Reduce heat to low, cover and simmer 10-15 minutes, until vegetables are tender. Add cabbage, corn, zucchini, beans and orzo pasta to pot; bring to a boil over high heat. Reduce heat to low, cover and simmer until pasta is cooked and vegetables are tender. Sprinkle with Parmesan cheese just before serving.

Serves: 6

Nutrition per Serving		Exchanges
Calories	300	3 starch
Carbohydrate	60 grams	3 vegetable
Cholesterol	0 milligrams	
Dietary Fiber	6 grams	
Fat	< 1 gram	
Protein	17 grams	
Sodium	748 milligrams	

Shopping List: 4 (16-ounce) cans fat-free beef broth, 8-ounce package baby carrots, celery, 14 1/2-ounce can Italian crushed tomatoes, 12-ounce package shredded cabbage, 15-ounce can corn kernels, 2 small zucchini, 15-ounce can fat-free kidney beans, orzo pasta, 2 ounces fat-free Parmesan cheese, Italian seasoning, onion flakes, garlic powder

ITALIAN

ANTIPASTO SALAD

EASY - DO AHEAD

ingredients:
8 cups romaine lettuce leaves
3 medium Italian plum tomatoes, sliced thin
1 medium red onion, sliced thin
3/4 cup roasted red peppers, drained
3 oz. fat-free whole Mozzarella, cut into strips
3 oz. fat-free ham
3 oz. fat-free roast beef
6 pepperoncini peppers
9 oz. package frozen artichoke hearts, thawed
    and drained
1 cup canned fat-free kidney beans, drained
3/4 cup fat-free Italian salad dressing

directions:
Arrange lettuce on the bottom of a large serving platter. Top with sliced tomatoes, onions and red peppers, overlapping as needed. Arrange the cheese, ham and roast beef on top of onions. Alternate pepperoncini peppers, artichoke hearts and beans around the outer edge of platter. Serve with salad dressing.

Serves: 6

Nutrition per Serving

Calories	179
Carbohydrate	28 grams
Cholesterol	10 milligrams
Dietary Fiber	5 grams
Fat	< 1 gram
Protein	15 grams
Sodium	984 milligrams

Exchanges
1 meat
1 starch
3 vegetable

Shopping List:
romaine lettuce, 3 Italian plum tomatoes, 1 red onion, 3 ounces fat-free Mozzarella cheese (whole or sliced), 3 ounces fat-free ham, 3 ounces fat-free roast beef, pepperoncini peppers, roasted red peppers, 9 ounces frozen artichoke hearts, canned kidney beans, 6 ounces fat-free Italian salad dressing

CAESAR SALAD

EASY - DO AHEAD

ingredients:

12 cups romaine lettuce, torn into bite-size pieces
1 cup cherry tomatoes, cut in half
3/4 cup chopped artichoke hearts
3/4 cup fat-free croutons
1/4 cup + 1 1/2 tbsp. fat-free Parmesan cheese, divided
1/2 cup fat-free chicken broth
1/4 cup white wine vinegar
6 whole anchovies
1 1/4 tsp. lemon juice
2 1/2 tsp. Dijon mustard
1/4 tsp. dry mustard
2 tbsp. egg substitute

directions:

Remove core from romaine lettuce and wash leaves under cold water. Place lettuce in colander and drain well. Wrap lettuce in paper towels and re-frigerate several hours or overnight. Tear lettuce into bite-size pieces and place in large salad bowl. Add tomatoes, artichokes, croutons and 1/4 cup Parmesan cheese to lettuce, and toss until well mixed. Combine chicken broth, vinegar, ancho-vies, lemon juice, Dijon mustard, remaining Parmesan cheese, dry mustard and egg substitute in a food processor or blender, and process until creamy and smooth. Pour dressing over salad and toss until well mixed. Serve immediately.

Serves: 6

Nutrition per Serving		Exchanges
Calories	85	3 1/2 vegetable
Carbohydrate	15 grams	
Cholesterol	3 milligrams	
Dietary Fiber	2 grams	
Fat	< 1 gram	
Protein	7 grams	
Sodium	513 milligrams	

Shopping List: 1 head romaine lettuce, 1/2 pint cherry tomatoes, canned or frozen artichoke hearts, fat-free croutons, 3 ounces fat-free Parmesan cheese, 4 ounces fat-free chicken broth, 2 ounces white wine vinegar, whole anchovies, lemon juice, Dijon mustard, dry mustard, egg substitute

ITALIAN

234

CAESAR PASTA SALAD
EASY - DO AHEAD

ingredients: 10 ounces fat-free angel hair pasta,
cooked and drained
1/2 cup chopped red onion
1/4 cup chopped red or green bell pepper
1/4 cup fat-free Parmesan cheese
2 tbsp. fresh parsley, snipped
8 oz. fat-free Caesar salad dressing
1 head romaine lettuce, shredded
1 small tomato, sliced (optional)

directions: Prepare pasta according to package directions; drain well and place in a large bowl.
Add onion, bell pepper, Parmesan cheese and parsley to pasta and mix lightly.
Pour salad dressing over mixture and toss until mixed.
Line serving platter with lettuce and spoon pasta salad over top.
Garnish with tomato slices and serve.

Serves: 6

ITALIAN

Nutrition per Serving
Calories	168
Carbohydrate	34 grams
Cholesterol	0 milligrams
Dietary Fiber	3 grams
Fat	< 1 gram
Protein	7 grams
Sodium	386 milligrams

Exchanges
1 starch
4 vegetable

Shopping List: 10 ounce fat-free angel hair pasta, red onion, red or green bell pepper, fat-free Parmesan cheese, fresh parsley, 8 ounces fat-free Caesar salad dressing, 1 head romaine lettuce, 1 small tomato

CREAMY SEAFOOD PASTA SALAD

EASY - DO AHEAD

ingredients: 10 ounces fat-free pasta, cooked and drained
6 ounces fat-free frozen cooked shrimp,
    thawed and drained
6 oz. can crabmeat, drained
3/4 cup frozen artichoke hearts, thawed
    and drained
3/4 cup frozen peas, thawed and drained
1/3 cup chopped celery
1/2 cup chopped red bell pepper
1/4 cup chopped green onions
1/2 cup fat-free creamy Italian salad dressing

directions: Cook pasta according to package directions and drain well; place pasta in a large serving bowl.
Add shrimp, crabmeat, artichokes, peas, celery, red pepper and green onions; mix well.
Pour salad dressing over pasta salad and toss until mixed and coated.
Cover and refrigerate several hours, or overnight, before serving.

Serves: 6

Nutrition per Serving		Exchanges
Calories	272	2 starch
Carbohydrate	50 grams	1 meat
Cholesterol	6 milligrams	3 vegetable
Dietary Fiber	3 grams	
Fat	< 1 gram	
Protein	15 grams	
Sodium	477 milligrams	

Shopping List: 10 ounces fat-free pasta (fusilli, shells, rotini, rotelle), 6 ounces frozen cooked shrimp, 6-ounce can crabmeat, 9-ounce package frozen artichoke hearts, frozen peas, celery, red bell pepper, green onions, 4 ounces fat-free creamy Italian salad dressing
*For quick preparation, purchase cut-up vegetables at supermarket salad bar

ITALIAN BREAD SALAD
EASY - DO AHEAD

ingredients:
3 1/2 cups fat-free Italian bread, cut in
   1-inch pieces
2 cups chopped Italian plum tomatoes
9 ounces frozen artichoke hearts,
   thawed and drained
1 medium red onion, sliced thin
1 small cucumber, peeled and sliced
1 1/2 tsp. minced garlic
1 1/2 tsp. dried basil
6 cups mixed greens
3/4 cup fat-free red wine vinegar
   salad dressing
1/4 cup fat-free Parmesan cheese (optional)

directions:
Combine all ingredients, except salad dressing, in a large bowl and mix well.
Pour salad dressing over salad and toss to coat all ingredients.
Let salad stand at room temperature 10-15 minutes.
Sprinkle with Parmesan cheese before serving, if desired.

Serves: 6

Nutrition per Serving		Exchanges
Calories	163	1 starch
Carbohydrate	34 grams	3 1/2 vegetable
Cholesterol	0 milligrams	
Dietary Fiber	3 grams	
Fat	< 1 gram	
Protein	6 grams	
Sodium	325 milligrams	

Shopping List: fat-free Italian bread, 9 ounces frozen artichoke hearts, 4 Italian plum tomatoes, 1 red onion, 1 cucumber, minced garlic, dried basil, 6 ounces fat-free red wine vinegar, 2 (8-ounce) packages mixed greens, fat-free Parmesan cheese

ITALIAN

ITALIAN BEAN SALAD

EASY

ingredients: 8 cups romaine lettuce, torn into bite-size pieces
1 cup shredded red cabbage
1/2 medium red onion, sliced thin
1 cup sliced mushrooms
3/4 cup canned garbanzo beans, drained
3 small Italian plum tomatoes, quartered
1/2 medium cucumber, sliced thin
1/2 cup shredded carrots
1/3 cup fat-free Parmesan cheese
1 tsp. dried oregano
1/8 tsp. pepper
3/4 cup fat-free Italian salad dressing

directions: Combine lettuce, cabbage, onion, mushrooms, beans, tomatoes, cucumber, carrots and cheese in a large salad bowl and toss until well mixed. Sprinkle with oregano and pepper; pour salad dressing over salad and toss until well mixed. Serve immediately.

Serves: 6

Nutrition per Serving		Exchanges
Calories	106	4 vegetable
Carbohydrate	19 grams	
Cholesterol	0 milligrams	
Dietary Fiber	5 grams	
Fat	< 1 gram	
Protein	6 grams	
Sodium	292 milligrams	

Shopping List: 2 heads romaine lettuce, 8-ounce package shredded red cabbage, red onion, 4 ounces sliced mushrooms, canned garbanzo beans, 3 small Italian plum tomatoes, cucumber, shredded carrots, fat-free Parmesan cheese, 6 ounces fat-free Italian salad dressing, dried oregano, pepper

ITALIAN SALAD

EASY - DO AHEAD

ingredients:
1 lb. mixed greens
3/4 cup red onions, sliced into rings
1 cup red and green bell peppers, cut into strips
1 cup cherry tomatoes
4 medium radishes
1 cup fat-free croutons
1/2 cup fat-free creamy Italian salad dressing
1/4 cup fat-free Parmesan cheese

directions;
Combine greens, onion, peppers, tomatoes, radishes and croutons in a large bowl.
Sprinkle with Parmesan cheese and toss with dressing.

Serves: 4

Nutrition per Serving

Calories	127
Carbohydrate	27 grams
Cholesterol	0 milligrams
Dietary Fiber	3 grams
Fat	< 1 gram
Protein	6 grams
Sodium	490 milligrams

Exchanges
5 vegetable

ITALIAN

Shopping List:
16-ounce package mixed greens, 1 red onion, 1 red bell pepper, 1 green bell pepper, 8-ounce package cherry tomatoes, 4 radishes, fat-free croutons, 4 ounces fat-free creamy Italian salad dressing, fat-free Parmesan cheese

SHRIMP PASTA SALAD
EASY - DO AHEAD

ingredients: 6 oz. fat-free pasta, cooked and drained
1 lb. fat-free frozen cooked shrimp,
    thawed and drained
1 small zucchini, sliced thin
1 small yellow squash, sliced thin
3 oz. fat-free Mozzarella cheese, cubed
3/4 cup broccoli florets
1 cup frozen pepper strips, thawed and drained
3 tsp. dried parsley
1/2 tsp. dried oregano
2 tbsp. sliced black olives
1/4 cup fat-free Parmesan cheese
3/4 cup *Parmesan Salad Dressing (see recipe*)*

directions: Prepare *Parmesan Salad Dressing* according to directions (see recipe). Cook pasta according to package directions; drain well and place in a large bowl. Add shrimp, zucchini, squash, Mozzarella cheese, broccoli, peppers, red onion, parsley, oregano and olives to pasta and mix well. Sprinkle Parmesan cheese over pasta mixture and toss to coat. Gradually pour salad dressing over salad, tossing to mix in between additions. Add just enough dressing to coat pasta and vegetables. Cover and refrigerate 2 hours or overnight; add additional salad dressing if salad seems a bit dry.

Serves: 6

Nutrition per Serving		Exchanges
Calories	150	1 starch
Carbohydrate	25 grams	3 vegetable
Cholesterol	0 milligrams	
Dietary fiber	2 grams	
Fat	< 1 gram	
Protein	9 grams	
Sodium	532 milligrams	

Shopping List: 6 ounces fat-free pasta, 1 pound fat-free frozen cooked shrimp, 1 zucchini, 1 yellow squash, broccoli florets, 3 ounces fat-free Mozzarella cheese, 10 ounce package frozen pepper strips, sliced black olives, dried oregano, dried parsley, *Parmesan Salad Dressing* (or any creamy fat-free dressing), fat-free Parmesan cheese

TUNA PASTA SALAD

EASY - DO AHEAD

ingredients: 10 oz. rotini pasta, cooked and drained
16 ounces frozen green beans, thawed and
    drained
12 oz. fat-free tuna, drained
3/4 cup chopped tomatoes, drained well
2 tbsp. chopped black olives
1/2 cup fat-free red wine vinegar salad dressing
2 tbsp. fat-free Parmesan cheese

directions: Cook pasta according to package directions and
drain well; place pasta in a large serving bowl.
Add beans, tuna, tomatoes and olives to pasta, and
mix well.
Pour salad dressing over mixture and toss until
well mixed.
Cover and refrigerate several hours or overnight;
sprinkle with Parmesan cheese just before serving.

Serves: 6

Nutrition per Serving		Exchanges
Calories	248	2 starch
Carbohydrate	36 grams	1 vegetable
Cholesterol	10 milligrams	2 meat
Dietary Fiber	3 grams	
Fat	< 1 gram	
Protein	24 grams	
Sodium	393 milligrams	

Shopping List: 10 ounces rotini pasta, 16 ounces frozen cut green beans,
12 ounces fat-free tuna, 1 tomato, chopped black olives,
4 ounces fat-free red wine vinegar salad dressing, fat-
free Parmesan cheese

CREAMY CAESAR SALAD DRESSING

EASY - DO AHEAD

ingredients: 3/8 cup fat-free sour cream
1/4 cup egg substitute
1/3 cup fat-free Parmesan cheese
3 tbsp. white wine vinegar
1 tbsp. lemon juice
2 tsp. chopped anchovies
1/2 tsp. garlic powder

directions: Combine all ingredients in a food processor or blender and process until smooth.

Serves: 6

Nutrition per Serving

Calories	30
Carbohydrate	4 grams
Cholesterol	1 milligram
Dietary Fiber	0 grams
Fat	< 1 gram
Protein	4 grams
Sodium	88 milligrams

Exchanges
1/3 milk

Shopping List: 3 ounces fat-free sour cream, 2 ounces egg substitute, fat-free Parmesan cheese, white wine vinegar, lemon juice, anchovies, garlic powder

ITALIAN

PARMESAN SALAD DRESSING

EASY - DO AHEAD

ingredients:
1/3 cup fat-free plain yogurt
2/3 cup fat-free sour cream
1/4 cup fat-free Parmesan cheese
1 tsp. skim milk
2 tsp. lemon juice
1/2 tsp. garlic powder

directions:
Combine all ingredients in a food processor or blender; process until creamy and smooth. Refrigerate several hours before serving. Great on pasta salads or assorted greens.

Serves: 6

Nutrition per Serving		Exchanges
Calories	27	1/3 milk
Carbohydrate	3 grams	
Cholesterol	< 1 milligram	
Dietary Fiber	0 grams	
Fat	< 1 gram	
Protein	3 grams	
Sodium	43 milligrams	

Shopping List: 3 ounces fat-free plain yogurt, 6 ounces fat-free sour cream, 1 ounce fat-free Parmesan cheese, skim milk, lemon juice, garlic powder

ITALIAN

BACON-TOMATO FRITTATA

AVERAGE

ingredients:
1 1/2 cups egg substitute
4 large egg whites
2 tbsp. fat-free cottage cheese, blended smooth
1/2 tsp. garlic powder
3/4 tsp. Italian seasoning
1/8 tsp. pepper
1 medium tomato, chopped and drained
6 pieces fat-free turkey bacon, cooked and drained
1/4 cup fat-free finely-shredded Cheddar cheese
1/2 cup fat-free finely-shredded Mozzarella cheese

directions:
Combine egg substitute, egg whites, cottage cheese, garlic powder, Italian seasoning and pepper in a medium bowl, and blend until smooth. Lightly spray large nonstick skillet with nonfat cooking spray and heat over medium-high heat. Add tomatoes to skillet and cook, stirring constantly, 1-2 minutes until soft. Add bacon to skillet and mix with tomatoes; spread mixture evenly over bottom of skillet. Reduce heat to low; pour egg mixture over tomatoes and bacon; cook, without stirring, 10-12 minutes, until eggs are almost set. Preheat broiler on high heat. Remove skillet from stove and place under broiler 3-4 minutes, until eggs are completely set. Sprinkle Cheddar and Mozzarella cheese over top and broil 1-2 minutes, until cheese is completely melted.

Serves: 4

Nutrition per Serving		Exchanges
Calories	128	1 vegetable
Carbohydrate	23 grams	3 meat
Cholesterol	23 milligrams	
Dietary Fiber	< 1 gram	
Fat	< 1 gram	
Protein	23 grams	
Sodium	550 milligrams	

Shopping List: 12 ounces egg substitute, large eggs, fat-free cottage cheese, 1 ounce fat-free finely shredded Cheddar cheese, 2 ounces fat-free finely-shredded Mozzarella cheese, 1 tomato, fat-free turkey bacon, garlic powder, Italian seasoning, pepper

MUSHROOM-HAM-CHEESE OMELET

AVERAGE

ingredients: 1 ounce fat-free ham
1/3 cup sliced mushrooms
1/2 cup egg substitute
2 large egg whites
2 tsp. skim milk
1/8 tsp. pepper
1/4 cup fat-free finely-shredded Cheddar cheese
1 tbsp. chopped Italian parsley

directions: Lightly spray 8-inch nonstick skillet or omelet pan with nonfat cooking spray and heat over medium-high heat. Add ham and mushrooms to skillet and cook, stirring frequently, 3-4 minutes, until lightly browned. Remove from skillet and set aside. Remove skillet from heat and respray with cooking spray. Combine egg substitute, egg whites, milk and pepper in a medium bowl and mix until blended smooth. Place skillet over medium-high heat; pour egg mixture into skillet and cook, without stirring, 2-3 minutes, until eggs are set around the edges. Carefully lift the omelet and let the uncooked eggs flow to the bottom of the skillet; continue cooking, without stirring, until eggs are set. Sprinkle ham, mushrooms and cheese over half the omelet. Fold omelet in half, and cook until cheese is melted and eggs are cooked through. Slide onto plate and sprinkle with parsley.

Serves: 1

Nutrition per Serving		Exchanges
Calories	166	4 meat
Carbohydrate	8 grams	1 vegetable
Cholesterol	10 milligrams	
Dietary Fiber	1 gram	
Protein	30 grams	
Sodium	862 milligrams	

Shopping List: 4 ounces egg substitute, large eggs, skim milk, 1 ounce fat-free ham, mushroom, 1 ounce fat-free finely-shredded Cheddar cheese, pepper, Italian parsley

ITALIAN

SPINACH-ARTICHOKE FRITTATA

AVERAGE

ingredients:
1 cup egg substitute
8 large egg whites
2 tbsp. skim milk
1/2 tsp. garlic powder
2 tsp. Dijon mustard
2 cups fresh spinach, cleaned and chopped
9 oz. package frozen artichoke hearts,
    thawed, drained and chopped
1/2 cup fat-free finely-shredded Cheddar cheese
1/2 cup fat-free finely-shredded Mozzarella cheese

directions:
Combine egg substitute, egg whites, milk, garlic powder and mustard in a large bowl and beat until completely blended. Lightly spray a large nonstick skillet with nonfat cooking spray and heat over medium- high heat. Add spinach and artichokes to skillet and cook, stirring constantly, until spinach begins to wilt and artichokes are lightly browned. Spread the vegetables evenly over the bottom of skillet; reduce heat to low. Pour egg mixture into skillet and cook, without stirring, until eggs are set. Sprinkle Cheddar and Mozzarella cheese over top and broil 1-2 minutes until cheese is completely melted. Cut the frittata into 4 equal pieces and serve immediately.

Serves: 4

Nutrition per Serving
Calories	154
Carbohydrate	13 grams
Cholesterol	0 milligrams
Dietary Fiber	4 grams
Fat	< 1 gram
Protein	24 grams
Sodium	556 milligrams

Exchanges
3 vegetable
2 meat

Shopping List:
8 ounces egg substitute, eggs, skim milk, 9-ounce package frozen artichoke hearts, fresh spinach leaves, Dijon mustard, garlic powder, 2 ounces fat-free finely-shredded Cheddar cheese, 2 ounces fat-free finely-shredded Mozzarella cheese

ZUCCHINI-MUSHROOM FRITTATA

AVERAGE

ingredients:
1 cup egg substitute
8 large egg whites
2 tbsp. fat-free ricotta cheese, blended smooth
1/4 cup fat-free Parmesan cheese
2 cups sliced mushrooms
1 medium zucchini, sliced 1/4-inch thick
1 small tomato, seeded and chopped
1 tsp. dried basil
1/2 tsp. dried thyme
3/4 tsp. onion powder
1/4 tsp. pepper
3/4 cup fat-free finely-shredded Mozzarella cheese

directions: Combine egg substitute, egg whites, ricotta cheese and Parmesan cheese in a medium bowl; beat until ingredients are blended smooth. Lightly spray large nonstick skillet with nonfat cooking spray and heat over medium-high heat. Add mushrooms, zucchini and tomatoes to skillet. Sprinkle with basil, thyme, onion powder and pepper; mix well. Cook, stirring frequently, 3-4 minutes, until vegetables are soft. Spread the vegetable mixture over bottom of skillet. Reduce heat to low; pour egg mixture into skillet and cook without stirring 8-10 minutes, until eggs are almost set. Preheat broiler on high heat. Remove skillet from stove and place under broiler 3-5 minutes, until eggs are set. Sprinkle cheese over top and broil 30-60 seconds, until cheese is completely melted. Cut frittata into four equal pieces and serve immediately.

Serves: 4

Nutrition per Serving		Exchanges
Calories	137	1 1/2 vegetable
Carbohydrate	9 grams	3 meat
Cholesterol	1 milligram	
Dietary Fiber	1 gram	
Fat	< 1 gram	
Protein	23 grams	
Sodium	408 milligrams	

Shopping List: 8 ounces egg substitute, large eggs, fat-free ricotta cheese, 1 ounce fat-free Parmesan cheese, 8 ounces sliced mushrooms, 1 zucchini, 1 tomato, 3 ounces fat-free finely-shredded Mozzarella cheese, dried basil, dried thyme, pepper, onion flakes

CHICKEN CACCIATORE

EASY - DO AHEAD - FREEZE

ingredients:
2 tbsp. fat-free chicken broth
2 lb. fat-free chicken breasts
1 tsp. garlic powder
1 tsp. onion powder
1/4 tsp. pepper
2 cups sliced mushrooms
2 tsp. minced garlic
3 cups canned crushed tomatoes with purée
2 tsp. Italian seasoning

directions:
Lightly spray a large nonstick skillet with nonfat cooking spray; pour chicken broth into skillet and heat over medium-high heat. Sprinkle chicken breasts with garlic powder, onion powder and pepper. Add to skillet and cook 3-4 minutes, turning frequently, until browned. Remove chicken from skillet and set aside. Reduce heat to medium; add mushrooms and garlic to skillet and cook, stirring frequently, until mushrooms are softened and lightly browned. Stir in tomatoes and Italian seasoning. Return chicken to skillet; increase heat to high and bring to a boil. Reduce heat to medium-low and simmer, uncovered, 5-7 minutes, until chicken is cooked through.

Serves: 8

Nutrition per Serving

Calories	135
Carbohydrate	8 grams
Cholesterol	71 milligrams
Dietary Fiber	1 gram
Fat	< 1 gram
Protein	25 grams
Sodium	530 milligrams

Exchanges
1 1/2 vegetable
3 meat

Shopping List: 2 pounds fat-free chicken breasts, 8 ounces sliced mushrooms, 24 ounces crushed tomatoes with purée, fat-free chicken broth, garlic powder, onion powder, pepper, minced garlic, Italian seasoning

CHICKEN MARSALA

AVERAGE

ingredients: 3/8 cup flour
3/8 tsp. dried marjoram
1/8 tsp. pepper
1/2 cup fat-free chicken broth
1/2 cup Marsala wine
2 1/4 cups sliced mushrooms
1/4 cup chopped green onions
1 1/2 lb. fat-free chicken breasts

directions: Combine flour, marjoram and pepper in a shallow dish and mix well.
Combine chicken broth and wine in a small bowl and mix well.
Lightly spray large nonstick skillet with nonfat cooking spray and heat over medium-high heat. Add mushrooms and onions to skillet and cook, stirring frequently, until vegetables are tender. Remove from skillet and set aside. Dip chicken in flour mixture and coat on both sides. Place chicken in skillet and cook 3-4 minutes per side, until lightly browned. Return mushrooms and onions to skillet. Gradually add broth mixture to skillet; cook 3-4 minutes, stirring frequently, until sauce thickens. Remove chicken from skillet and arrange on platter. Spoon sauce over top and serve.

Serves: 6

ITALIAN

Nutrition per Serving

		Exchanges
Calories	152	2 vegetable
Carbohydrate	8 grams	3 meat
Cholesterol	71 milligrams	
Dietary Fiber	1 gram	
Fat	< 1 gram	
Protein	25 grams	
Sodium	351 milligrams	

Shopping List: 1 1/2 pounds fat-free chicken breasts, 4 ounces fat-free chicken broth, 4 ounces dry Marsala wine, 1/2 pound mushrooms, green onions, flour, dried marjoram, pepper

CHICKEN TENDERS MARSALA

AVERAGE

ingredients:
1 lb. fat-free chicken tenders
Flour (enough to lightly coat turkey)
3 cups sliced button mushrooms
1/2 cup Marsala wine
3/4 cup fat-free chicken broth
3 tbsp. fat-free plain yogurt
Salt and pepper, to taste

directions:
Coat chicken tenders with flour.
Lightly spray large nonstick skillet with nonfat cooking spray; add chicken tenders and sauté for about 2 minutes on each side.
Remove from pan and blot with a paper towel. Add mushrooms to skillet and sauté until all the liquid is evaporated.
Add Marsala wine and reduce by half. Add broth and bring to a boil over medium-high heat.
Add yogurt and salt and pepper; mix well. Add chicken to sauce, heat and serve.

Serves: 4

Nutrition per Serving		Exchanges
Calories	153	2 meat
Carbohydrate	8 grams	2 vegetable
Cholesterol	41 milligrams	
Dietary Fiber	1 gram	
Fat	< 1 gram	
Protein	18 grams	
Sodium	1414 milligrams	

Shopping List: 1 pound fat-free chicken tenders, 3 cups button mushrooms, flour, 4 ounces Marsala wine, 6 ounces fat-free chicken broth, fat-free plain yogurt, salt, pepper

ITALIAN

CHICKEN TETRAZZINI
AVERAGE - DO AHEAD - FREEZE

ingredients:

8 oz. spaghetti, cooked and drained
1 1/2 cups fat-free chicken broth
2 1/2 cup sliced mushrooms
1/2 cup chopped celery
3 tbsp. dry white wine
3 tbsp. cornstarch
1 cup evaporated skim milk
3 cups fat-free chicken tenders, cooked and cubed
1/4 cup fat-free Parmesan cheese

directions:

Cook spaghetti according to package directions and drain well. Preheat oven to 375 degrees. Lightly spray 9x13-inch baking dish with nonfat cooking spray. Pour broth into large saucepan and bring to a boil over high heat. Add mushrooms and celery to broth; reduce heat to low and simmer 3-4 minutes, until vegetables are tender. Combine wine and cornstarch in a small bowl and mix until cornstarch is dissolved and mixture is blended. Gradually add milk to broth, stirring constantly. Stir in cornstarch mixture. Bring to a boil over medium-high heat; cook, stirring constantly, until mixture thickens. Remove pan from heat. Add chicken, pasta and 2 tablespoons Parmesan cheese to sauce, and mix well. Turn mixture into prepared baking pan; sprinkle with remaining Parmesan cheese. Bake in preheated oven 25-30 minutes, until golden brown and cooked through.

Serves: 6

Nutrition per Serving		Exchanges
Calories	326	2 starch
Carbohydrate	40 grams	3 1/4 meat
Cholesterol	57 milligrams	2 vegetable
Dietary Fiber	1 gram	
Fat	< 1 gram	
Protein	36 grams	
Sodium	537 milligrams	

Shopping List: 1 3/4 pounds fat-free chicken tenders, 8 ounces spaghetti, 15 ounces fat-free chicken broth, 8 ounces sliced mushrooms, celery, 8 ounces evaporated skim milk, white wine, 1 ounce fat-free Parmesan cheese, cornstarch

ITALIAN GARLIC CHICKEN
EASY - DO AHEAD

ingredients: 1/2 cup fat-free mayonnaise
1/2 cup fat-free Italian salad dressing
1/4 tsp. garlic powder
1/8 tsp. ground red pepper
4 fat-free chicken breast halves (1-1 1/2 lb.)

directions: Combine mayonnaise, salad dressing, garlic powder and red pepper in a small bowl; mix well. Pour over chicken.
Cover and refrigerate 20 minutes; drain.
Place chicken on grill over medium-hot coals, or on rack of broiler pan sprayed with nonfat cooking spray.
Grill or broil 10-12 minutes per side, until tender.

Serves: 4

ITALIAN

Nutrition per Serving		Exchanges
Calories	233	1/3 starch
Carbohydrate	8 grams	6 meat
Cholesterol	96 milligrams	
Dietary Fiber	0 grams	
Fat	< 1 gram	
Protein	46 grams	
Sodium	715 milligrams	

Shopping List: 1 to 1 1/2 pounds fat-free chicken breasts, 4 ounces fat-free mayonnaise, 4 ounces fat-free Italian salad dressing, garlic powder, ground red pepper

MEAT LOAF ITALIANO
EASY - DO AHEAD - FREEZE

ingredients: 1 1/2 lb. fat-free ground turkey (or chicken)
3/8 cup egg substitute
2 tsp. minced garlic
1 1/4 tsp. dried basil
3/4 tsp. dried rosemary
1/2 tsp. crushed red pepper
1 tbsp. onion flakes
3/4 cup fat-free bread crumbs
1 cup fat-free pasta sauce
1/4 cup fat-free Parmesan cheese

directions: Preheat oven to 350 degrees. Lightly spray 5x9-inch loaf pan with nonfat cooking spray. Combine turkey, egg substitute, garlic, basil, rosemary, red pepper, onion flakes and bread crumbs in a large bowl and mix until all ingredients are blended. Pat mixture into prepared pan and bake in preheated oven 15 minutes. Spread pasta sauce over turkey loaf and bake 20-25 minutes, until turkey is no longer pink. Sprinkle Parmesan cheese over top and bake 1-2 minutes, until cheese is lightly brown. Slice turkey loaf and serve.
Great with Garlic Mashed Potatoes.

Serves: 6

Nutrition per Serving		Exchanges
Calories	153	3 1/2 meat
Carbohydrate	8 grams	1 vegetable
Cholesterol	50 milligrams	
Dietary Fiber	< 1 gram	
Fat	< 1 gram	
Protein	28 grams	
Sodium	442 milligrams	

Shopping List: 3 ounces egg substitute, 1 1/2 pounds fat-free ground turkey (or chicken), 8 ounces fat-free pasta sauce, 1 ounce fat-free Parmesan cheese, fat-free bread crumbs, minced garlic, dried basil, dried rosemary, crushed red pepper, onion flakes

ITALIAN

PERCH FLORENTINE

AVERAGE

ingredients: 1 lb. yellow freshwater perch fillets, skinned
10 oz. package frozen chopped spinach, thawed
and drained
1/2 cup fat-free ricotta cheese
3 tbsp. fat-free Parmesan cheese
2 tbsp. egg substitute
2 tbsp. minced onions
1/2 tsp. dried basil
Ground black pepper, to taste
Dash of garlic powder

directions: Preheat oven to 375 degrees. Lightly spray a
1 1/2-quart baking dish with nonfat cooking spray.
Lay fillets flat and set aside.
In a medium bowl, combine spinach, ricotta,
Parmesan cheese, egg substitute, onions, basil,
pepper and garlic powder.
Spread some of the mixture on each fillet. Roll up
fish around spinach and fasten with a toothpick.
Stand the fish rolls on end in the baking dish.
Cover and bake in preheated oven until fish flakes
easily with a fork, 10-15 minutes.

Serves: 6

Nutrition per Serving   **Exchanges**
Calories   106   1 vegetable
Carbohydrate   5 grams   2 1/2 meat
Cholesterol   70 milligrams
Dietary Fiber   1 gram
Fat   < 1 gram
Protein   20 grams
Sodium   151 milligrams

Shopping List: 10-ounce package frozen chopped spinach, 1 pound
yellow fresh-water perch fillets, 4 ounces fat-free ricotta
cheese, fat-free grated Parmesan cheese, fat-free egg
substitute, minced onions, dried basil, ground black
pepper, garlic powder

SEAFARER'S ITALIAN PASTA

AVERAGE

ingredients:
1 lb. fat-free angel hair pasta, cooked and drained
1 cup fat-free chicken broth
5 cloves garlic, peeled and slivered
1 lb. fat-free shrimp, peeled and deveined
Salt and pepper, to taste
4 oz. can minced clams, undrained
28 oz. can Italian-style tomatoes, undrained
1 tsp. oregano
1/4 cup dry white wine
1/4 cup chopped fresh parsley
1/2 cup fat-free Parmesan cheese

directions:
Prepare pasta according to package directions and drain well; set aside and keep warm on large serving platter. Pour chicken broth into large nonstick skillet and heat over medium-high heat; add garlic, shrimp, salt and pepper to broth and cook, stirring frequently, until shrimp turn pink and are cooked through.
Remove shrimp from skillet and set aside. Add clams (with liquid), tomatoes, oregano and wine to skillet; cook until sauce thickens.
Return shrimp to skillet and cook over low heat 10 minutes, until heated through. Sprinkle with parsley. Spoon shrimp mixture over pasta; sprinkle with Parmesan cheese and serve.

Serves: 8

ITALIAN

Nutrition per Serving
Calories	259
Carbohydrate	46 grams
Cholesterol	16 milligrams
Dietary Fiber	3 grams
Protein	17 grams
Sodium	650 milligrams

Exchanges
3 vegetable
2 starch
1 meat

Shopping List:
1 pound fat-free shrimp, 4-ounce can minced clams, 8 ounces fat-free chicken broth, 28-ounce can Italian-style tomatoes, dry white wine, fresh parsley, whole garlic, fat-free Parmesan cheese, oregano, salt, pepper

SEAFOOD STEW
EASY - DO AHEAD

ingredients:
1/4 cup chopped onion
1/4 cup chopped celery
2 tsp. fat-free chicken broth
1 cup dry white wine
28 oz. can Italian plum tomatoes with juice
1 bay leaf
1/2 tsp. dried oregano
Fresh ground pepper
1 lb. cod, cut into 1-inch pieces
12 medium fat-free shrimp,
    peeled and deveined
Parsley

directions:
Combine onion, celery and broth in a large saucepan.
Cook, stirring, over low heat until the vegetables are tender, about 10 minutes.
Add the wine and heat to boiling; boil 5 minutes.
Add the tomatoes, bay leaf, oregano and pepper; stir to break up tomatoes.
Cook, uncovered, 5 minutes. Add the fish and shrimp. Cover and cook over low heat until the fish is cooked through, about 5 minutes.
Divide fish and broth evenly among the bowls.
Sprinkle with parsley.

Serves: 6

Nutrition per Serving

		Exchanges
Calories	160	3 vegetable
Carbohydrate	13 grams	2 1/2 meat
Cholesterol	71 milligrams	
Dietary Fiber	1 gram	
Fat	< 1 gram	
Protein	19 grams	
Sodium	581 milligrams	

Shopping List: onion, celery, dry white wine, chicken broth, 28-ounce can plum tomatoes, bay leaf, oregano, black pepper, 1 pound cod, 12 medium shrimp

SPICY ANGEL HAIR PASTA PUTTANESCA

EASY

ingredients:
1/4 cup red wine
1/2 tsp. minced garlic
1 oz. red onion, julienned
4 cups fat-free pasta sauce (marinara)
1 tbsp. capers
1 tbsp. sliced black olives
1 tsp. Cajun spice
6 oz. fat-free shrimp, uncooked
6 oz. sole, cubed
2 tbsp. sun-dried tomato, chopped
8 oz. fat-free angel hair pasta, cooked and drained

directions:
Pour wine into large nonstick skillet and heat over medium heat.
Add garlic and onion and cook until soft.
Add pasta sauce, capers, olives and Cajun spice.
Add shrimp, sole and tomato; simmer 2-3 minutes. Toss with cooked pasta and serve immediately.

Serves: 4

Nutrition per Serving
		Exchanges
Calories	481	3 starch
Carbohydrate	86 grams	1 meat
Cholesterol	25 milligrams	8 vegetable
Dietary Fiber	3 grams	
Fat	< 1 gram	
Protein	27 grams	
Sodium	1038 milligrams	

Shopping List: 6 ounces sole, 6 ounces fat-free shrimp (uncooked), red onion, minced garlic, sun-dried tomato (not oil-packed), 32 ounces fat-free marinara sauce, 2 ounces red wine, capers, black olives, Cajun spice, 8 ounces fat-free angel hair pasta

ITALIAN

257

ANGEL HAIR PASTA WITH SPINACH AND CREAM SAUCE

EASY

ingredients:
12 oz. fat-free angel hair pasta, cooked and drained
3/4 cup fat-free cottage cheese
3/4 cup fat-free ricotta cheese
1 tbsp. fat-free chicken broth
1 tsp. minced garlic
16 oz. package frozen chopped spinach,
    thawed and drained
3/4 cup fat-free Parmesan cheese

directions:
Cook pasta according to package directions and drain well. Combine cottage cheese and ricotta cheese in a medium bowl and mix until blended smooth. Lightly spray large nonstick skillet with nonfat cooking spray; add chicken broth and heat over medium-high heat. Add garlic and cook, stirring constantly, 30 seconds. Add spinach and cook 1-2 minutes, until heated through. Gradually add cottage cheese mixture and Parmesan cheese to spinach; cook, stirring constantly, until sauce is blended smooth and thick. Add cooked pasta; toss lightly and serve. Sprinkle with additional Parmesan cheese, if desired.

Serves: 6

Nutrition per Serving		Exchanges
Calories	233	2 starch
Carbohydrate	41 grams	2 vegetable
Cholesterol	6 milligrams	1 meat
Dietary Fiber	3 grams	
Fat	< 1 gram	
Protein	18 grams	
Sodium	250 milligrams	

Shopping List:
12 ounces fat-free angel hair pasta, 16 ounces frozen chopped spinach, 6 ounces fat-free cottage cheese, 6 ounces fat-free ricotta cheese, 3 ounces fat-free Parmesan cheese, minced garlic, fat-free chicken broth

ITALIAN

EGGPLANT CASSEROLE
EASY - DO AHEAD

ingredients:
1 1/2 cups fat-free rice (raw)
4 1/2 cups Italian-style chopped tomatoes
1 tbsp. onion powder
1 1/2 tsp. garlic powder
1 1/2 tbsp. sugar
1 tbsp. Italian seasoning
1 1/2 lb. eggplant, sliced 1/2-inch thick
2 cups fat-free finely-shredded Mozzarella cheese
2 cups fat-free Parmesan cheese

directions:
Cook rice according to package directions and set aside. Combine tomatoes, onion powder, garlic powder, sugar and Italian seasoning in a medium saucepan; bring to a boil over high heat. Reduce heat to low, cover and simmer 15 minutes. Preheat oven to 350 degrees. Lightly spray 10-inch baking dish with nonfat cooking spray. Spoon enough tomato mixture into baking dish just to cover the bottom of dish. Arrange half the eggplant slices on top of sauce; top with 1/2 the sauce, 1/2 the rice, 1/2 the Mozzarella cheese and 1/2 the Parmesan cheese. Repeat layers, ending with Parmesan cheese. Bake in preheated oven 20-25 minutes, until cheese is completely melted and casserole is bubbly and hot. Let stand at room temperature for 5-8 minutes; cut and serve.

Serves: 6

ITALIAN

Nutrition per Serving

Calorie	363	
Carbohydrate	63 grams	
Cholesterol	0 milligrams	
Dietary Fiber	6 grams	
Fat	< 1 gram	
Protein	28 grams	
Sodium	1238 milligrams	

Exchanges
3 starch
3 vegetable
1 1/2 meat

Shopping List: fat-free rice, 1 1/2 pounds eggplant, 2 (28-ounce) cans Italian-style chopped tomatoes, 8 ounces fat-free finely-shredded Mozzarella cheese, 8 ounces fat-free Parmesan cheese, Italian seasoning, sugar, onion powder, garlic powder

EGGPLANT STUFFED
WITH RICE
AVERAGE

ingredients: 2 small eggplants, about 8 oz. each
1/4 cup chopped onion
2 tsp. fat-free chicken broth
1 roma tomato, diced
2 tbsp. chopped parsley
1/2 cup seedless raisins
2 cups cooked rice
1/2 cup chopped yellow bell pepper
1 medium apple, chopped
1 1/2 tbsp. curry powder
1 tsp. fat-free Parmesan cheese

directions: Preheat oven to 400 degrees. Cut eggplants in half lengthwise. Spray insides with nonfat cooking spray and place cut-side down on baking sheet. Bake until browned, and eggplant is tender when pierced with fork, about 15 minutes. Reduce oven temperature to 350 degrees. Combine onion and chicken broth in a large skillet. Cook, stirring, until onion is tender, about 5 minutes. Stir in the remaining ingredients until well blended; remove from heat. Using a spoon, carefully remove the eggplant flesh, leaving a 1/2-inch-thick shell intact. Chop the flesh and add to rice mixture. Pack the rice mixture into the eggplant shells. Sprinkle with Parmesan cheese. Arrange on baking sheet, cover lightly with foil and bake 20 minutes. Uncover and bake until tops are browned, about 10 minutes.

Serves: 4

Nutrition per Serving		Exchanges
Calories	202	1 starch
Carbohydrate	48 grams	1 fruit
Cholesterol	0 milligrams	3 vegetable
Dietary Fiber	4 grams	
Fat	< 1 gram	
Protein	4 grams	
Sodium	24 milligrams	

Shopping List: 2 eggplants, roma tomato, onion, yellow bell pepper, parsley, 1 medium apple, seedless raisins, curry powder, cooked rice, chicken broth, Parmesan cheese

GARDEN PASTA

EASY

ingredients:	1 medium onion, finely chopped
	1 clove garlic, peeled and chopped
	3 medium ripe tomatoes, peeled and chopped
	3 medium zucchini, shredded
	1 carrot, peeled and shredded
	1 tsp. salt
	Freshly ground pepper, to taste
	2 tsp. chopped fresh basil (or 1 tsp. dried basil)
	1 tsp. fresh oregano, chopped (or 1/2 tsp. dried oregano)
	1/2 tsp. fresh thyme, chopped (or 1/4 tsp. dried thyme)
	1/4 cup fat-free chicken broth
	12 oz. fat-free pasta, cooked and drained
	1 cup fat-free Parmesan cheese, freshly grated

directions: Combine onion, garlic, tomatoes, zucchini and carrot in a large bowl. Add salt, pepper, basil, oregano and thyme; toss lightly. Heat chicken broth in a large nonstick skillet. Add vegetable mixture and sauté over medium heat.
Reduce heat and simmer 15 minutes. Cook pasta according to package directions and drain well. Serve vegetables over hot pasta with generous spoonfuls of fresh Parmesan cheese.

Serves: 4

Nutrition per Serving		Exchanges
Calories	351	3 starch
Carbohydrate	68 grams	5 vegetable
Cholesterol	0 milligrams	
Dietary Fiber	6 grams	
Fat	< 1 gram	
Protein	21 grams	
Sodium	799 milligrams	

Shopping List: 1 medium onion, 1 clove garlic, 3 medium tomatoes, 3 medium zucchini, 1 carrot, salt, pepper, fresh basil, fresh oregano, fresh thyme, chicken broth, 12 ounces fat-free pasta, 1 cup fat-free Parmesan cheese

ITALIAN

GARLIC ESCAROLE POTATOES

AVERAGE

ingredients: 1 1/2 lb. small new potatoes, quartered
1 1/4 cups boiling water
6 medium cloves garlic
1 chicken bouillon cube
1/2 cup fresh parsley
1 small bunch escarole, torn into bite-size pieces
1/2 tsp. pepper

directions: In a large saucepan, cook potatoes in boiling water for 10 minutes, or until tender.
Remove potatoes and place in a bowl. Add garlic and bouillon to water; stir to dissolve bouillon. Simmer 10 minutes, until garlic is tender.
In food processor, chop parsley. With machine running, pour bouillon mixture through feed tube and process until puréed.
Return to saucepan and heat to boiling; stir in escarole.
Cook, covered, 3 minutes, or until escarole is tender. Stir in potatoes and pepper; heat through. Serve immediately.

Serves: 4

Nutrition per Serving		Exchanges
Calories	172	1 starch
Carbohydrate	40 grams	4 vegetable
Cholesterol	0 milligrams	
Dietary Fiber	4 grams	
Fat	< 1 gram	
Protein	4 grams	
Sodium	240 milligrams	

Shopping List: 1 1/2 pounds small new potatoes, 6 medium cloves garlic, 1 chicken bouillon cube, fresh parsley, 1 small bunch escarole, pepper

GARLIC MASHED POTATOES

EASY - DO AHEAD

ingredients: 2 lb. baking potatoes, peeled and quartered
2 tbsp. Butter Buds, reconstituted
1 1/2 tsp. crushed garlic
1/3 cup skim milk
1/8 tsp. white pepper

directions: Place cut and peeled potatoes in a large pot; cover with water and bring to a boil over high heat.
Reduce heat to medium-low, cover and cook 8-10 minutes, until potatoes are soft.
Drain potatoes and place in a large bowl.
Combine Butter Buds and crushed garlic in a small cup and mix well.
Pour butter mixture and milk into potatoes and mash with fork or potato masher until creamy and smooth. If you want a creamy, smooth texture, blend potatoes with electric mixer.
Sprinkle with pepper and mix lightly.

Serves: 6

Nutrition per Serving		Exchanges
Calories	161	2 starch
Carbohydrate	36 grams	
Cholesterol	< 1 milligram	
Dietary Fiber	4 grams	
Fat	< 1 gram	
Protein	4 grams	
Sodium	145 milligrams	

Shopping List: 2 pounds baking potatoes, skim milk, Butter Buds, crushed garlic, white pepper

ITALIAN

ITALIAN GREEN BEANS

EASY

ingredients: 2 tsp. chicken broth
2 (15 oz.) package frozen French-style
    green beans
3/4 cup fat-free Italian bread crumbs
1/2 tsp. garlic powder
1/2 tsp. pepper
1/2 tsp. salt
1/2 cup fat-free Parmesan cheese, divided

directions: Preheat oven to 350 degrees. Heat broth in a skillet over medium-high heat.
Add the beans and sauté until thawed through.
Add the bread crumbs, garlic, pepper and salt and stir to combine.
Add 1/4 cup of cheese and mix well.
Transfer the mixture to an 8x8-inch baking pan.
Sprinkle the remaining cheese on top and bake for 15-20 minutes, until top is lightly browned.

Serves: 6

Nutrition per Serving		Exchanges
Calories	73	1/2 starch
Carbohydrate	14 grams	1 vegetable
Cholesterol	0 milligrams	
Dietary Fiber	2 grams	
Fat	< 1 gram	
Protein	5 grams	
Sodium	291 milligrams	

Shopping List: fat-free chicken broth, 2 (15-ounce) packages frozen French-style green beans, fat-free Italian bread crumbs, garlic powder, pepper, salt, fat-free Parmesan cheese

ITALIAN ROASTED PEPPERS

EASY - DO AHEAD - FREEZE*

ingredients:
2 large red bell peppers
2 large yellow bell peppers
2 large green bell peppers
1/3 cup fat-free Italian salad dressing

directions:
Wash peppers and dry well. Cut peppers in half lengthwise; thoroughly clean out the inside of each pepper (removing seeds and membranes). Preheat oven to 425 degrees.
Line baking sheet with foil and lightly spray with nonfat cooking spray.
Arrange peppers in a single layer, skin-side up, on baking sheet.
Bake in preheated oven 25-30 minutes, until skin becomes blistered and charred.
Remove from oven and transfer peppers to bowl; immediately cover tightly with plastic wrap and let stand 15 minutes.
When peppers are cool enough to handle, carefully remove skins with knife or fingers.
Cut peppers into thin slices and return to bowl. Pour salad dressing over peppers and toss until coated.
Cover the bowl and refrigerate several hours, or overnight, before serving.
*You can prepare peppers without marinating, and freeze; slice or chop before freezing.

Serves: 6

ITALIAN

Nutrition per Serving

Calories	29	
Carbohydrate	7 grams	
Cholesterol	0 milligrams	
Dietary Fiber	1 gram	
Fat	< 1 gram	
Protein	1 gram	
Sodium	55 milligrams	

Exchanges
1 vegetable

Shopping List: 2 each red, yellow and green bell peppers, fat-free Italian salad dressing

ITALIAN-STYLE GREEN BEANS

EASY

ingredients: 2 lb. fresh green beans, trimmed
2 tsp. crushed garlic
28 oz. can Italian-style stewed tomatoes
3/4 tsp. Italian seasoning
2 tbsp. fat-free Parmesan cheese

directions: Wash, trim and cut beans into 2-inch pieces.
Lightly spray large nonstick skillet with nonfat cooking spray and heat over medium-high heat.
Add garlic to skillet and cook 30-45 seconds, until heated.
Add green beans, tomatoes with liquid, and Italian seasoning to skillet and mix well.
Bring mixture to a boil; reduce heat to low, cover and simmer 20-25 minutes, until green beans are tender-crisp.
Remove from skillet; sprinkle with cheese just before serving.

Serves: 6

ITALIAN

Nutrition per Serving		Exchanges
Calories	66	3 vegetable
Carbohydrate	15 grams	
Cholesterol	0 milligrams	
Dietary Fiber	3 grams	
Fat	< 1 gram	
Protein	4 grams	
Sodium	565 milligrams	

Shopping List: 2 pounds fresh green beans, 28-ounce can Italian-style tomatoes, Italian seasoning, fat-free Parmesan cheese, crushed garlic

POLENTA AND RED PEPPER SAUCE

AVERAGE - DO AHEAD

ingredients: 2 large red bell peppers, halved and seeded
2 tsp. sugar
2 tsp. red wine vinegar
24 oz. fat-free basil-garlic polenta, cut
into 1/2-inch slices

directions: Preheat oven to 425 degrees. Line baking sheet with foil and lightly spray with nonfat cooking spray.
Arrange pepper halves, cut-side down, on baking sheet. Bake in preheated oven 20-25 minutes, until browned.
Immediately place peppers in brown paper bag to cool. Remove skins when completely cooled.
Combine peppers, sugar and vinegar in a food processor or blender and process until smooth.
Pour mixture into small saucepan; cook over medium-low heat 5-10 minutes, until heated through.
Reduce oven temperature to 375 degrees.
Arrange polenta slices in a single layer on baking sheet.
Bake 15-20 minutes, until golden brown.
Serve polenta slices with warm red pepper sauce.

Serves: 6

Nutrition per Serving

		Exchanges
Calories	99	1 1/2 starch
Carbohydrate	22 grams	
Cholesterol	0 milligrams	
Dietary Fiber	2 grams	
Fat	< 1 gram	
Protein	3 grams	
Sodium	352 milligrams	

Shopping List: 24-ounce package basil-garlic polenta, 2 large peppers, sugar, red wine vinegar

POLENTA WITH MUSHROOM RAGOUT

AVERAGE - DO AHEAD

ingredients:
24 oz. fat-free polenta, sliced 1/2-inch thick
3 tbsp. fat-free chicken broth
1 1/2 lb. mushrooms, cut in half
1 cup chopped onions
1/2 tsp. oregano
1/2 tsp. basil
1/2 tsp. thyme
1/4 tsp. garlic powder
1 1/2 cups Italian-style stewed tomatoes
15 oz. can kidney beans, rinsed and drained
1/3 cup fat-free Parmesan cheese

directions:
Preheat oven to 375 degrees. Line baking sheet with foil and lightly spray with nonfat cooking spray. Arrange sliced polenta on baking sheet and bake in preheated oven 15 minutes. Remove from oven and keep warm. Lightly spray large nonstick skillet with nonfat cooking spray; add chicken broth to skillet and heat over medium-high heat. Add mushrooms, onions, oregano, basil, thyme and garlic powder to skillet and cook 5-6 minutes, stirring frequently, until mushrooms are tender. Add tomatoes and beans to mushrooms and cook over medium heat until heated through. Stir in cheese and mix well. Spoon sauce over polenta and serve.

Serves: 6

Nutrition per Serving		Exchanges
Calories	211	2 vegetable
Carbohydrate	42 grams	2 starch
Cholesterol	0 milligrams	
Dietary Fiber	7 grams	
Fat	< 1 gram	
Protein	11 grams	
Sodium	666 milligrams	

Shopping List:
24 ounces fat-free polenta, 1 1/2 pounds mushrooms, 1 large onion, fat-free chicken broth, 14 1/2-ounce can Italian-style stewed tomatoes, 15-ounce can kidney beans, fat-free Parmesan cheese, oregano, basil, thyme, garlic powder

RISOTTO

AVERAGE

ingredients:　　3 cups fat-free chicken broth
1 large carrot, peeled and chopped
2 tsp. onion powder
1/2 tsp. garlic powder
1/4 cup dry white wine
1 cup Arborio rice
3 tsp. dried parsley

directions:　　Pour chicken broth into medium saucepan and simmer over medium-low heat.
Lightly spray a large nonstick skillet with nonfat cooking spray and heat over medium-high heat.
Add carrots to skillet and sprinkle with onion and garlic powder; stir-fry 1-2 minutes, until carrots are tender.
Pour wine into skillet and cook, stirring frequently, until most of the wine has evaporated.
Add rice to skillet and mix well; pour 1 cup of the hot broth into skillet.
Cook, stirring frequently, 10 minutes, until most of the liquid has been absorbed.
Repeat with remaining broth, cooking 10 minutes for each cup of broth added.
Transfer to bowl; sprinkle with parsley and serve.

Serves: 6

Nutrition per Serving

Calories	131	
Carbohydrate	27 grams	
Cholesterol	0 milligrams	
Dietary Fiber	1 gram	
Fat	< 1 gram	
Protein	3 grams	
Sodium	439 milligrams	

Exchanges
2 vegetable
1 starch

Shopping List:　　24 ounces fat-free chicken broth, 1 carrot, 2 ounces dry white wine, Arborio rice, onion powder, garlic powder, dried parsley

RISOTTO-STYLE POTATOES
EASY

ingredients: 14 oz. fat-free chicken broth
1 onion, finely chopped
1/2 tsp. salt
1/2 tsp. dried thyme
2 lb. all-purpose potatoes, peeled and shredded
1/4 cup fat-free sour cream
1/4 cup fat-free Parmesan cheese
1/4 tsp. pepper

directions: Bring broth, onion, salt and thyme to a boil in saucepan.
Stir in potatoes and simmer, uncovered, stirring frequently, for 20 minutes or until tender.
Remove from heat. Stir in sour cream, Parmesan cheese and pepper.
Serve hot.

Serves: 8

Nutrition per Serving

		Exchanges
Calories	127	1 1/2 starch
Carbohydrate	28 grams	
Cholesterol	0 milligrams	
Dietary Fiber	3 grams	
Fat	< 1 gram	
Protein	4 grams	
Sodium	280 milligrams	

Shopping List: 2 pounds all-purpose potatoes, 14 ounce can fat-free chicken broth, 1 onion, 2 ounces fat-free sour cream, 1 ounce fat-free Parmesan cheese, salt, pepper, dried thyme

SPINACH GNOCCHI
AVERAGE

ingredients: 10 oz. package frozen chopped spinach, thawed and drained
1 lb. fat-free ricotta cheese
1/4 cup egg substitute
1/2 cup fat-free Parmesan cheese
1/2 tsp. salt
1/4 tsp. pepper
1/4 tsp. freshly-grated nutmeg
3/4 cup flour, divided
4 cups salted water
freshly-grated fat-free Parmesan cheese

directions: Place spinach in a sieve; press with back of spoon to push out water. Combine ricotta, spinach and egg substitute in a bowl and mix well. Stir in 1/2 cup Parmesan cheese, salt, pepper and nutmeg. Add 1/2 cup flour; mix well. Place 1/4 cup flour on plate. Form rounded teaspoon of spinach-cheese mixture into gnocchi dumplings by coating lightly with flour and rolling between palms of hands to form round balls. Place on waxed paper in single layer until ready to cook. Bring salted water to a boil in a large saucepan. Drop gnocchi one by one into boiling water until bottom of pan is filled with single layer of gnocchi. Cook about 5 minutes. Gnocchini will rise to surface of water when done. Remove with slotted spoon; drain well. Place gnocchini in heated serving bowl. Sprinkle with grated Parmesan cheese or serve with your favorite fat-free sauce.

Serves: 6

Nutrition per Serving

Calories	150	
Carbohydrate	21 grams	
Cholesterol	0 milligrams	
Dietary Fiber	1 gram	
Fat	< 1 gram	
Protein	18 grams	
Sodium	438 milligrams	

Exchanges
4 vegetable
1 1/2 meat

Shopping List: 10-ounce package frozen chopped spinach, 1 pound fat-free ricotta cheese, 2 ounces egg substitute, 8 ounces fat-free Parmesan cheese, salt, pepper, freshly-grated nutmeg, flour

SQUASH CASSEROLE

EASY - DO AHEAD

ingredients: 3 tbsp. uncooked rice
2 yellow squash, sliced
1 onion, sliced
2 tomatoes, sliced
2 ribs celery, chopped
1 green bell pepper, sliced thin
3/4 tsp. salt
1/2 tsp. pepper
2 tbsp. reconstituted Butter Buds
1 tbsp. brown sugar

directions: Preheat oven to 350 degrees.
Lightly spray a 2-quart casserole dish with nonfat cooking spray.
Layer the rice, squash, onion, tomatoes, celery and green pepper. Sprinkle salt and pepper over top layer.
Sprinkle Butter Buds and brown sugar over vegetables and bake 1 hour.

Serves: 6

Nutrition per Serving		Exchanges
Calories	98	1 starch
Carbohydrate	22 grams	1 vegetable
Cholesterol	0 milligrams	
Dietary Fiber	5 grams	
Fat	< 1 gram	
Protein	3 grams	
Sodium	862 milligrams	

Shopping List: rice, 2 yellow squash, 1 onion, 2 tomatoes, 2 ribs celery, 1 green bell pepper, Butter Buds, brown sugar, salt, pepper

STRING BEANS IN TOMATO SAUCE

EASY

---

ingredients: 1 lb. fresh string beans
2 tbsp. fat-free chicken broth
2 large cloves garlic, mashed
2 large tomatoes, peeled, seeded and chopped;
    or 15 oz. can chopped tomatoes
Salt and pepper, to taste

directions: Wash and trim the beans of any blemishes or strings, and break or cut into 3-inch lengths. Boil them in rapidly boiling, salted water for about 2 minutes.
Drain them well and scatter them on a plate or a towel to dry and cool slowly. Set them aside.
In a large heavy pan, heat the broth and sauté the garlic.
Add salt, pepper and tomatoes; cook for 15 minutes over high heat. Lower the heat; add the beans, stirring them well.
Cover and cook 5-6 minutes, or until they are just tender.
Watch that they don't get overcooked, they should be al denté.
Serve hot.

Serves: 4

Nutrition per Serving
Calories	59
Carbohydrate	13 grams
Cholesterol	0 milligrams
Dietary Fiber	1 gram
Fat	< 1 gram
Protein	3 grams
Sodium	35 milligrams

Exchanges
2 1/2 vegetable

Shopping List: 1 pound fresh string beans, fat-free chicken broth, 2 large cloves garlic, 2 large tomatoes or 15-ounce can chopped tomatoes, salt, pepper

STUFFED EGGPLANT

AVERAGE

ingredients: 1 eggplant
1 cup fat-free bread crumbs
2 tbsp. fat-free vegetable broth
1 1/2 tsp. chopped onion
1/4 cup egg substitute
Salt and pepper, to taste

directions: Preheat oven to 400 degrees.
Place eggplant in saucepan and cover with water;
bring to a boil over high heat and cook until tender.
Remove eggplant from saucepan and cut a slice
from the top of the eggplant.
Remove the pulp from the center of the eggplant,
being careful not to tear or puncture the skin.
Chop the pulp and combine it with bread crumbs.
Pour vegetable broth into large skillet and heat
over medium-high heat. Add the onion and sauté
for 5 minutes, until soft.
Add the pulp mixture, egg substitute, salt and
pepper.
Add a little water to moisten, if too dry.
Spoon the mixture into the eggplant shells; place
on baking sheet and bake for 25 minutes.

Serves: 2-4

Nutrition per Serving		Exchanges
Calories	58	1/2 starch
Carbohydrate	10 grams	1 vegetable
Cholesterol	0 milligrams	
Dietary Fiber	< 1 gram	
Fat	< 1 gram	
Protein	3 grams	
Sodium	125 milligrams	

Shopping List: 1 eggplant, 1 cup fat-free bread crumbs, fat-free vegetable broth, onion, 2 ounces egg substitute, salt, pepper

ITALIAN

ANISE BISCOTTI
AVERAGE - DO AHEAD - FREEZE

ingredients:
2 cups flour
1 cup sugar
1 tsp. baking powder
1/2 tsp. baking soda
1 tbsp. crushed anise seed
1/2 cup egg substitute
2 large egg whites
1/2 tsp. vanilla
1 tbsp. lemon juice

directions:
Preheat oven to 325 degrees. Line baking sheet(s) with foil and lightly spray with nonfat cooking spray. Combine flour, sugar, baking powder, baking soda and anise seed in a large bowl and mix well. Combine egg substitute, egg whites, vanilla and lemon juice in a medium bowl, and blend until smooth. Add egg mixture to flour mixture and blend until dry ingredients are moistened. Divide dough in half and shape into logs. Place logs on baking sheet(s) and bake in preheated oven 20-25 minutes. Remove from oven and cool at room temperature 15 minutes. Cut logs diagonally into 1/2-inch-thick slices and place, cutside up, on baking sheet. Bake 5-8 minutes, until lightly browned and crisp; turn slices over and bake an additional 5-10 minutes, until crisp. Cool completely before serving.

Serves: 24

ITALIAN

Nutrition per Serving		Exchanges
Calories	73	1 starch
Carbohydrate	16 grams	
Cholesterol	0 milligrams	
Dietary Fiber	< 1 gram	
Fat	< 1 gram	
Protein	2 grams	
Sodium	42 milligrams	

Shopping List: flour, sugar, 4 ounces egg substitute, large eggs, baking powder, baking soda, anise seed, vanilla, lemon juice

CHOCOLATE-CHIP BISCOTTI

EASY - DO AHEAD - FREEZE

ingredients:
2 1/2 cups flour
3/4 cup sugar
1/4 cup brown sugar
1 tsp. baking powder
1/2 tsp. baking soda
2 tbsp. unsweetened cocoa powder
1 tsp. vanilla
3/4 cup egg substitute
3 tbsp. mini chocolate chips

directions:
Preheat oven to 350 degrees. Line baking sheet with foil and lightly spray with nonfat cooking spray. Combine flour, sugar, brown sugar, baking powder, baking soda and cocoa in a large bowl and mix well. Add vanilla and egg substitute and mix until dry ingredients are moistened and blended. Fold in chocolate chips. Turn dough onto lightly-floured surface and roll into 2 logs. Place logs on baking sheet and bake in preheated oven 20-25 minutes. Remove from oven and cool at room temperature 15 minutes. Cut logs into 1/2-inch slices and arrange, cut-side down, on baking sheet. Bake 5 minutes; turn slices over and bake an additional 5 minutes, until crisp. Cool completely before storing in sealed container.

Serves: 18

Nutrition per Serving		Exchanges
Calories	121	1 1/2 starch
Carbohydrate	27 grams	
Cholesterol	0 milligrams	
Dietary Fiber	< 1 gram	
Fat	< 1 gram	
Protein	3 grams	
Sodium	56 milligrams	

Shopping List: flour, sugar, brown sugar, unsweetened cocoa powder, 6 ounces egg substitute, baking powder, baking soda, vanilla, mini chocolate chips

CHOCOLATE-ORANGE BISCOTTI

AVERAGE - DO AHEAD

ingredients:

1/2 cup corn syrup
1/2 cup sugar
1/2 cup brown sugar
1/4 cup orange juice
1 1/8 cups egg substitute
3 cups flour
1/3 cup unsweetened cocoa powder
2 tsp. baking powder

directions:

Preheat oven to 350 degrees. Lightly spray baking sheet with nonfat cooking spray. In a large bowl, combine corn syrup, sugar, brown sugar, orange juice and egg substitute, and mix until ingredients are blended smooth. Add flour, cocoa and baking powder; mix until dry ingredients are moistened and blended. Turn dough onto lightly-floured surface and gently roll into 4x16-inch loaf. Place on baking sheet and bake in preheated oven 25-30 minutes. Remove from oven and reduce oven temperature to 275 degrees. Cool loaf at room temperature 15-20 minutes. Using a serrated knife, cut 1/2-inch diagonal slices and place in a single layer on baking sheet. Bake in oven 15 minutes; turn cookies over and bake an additional 15 minutes. Remove from oven; cool completely, and roll in powdered sugar, if desired.

Serves: 18

Nutrition per Serving

Calories	157
Carbohydrate	35 grams
Cholesterol	0 milligrams
Dietary Fiber	1 gram
Protein	4 grams
Sodium	66 milligrams

Exchanges
2 starch

Shopping List: 4 ounces corn syrup, sugar, brown sugar, 2 ounces orange juice, 10 ounces egg substitute, flour, unsweetened cocoa powder, baking powder

ITALIAN SPICE CAKE

EASY - DO AHEAD

ingredients:
3/4 cup raisins
1/3 cup + 1 tbsp. Baking Healthy (Smucker's)
1/2 cup granulated sugar
1/4 cup egg substitute
1 3/4 cup + 3 tsp. flour, divided
1/2 cup + 3 tbsp. unsweetened cocoa powder, divided
2 tsp. baking powder
1 tsp. cinnamon
1 tsp. nutmeg
1/4 tsp. cloves
3/4 tsp. salt
3/4 cup coffee
1/4 cup powdered sugar

directions:
Preheat oven to 350 degrees. Lightly spray 8-inch cake pan with nonfat cooking spray and sprinkle with flour (1-2 teaspoons) to coat. Soak raisins in warm water for 30 minutes; drain. Combine Baking Healthy and sugar in a large bowl and mix until light and fluffy. Add egg substitute; mix until blended. Sift 1 3/4 cups flour with cocoa, baking powder, cinnamon, nutmeg, cloves and salt. Add flour mixture alternately with coffee, in 3 additions, to sugar mixture; blend well. Toss raisins with 1 teaspoon flour and fold into batter. Spoon batter into cake pan; bake in preheated oven 35-40 minutes, until cake pulls away from sides of pan. Cool on rack; sift powdered sugar on top before serving.

Serves: 8

Nutrition per Serving		Exchanges
Calories	253	2 starch
Carbohydrate	58 grams	1 2/3 fruit
Cholesterol	0 milligrams	
Dietary Fiber	3 grams	
Fat	< 1 gram	
Protein	6 grams	
Sodium	113 milligrams	

Shopping List: flour, sugar, powdered sugar, unsweetened cocoa powder, fat-free margarine, egg substitute, 6 ounces raisins, coffee, cloves, nutmeg, baking powder, cinnamon, salt

RASPBERRY-ALMOND MANICOTTI DESSERT

AVERAGE - DO AHEAD

ingredients:
6 oz. manicotti shells
1 cup fat-free ricotta cheese
1/2 cup fat-free cottage cheese
1/3 cup sugar
1/2 tsp. almond extract
1/2 tsp. vanilla
1/2 cups raspberries
3/4 cup lite chocolate syrup

directions:
Cook pasta according to package directions and drain well.

Combine ricotta cheese, cottage cheese, sugar, almond extract and vanilla in a food processor or blender; process just until smooth.

Spoon mixture into medium bowl; fold in 1 cup raspberries.

Line baking sheet with plastic wrap. Carefully fill each manicotti shell with 1/3 to 1/2 cup filling and place on baking sheet.

Cover and refrigerate 6 hours, or overnight.

Just before serving, drizzle with chocolate sauce and garnish with remaining raspberries.

Serves: 6

Nutrition per Serving		Exchanges
Calories	210	1 milk
Carbohydrate	46 grams	2 fruit
Cholesterol	17 milligrams	
Dietary Fiber	2 grams	
Fat	< 1 gram	
Protein	9 grams	
Sodium	133 milligrams	

Shopping List:
6 ounces manicotti shells, 8 ounces fat-free ricotta cheese, 4 ounces fat-free cottage cheese, fresh or frozen raspberries, 6 ounces lite chocolate syrup, sugar, almond extract, vanilla

ITALIAN

CANTALOUPE-BANANA SMOOTHIE

EASY - DO AHEAD

ingredients:
1 1/2 cups cantaloupe balls
1 small banana, sliced
3/4 cup fat-free banana yogurt
1/3 cup orange juice

directions:
Combine all the ingredients in a food processor or blender and process until blended smooth.
Add 4 to 5 ice cubes and process until thick and creamy.

Serves: 2

Nutrition per Serving		Exchanges
Calories	147	2 1/3 fruit
Carbohydrate	33 grams	
Cholesterol	2 milligrams	
Dietary Fiber	2 grams	
Fat	< 1 gram	
Protein	5 grams	
Sodium	64 milligrams	

Shopping List: prepackaged cubed cantaloupe, 1 banana, 6 ounces fat-free banana yogurt, orange juice

**Cantaloupe is a favorite Italian fruit. Its name comes from Cantalupo, a city near Rome.

SANGRIA

EASY - DO AHEAD - FREEZE

ingredients: 750 milliliters dry red wine
16 oz. seltzer water
6 tbsp. orange juice
2 tbsp. lemon juice
1/2 cup sugar
1 medium orange, sliced
1 medium lemon, sliced

directions: Refrigerate wine and seltzer water separately several hours or overnight, until well chilled.
Combine orange and lemon juices in a large pitcher; stir in sugar until dissolved.
Pour wine into pitcher and mix well.
Add seltzer water and sliced fruit. Stir until ingredients are blended.
Serve immediately, or pour into freezer-safe container and freeze up to 3 months.
Thaw and serve over ice.

Serves: 8

Nutrition per Serving

		Exchanges
Calories	128	2 fruit
Carbohydrate	18 grams	
Cholesterol	0 milligrams	
Dietary Fiber	1 gram	
Fat	< 1 gram	
Protein	1 gram	
Sodium	18 milligrams	

Shopping List: 750 milliliter bottle dry red wine, 16-ounce bottle seltzer water, 1 ounce lemon juice, 3 ounces orange juice, 1 medium orange, 1 lemon, sugar

JEWISH

JEWISH

JEWISH

Food has always played an important role in Jewish culture as the center of the Sabbath observance, and an important part of holiday celebrations. Jewish cooking is firmly grounded in tradition, recipes that have been passed down through the generations. Jewish food is far more than bagels with lox, gefilte fish and chopped liver; it has been strongly influenced by European, Mediterranean and Middle Eastern cultures and is becoming increasingly mainstream with healthy-choice alternatives.

What's a better choice?

Instead of...	Substitute...
schmaltz (chicken fat)	fat-free broth, wine, or fruit juice
oil (for frying)	nonfat cooking spray
sour cream	fat-free sour cream
whole or 2% milk	skim milk
cream cheese	fat-free cream cheese
cottage cheese	fat-free cottage cheese
whole chicken	fat-free chicken breasts of tenders
buttered cracker crumbs	matzo meal
ground beef	fat-free ground turkey or chicken
butter (for baking)	applesauce, puréed fruit, or fat substitutes (i.e. Lighter Bake, Smucker's Baking Healthy)
egg noodles	yolk-free noodles

So you can have your blintzes, kugel, and potato latkes. You can even eat them without an ounce of "Jewish guilt." Start new and healthy family traditions as you make simple changes to Grandma's recipes--keep the tradition and flavor, but get rid of the fat! As the Israelis say, "B'tayavon! Eat well and enjoy!"

BROCCOLI MUSHROOM CHEESE BAKE
EASY - DO AHEAD - FREEZE

ingredients: 2 cups fat-free cottage cheese
2 cups fat-free finely-shredded Cheddar cheese
10 oz. frozen, chopped broccoli, thawed and drained
3/4 cup sliced mushrooms
1/4 cup + 2 tbsp. matzo meal
1 tsp. garlic powder
1/2 tsp. onion powder
1/4 tsp. pepper
1 1/2 cups egg substitute
2 tbsp. fat-free Parmesan cheese

directions: Preheat oven to 350 degrees. Lightly spray 9x13-inch dish with nonfat cooking spray. Combine cottage cheese, Cheddar cheese, broccoli, mushrooms, matzo meal, garlic powder, onion powder and pepper in a large bowl, and mix until blended. Add egg substitute and mix well. Pour into baking dish and sprinkle with Parmesan cheese. Bake in preheated oven 45-60 minutes, until top is browned and eggs are cooked through. Great for Passover lunch!

Serves: 8

Nutrition per Serving		Exchanges
Calories	113	1 vegetable
Carbohydrate	11 grams	1/3 starch
Cholesterol	1 milligram	2 meat
Dietary Fiber	< 1 gram	
Fat	< 1 gram	
Protein	16 grams	
Sodium	405 milligrams	

Shopping List: 16 ounces fat-free cottage cheese, 8 ounces fat-free finely-shredded Cheddar cheese, 10 ounces frozen chopped broccoli, sliced mushrooms, 12 ounces egg substitute, fat-free Parmesan cheese, matzo meal, garlic powder, onion powder, pepper

PASSOVER SPINACH AND BROCCOLI SQUARES

EASY - DO AHEAD - FREEZE

Ingredients:
10 oz. frozen, chopped broccoli, thawed and drained
10 oz. frozen, chopped spinach, thawed and drained
1 1/2 tsp. garlic powder
1 1/2 tsp. onion powder
2 tsp. lemon juice
3/4 tsp. dried oregano
3 large egg whites

directions:
Preheat oven to 350 degrees.
Lightly spray 8-inch baking dish with nonfat cooking spray.
Combine broccoli, spinach, garlic powder, onion powder, lemon juice and oregano in a medium bowl, and mix well.
In a separate bowl, beat egg whites with electric mixer until foamy.
Fold into spinach mixture.
Pour into prepared pan and bake 30-35 minutes, until knife inserted in center comes out clean.

Serves: 4

JEWISH

Nutrition per Serving		Exchanges
Calories	60	1/2 meat
Carbohydrate	10 grams	2 vegetable
Cholesterol	0 milligrams	
Dietary Fiber	4 grams	
Fat	< 1 gram	
Protein	7 grams	
Sodium	120 milligrams	

Shopping List:
10-ounce package frozen chopped broccoli, 10-ounce package frozen chopped spinach, eggs, garlic powder, onion powder, lemon juice, dried oregano

BERRY COLD BERRY SOUP

EASY - DO AHEAD

ingredients: 1 1/2 cups strawberries, hulled and halved
1 cup raspberries, rinsed and drained
1 cup ice water
1/2 cup fat-free sour cream
1/2 cup dry red wine
1/3 cup sugar

directions: Combine 1 cup strawberries and raspberries in blender or food processor, and purée.
Pour berries into large bowl; add ice water, sour cream, wine and sugar, and mix well.
Cover and refrigerate several hours, or overnight.
Best served in chilled bowls.
Garnish with remaining strawberries and sprinkle with sugar, if desired.

Serves: 4

Nutrition per Serving		Exchanges
Calories	133	2 fruit
Carbohydrate	26 grams	
Cholesterol	0 milligrams	
Dietary Fiber	3 grams	
Fat	< 1 gram	
Protein	3 grams	
Sodium	22 milligrams	

Shopping List: 1 pint strawberries, 1 pint raspberries, 4 ounces fat-free sour cream, 4 ounces dry red wine, sugar

JEWISH

BORSCHT

EASY - DO AHEAD

ingredients:
2 quarts water
1 1/2 tsp. salt
10 small beets, peeled and shredded
1 cup shredded carrots
1 cup chopped onions
1 tbsp. lemon juice
1/2 cup sugar
1/2 cup fat-free sour cream

directions:
Combine water and salt in a large soup pot, and bring to a boil over high heat.
Add beets, carrots, and onions to boiling water. Reduce heat to medium and continue cooking, uncovered, 20-25 minutes, until vegetables are tender.
Add lemon juice and sugar, and mix well.
Cover and refrigerate overnight.
Garnish with sour cream just before serving.

Serves: 8

Nutrition per Serving		Exchanges
Calories	88	4 vegetable
Carbohydrate	20 grams	
Cholesterol	0 milligrams	
Dietary Fiber	2 grams	
Fat	< 1 gram	
Protein	2 grams	
Sodium	446 milligrams	

JEWISH

Shopping List: 10 small beets, 8 ounces packaged shredded carrots, 8 ounces packaged chopped onions, 4 ounces fat-free sour cream, lemon juice, sugar, salt

CREAMED CUCUMBER SOUP

EASY - DO AHEAD

ingredients: 4 large cucumbers, peeled and seeded
1 tbsp. minced garlic
2 cups fat-free sour cream
1 tbsp. dried dill

directions: Combine all ingredients in a food processor or blender, and process until smooth.
Refrigerate several hours before serving.

Serves: 6

Nutrition per Serving		Exchanges
Calories	95	2 vegetable
Carbohydrate	15 grams	1/2 milk
Cholesterol	0 milligrams	
Dietary Fiber	3 grams	
Fat	< 1 gram	
Protein	7 grams	
Sodium	60 milligrams	

Shopping List: 4 large cucumbers, 16 ounces fat-free sour cream, minced garlic, dried dill

JEWISH

GRANDMA'S "GET WELL" CHICKEN SOUP

EASY - DO AHEAD - FREEZE

ingredients: 7 cups fat-free chicken broth
7 cups water
2 large onions, quartered
8 large carrots, peeled and quartered
6 stalks celery, cut into thirds
2 lb. fat-free chicken tenders, cut into 1-inch
pieces
1 tbsp. parsley
1 tsp. lemon pepper

directions: Combine chicken broth, water, onions, carrots and
celery in a large soup pot; bring to a boil over high
heat.
Reduce heat to low and simmer 30 minutes.
Add chicken, parsley and lemon pepper to pot and
cook 20-25 minutes, until chicken is tender.
Flavor with additional onion powder or pepper, if
desired.

Serves: 8

Nutrition per Serving		Exchanges
Calories	155	2 vegetable
Carbohydrate	12 grams	3 meat
Cholesterol	71 milligrams	
Dietary Fiber	3 grams	
Fat	< 1 gram	
Protein	25 grams	
Sodium	730 milligrams	

Shopping List: 2 pounds fat free chicken tenders, 4 (16-ounce) cans fat-
free chicken broth, 2 large onions, 8 large carrots, celery,
parsley, lemon pepper

JEWISH

MATZO BALLS
EASY - DO AHEAD - FREEZE

ingredients: 1 cup matzo meal
1 1/2 tsp. instant chicken bouillon granules
1 tsp. onion powder
1/4 tsp. garlic powder
4 large egg whites
1/4 cup egg substitute
6 tbsp. club soda

directions: Combine matzo meal, bouillon granules, onion powder and garlic powder in a medium bowl, and mix well.
Add egg whites, egg substitute and club soda, and mix with a fork until ingredients are blended.
Cover and refrigerate 15-20 minutes.
Bring fat-free broth or water to a boil over high heat; form matzo mixture into 1-inch balls and drop into boiling liquid.
Reduce heat to low; cover and simmer 20-25 minutes, until matzo balls are cooked through, but slightly firm.

Serves: 8

Nutrition per Serving

		Exchanges
Calories	77	1 starch
Carbohydrate	14 grams	
Cholesterol	0 milligrams	
Dietary Fiber	< 1 gram	
Fat	< 1 gram	
Protein	4 grams	
Sodium	77 milligrams	

Shopping List: matzo meal, chicken bouillon granules, eggs, egg substitute, club soda, onion powder, garlic powder

JEWISH

BERRY APPLESAUCE

EASY - DO AHEAD - FREEZE

ingredients: 4 medium apples, peeled, cored and cut into
 chunks
1/4 cup strawberries, hulled and halved
2 tbsp. apple juice
2 tbsp. sugar
1/2 tsp. cinnamon

directions: Combine all ingredients in a large saucepan and
bring to a boil over medium-high heat.
Reduce heat to low; partially cover and simmer 20-
25 minutes, until tender.
Pour mixture into bowl and mash with a fork,
keeping apples somewhat chunky.
Great with potato latkes!

Serves: 4

Nutrition per Serving		Exchanges
Calories	111	2 fruit
Carbohydrate	29 grams	
Cholesterol	0 milligrams	
Dietary Fiber	3 gram	
Fat	< 1 gram	
Protein	< 1 gram	
Sodium	1 milligram	

Shopping List: 4 apples, strawberries, apple juice, sugar, cinnamon

JEWISH

CUCUMBER AND PEPPER SALAD

EASY - DO AHEAD

ingredients:
1/3 cup sugar
1/2 cup water
1/2 cup white wine vinegar
2 large cucumbers, peeled and sliced
1 large onion, sliced thin
1 large carrot, peeled and sliced
1 cup red bell pepper, sliced thin

directions:
Combine sugar, water and vinegar in a small saucepan, and bring to a boil over high heat.
Combine sliced cucumbers, onion slices, carrot and red pepper in a large bowl, and toss until mixed.
Pour dressing over mixture and toss until coated. Cover and refrigerate several hours before serving.

Serves: 6

Nutrition per Serving
Calories	82
Carbohydrate	21 grams
Cholesterol	0 milligrams
Dietary Fiber	3 grams
Fat	< 1 gram
Protein	1 gram
Sodium	11 milligrams

Exchanges
2 vegetable
1/2 fruit

Shopping List: 2 large cucumbers, 1 onion, 1 large carrot, 1 red bell pepper, sugar, white wine vinegar

HOT SPINACH-ORANGE SALAD

EASY - DO AHEAD

ingredients:
4 hard-boiled egg whites
8 cups fresh spinach, washed and chopped
1 medium red onion, sliced thin
8 oz. mandarin oranges in juice, drained
8 oz. sliced water chestnuts, drained
1 cup fat-free croutons
3/4 cup fat-free Italian salad dressing*

directions:
Hard-boil eggs; peel and discard yolks.
Chop egg whites and refrigerate while preparing salad.
Combine chopped spinach, onion, oranges, water chestnuts and croutons in a large bowl, and toss until well mixed.
Pour salad dressing into microwave-safe cup and heat 45-60 seconds, until thoroughly heated.
Sprinkle egg whites over salad and toss with dressing until mixed.

Serves: 6

Nutrition per Serving		Exchanges
Calories	105	1/2 fruit
Carbohydrate	21 grams	3 vegetable
Cholesterol	0 milligram	
Dietary Fiber	3 grams	
Fat	< 1 gram	
Protein	6 grams	
Sodium	241 milligrams	

Shopping List:
2 packages fresh spinach leaves (cut-up), 1 red onion, 8 ounces mandarin oranges in juice, 8-ounce can sliced water chestnuts, fat-free croutons, eggs, fat-free salad dressing (*do not use creamy style)

APPLE BLINTZES
AVERAGE - DO AHEAD - FREEZE

ingredients:
1 cup flour
1/2 cup water
1/2 cup skim milk
1/2 cup egg substitute
1 large egg white
3 cups canned cinnamon-spice apple slices,
   chopped

directions:
Combine flour, water, milk, egg substitute and
egg white together in a medium bowl, and mix
until smooth. Tear large sheet of foil and lightly
spray with nonfat cooking spray; set aside.
Lightly spray large nonstick skillet with nonfat
cooking spray, and heat over medium heat.
Add just enough batter to coat the bottom of
skillet; cook until top is dry. Turn onto foil sheet,
with cooked-side up. Repeat with remaining batter. Spoon 1 1/2-2 tablespoons apples into center
of crêpe. Fold up sides over the middle, and then
the top and bottom. Line baking sheet with foil and
lightly spray with nonfat cooking spray.
Arrange blintzes on baking sheet.
Preheat oven to 350 degrees.
Bake blintzes 20-25 minutes, until lightly browned.

Serves: 6

Nutrition per Serving

		Exchanges
Calories	163	1 1/4 fruit
Carbohydrate	34 grams	1 starch
Cholesterol	0 milligrams	1/2 meat
Dietary Fiber	3 grams	
Fat	< 1 gram	
Protein	5 grams	
Sodium	50 milligrams	

Shopping List: 4 ounces skim milk, 4 ounces egg substitute, large eggs, 28-ounce can cinnamon-spice apple slices, flour

BAKED CHICKEN BREASTS WITH VEGETABLES

EASY - DO AHEAD

ingredients:
2 lb. fat-free chicken breasts
1 1/2 tsp. garlic powder
1 tsp. onion powder
3/4 tsp. dried thyme
3/4 tsp. dried sage
1/2 tsp. pepper
1 large onion, thinly sliced
1 large red bell pepper, thinly sliced
1 large green bell pepper, thinly sliced
1 1/2 cups sliced mushrooms
3 small red potatoes, cut in half

directions:
Preheat oven to 350 degrees. Lightly spray 9x13-inch baking dish with nonfat cooking spray. Arrange chicken breasts in baking dish; sprinkle both sides with garlic powder, onion powder, thyme, sage and pepper. Top with sliced onion, bell peppers and mushrooms. Place potatoes around sides of baking dish and lightly spray with nonfat cooking spray. Cover with foil and bake in preheated oven 25-30 minutes, until chicken is cooked through and vegetables are tender.

Serves: 6

Nutrition per Serving		Exchanges
Calories	188	4 meat
Carbohydrate	12 grams	1/3 starch
Cholesterol	95 milligrams	1 vegetable
Dietary Fiber	2 grams	
Fat	< 1 gram	
Protein	32 grams	
Sodium	369 milligrams	

Shopping List: 2 pounds fat-free chicken breasts, 3 small red potatoes, 1 large onion, 1 large red bell pepper, 1 large green bell pepper, sliced mushrooms, garlic powder, onion powder, dried thyme, dried sage, pepper

BAKED FISH ROLL-UPS

EASY - DO AHEAD

ingredients: 1 lb. flounder fillets
3/4 cup frozen chopped spinach, thawed and
 drained
1/4 cup egg substitute
1/4 cup matzo meal
1/2 tsp. garlic powder
1/4 tsp. pepper
1 medium tomato, sliced 1-inch thick
2 tbsp. reconstituted Butter Buds

directions: Preheat oven to 325 degrees.
Lightly spray a 9x13-inch baking dish with nonfat
cooking spray. Arrange fillets in baking dish.
Combine spinach, egg substitute, matzo meal,
garlic powder and pepper in a medium bowl, and
mix until blended.
Divide mixture and place in center of fish fillets.
Roll each fish fillet, jellyroll fashion, and place,
seam-side down, in baking dish (secure with tooth-
pick, if desired).
Top fillets with tomato slices and drizzle with
Butter Buds.
Bake in preheated oven 25-30 minutes, until fish
flakes easily.

Serves: 4

Nutrition per Serving		Exchanges
Calories	153	3 meat
Carbohydrate	11 grams	1/3 starch
Cholesterol	41 milligrams	1 vegetable
Dietary Fiber	2 grams	
Fat	< 1 gram	
Protein	24 grams	
Sodium	136 milligrams	

Shopping List: 1 pound flounder fillets, 10 ounces frozen chopped
spinach, egg substitute, matzo meal, 1 tomato, garlic
powder, pepper, Butter Buds

JEWISH

HONEY DIJON CHICKEN
EASY - DO AHEAD - FREEZE

ingredients: 1/3 cup fat-free honey mustard
2 tsp. onion powder
1/2 tsp. garlic powder
3/4 tsp. dried dill
1 1/2 lb. fat-free chicken breasts

directions: Preheat oven to 350 degrees.
Lightly spray a 9-inch baking dish with nonfat cooking spray.
Combine honey mustard, onion powder, garlic powder and dill in a small bowl, and mix until blended.
Arrange chicken in baking dish and brush with honey-mustard sauce.
Bake in preheated oven 25-35 minutes, until chicken is cooked through.

Serves: 4

Nutrition per Serving		Exchanges	
Calories	210	5 meat	
Carbohydrate	15 grams	2/3 fruit	
Cholesterol	106 milligrams		
Dietary Fiber	0 grams		
Fat	< 1 gram		
Protein	35 grams		
Sodium	428 milligrams		

JEWISH

Shopping List: 1 1/2 pounds fat-free chicken breasts, fat-free honey mustard, onion powder, garlic powder, dried dill

LEMON CHICKEN

EASY - DO AHEAD - FREEZE

ingredients: 1 1/2 lb. fat-free chicken breasts
1/4 cup lemon juice
2 tsp. dried dill
1/4 tsp. pepper
2 tsp. garlic powder
1/2 tsp. onion powder

directions: Preheat oven to 350 degrees.
Lightly spray an 8-inch baking dish with nonfat cooking spray.
Arrange chicken breasts in dish; drizzle with lemon juice.
Sprinkle on both sides with garlic powder, onion powder, pepper and dill.
Bake in preheated oven 20-25 minutes, until lightly browned and cooked through.

Serves: 4

Nutrition per Serving		**Exchanges**
Calories	163	5 meat
Carbohydrate	3 grams	
Cholesterol	106 milligrams	
Dietary Fiber	0 grams	
Fat	< 1 gram	
Protein	35 grams	
Sodium	412 milligrams	

Shopping List: 1 1/2 pounds fat-free chicken breasts, 2 ounces lemon juice, dried dill, pepper, garlic powder, onion powder

JEWISH

STUFFED CABBAGE
DIFFICULT - DO AHEAD - FREEZE

ingredients:
1 large head of cabbage
2 large onions, sliced thin, divided
2 lb. fat-free ground turkey
1/2 cup fat-rice (uncooked)
1 tsp. onion powder
1/2 tsp. pepper
1 1/2 cups sugar
2 cups fat-free tomato sauce
1 tbsp. lemon juice

directions:
Cut core from cabbage. Fill large pan or soup pot with water and bring to a boil; place cabbage in boiling water. Reduce heat to low; cover and steam 5-8 minutes, until softened. Remove cabbage and drain well, but reserve cooking water. Preheat oven to 350 degrees. Lightly spray a 14x11-inch baking dish with nonfat cooking spray. Arrange half the onion slices on bottom of dish. Combine turkey, rice, onion powder and pepper in a medium bowl, and mix until ingredients are blended. Spoon 1/4-1/3 cup mixture into center of whole cabbage leaf; fold edges of cabbage around mixture and place on top of onions. Lightly spray medium saucepan with nonfat cooking spray. Combine sugar, remaining onions, tomato sauce and lemon juice in saucepan and cook, stirring frequently, over medium-low heat, until blended and heated through. Pour sauce over cabbage rolls; if more liquid is needed in the pan, gradually add reserved cooking water. Bake in preheated oven 1 1/2 hours, until browned and cooked through.

Serves: 6

Nutrition per Serving		Exchanges
Calories	429	1 meat
Carbohydrate	79 grams	4 starch
Cholesterol	54 milligrams	3 vegetables
Dietary Fiber	2 grams	
Fat	< 1 gram	
Protein	25 grams	
Sodium	919 milligrams	

Shopping List: 1 large head of cabbage, 2 pounds fat-free ground turkey (or chicken), fat-free rice, 16 ounces fat-free tomato sauce, 2 large onions, lemon juice, onion powder, pepper, sugar

TUNA SOUFFLÉ

EASY - DO AHEAD

ingredients:
7 oz. fat-free tuna, drained
1/4 cup diced celery
1/4 cup diced onion
2 tbsp. fat-free mayonnaise
3 whole matzo crackers
2 cups fat-free shredded Cheddar cheese
1 cup egg substitute
2 1/2 cups skim milk

directions:
Lightly spray a 9-inch square pan with nonfat cooking spray.
Combine tuna, celery, onion and mayonnaise in a small bowl, and mix until blended.
Place one matzo on bottom of baking dish.
Top with 1 cup cheese and half of the tuna mixture.
Repeat layers, ending with matzo on top.
Combine egg substitute and milk in a medium bowl and mix until blended.
Pour mixture over matzo; cover and refrigerate overnight.
Preheat oven to 325 degrees.
Bring casserole to room temperature; bake in preheated oven 40-50 minutes, until completely set.
Remove from oven and let stand 10 minutes before serving.

Serves: 4

Nutrition per Serving		Exchanges
Calories	321	4 1/2 meat
Carbohydrate	31 grams	1 milk
Cholesterol	11 milligrams	3 vegetable
Dietary Fiber	1 gram	
Fat	< 1 gram	
Protein	43 grams	
Sodium	955 milligrams	

Shopping List: 7-ounce can fat-free tuna, celery, onion, fat-free mayonnaise, matzo, 8 ounces fat-free shredded Cheddar cheese, 8 ounces egg substitute, 20 ounces skim milk

TUNA-STUFFED TOMATO

EASY - DO AHEAD

ingredients: 4 large tomatoes
12 oz. fat-free tuna, drained
1 1/2 tbsp. fat-free mayonnaise
1/2 cup chopped onions
3/4 cup chopped celery
1 1/2 tsp. mustard
1/2 tsp. pepper
2 tbsp. dill pickle relish
Paprika (optional)

directions: Cut tops off tomatoes and set aside. Scoop out pulp and drain well.
Combine tomato pulp, tuna, mayonnaise, onions, celery, mustard, pepper and pickle relish, and mix well.
Cover and refrigerate several hours before serving.
Just before serving, stuff tomato shells with tuna mixture. Sprinkle with paprika before serving, if desired.

Serves: 4

JEWISH

Nutrition per Serving
Calories	169
Carbohydrate	12 grams
Cholesterol	16 milligrams
Dietary Fiber	2 grams
Fat	< 1 gram
Protein	28 grams
Sodium	454 milligrams

Exchanges
2 vegetable
3 1/2 meat

Shopping List: 4 large tomatoes, 12 ounces fat-free tuna, fat-free mayonnaise, 1 small onion, celery, dill pickle relish, mustard, pepper, paprika (optional)

ALMOND BREAD

EASY - DO AHEAD - FREEZE

ingredients:

3/4 cup egg substitute
3/4 tsp. almond extract
1/2 cup sugar
1 1/2 cups flour
2 tsp. baking powder

directions:

Preheat oven to 350 degrees. Lightly spray a 9x5-inch loaf pan with nonfat cooking spray.
Combine all ingredients in a medium bowl and mix until well blended and smooth.
Spoon batter into prepared pan and bake in preheated oven 45-60 minutes, until knife inserted in center comes out clean.

Serves: 8

Nutrition per Serving

Calories	142	
Carbohydrate	31 grams	
Cholesterol	0 milligrams	
Dietary Fiber	1 gram	
Fat	< 1 gram	
Protein	4 grams	
Sodium	113 milligrams	

Exchanges
1 fruit
1 starch

Shopping List: 6 ounces egg substitute, flour, sugar, almond extract, baking powder

JEWISH

302

BAGELS

AVERAGE - DO AHEAD - FREEZE

ingredients:
3 1/2 cups bread flour, divided
2 tsp. + 1 tbsp. sugar
1 tsp. salt
2 1/2 tsp. active dry yeast
1 1/4 cups warm water
8 cups cold water
2 large egg whites
1 tbsp. water

directions: Combine 3 cups flour, 2 teaspoons sugar, salt, yeast and warm water in bread machine; process on dough cycle. Remove from machine and turn onto lightly floured surface. If dough is too sticky, gradually add remaining flour, 1 tablespoon at a time. Lightly spray medium bowl with nonfat cooking spray; place dough in bowl and turn to coat. Cover with a damp cloth and let rise about 45-60 minutes, until doubled in bulk. Line baking sheet with foil and lightly spray with nonfat cooking spray. Turn dough onto baking sheet(s) and knead lightly to remove air bubbles. Divide dough into 12 equal pieces. Roll each piece into a ball and press your thumb through the center to make a hole. Stretch and pull the dough to enlarge the hole. Place bagels onto baking sheets; cover with damp cloth and let rise 10-15 minutes, until slightly puffy. Preheat oven to 375 degrees. Fill large pot with 8 cups of water; add remaining sugar and bring to a boil over high heat. Reduce heat to medium-high and keep water at a low boil. Place 2 bagels at a time into pot; turn after 15 seconds and remove from pot with slotted spoon. Repeat with remaining dough, arranging bagels in a single layer. Combine egg whites and remaining water in a small bowl, and mix well; brush mixture over bagels. Bake in preheated oven 20-25 minutes, until lightly browned.

Serves: 12

Nutrition per Serving		Exchanges
Calories	128	1 2/3 starch
Carbohydrate	25 grams	
Cholesterol	0 milligrams	
Dietary Fiber	1 gram	
Fat	< 1 gram	
Protein	5 grams	
Sodium	20 milligrams	

Shopping List: bread flour, sugar, salt, eggs, active dry yeast

CHALLAH

DIFFICULT - DO AHEAD - FREEZE

ingredients:
6 tbsp. egg substitute
1 tbsp. Baking Healthy (Smucker's)
1/4 tsp. vanilla
1/2 cup warm water
1 1/2 tbsp. sugar
1 tsp. salt
2 3/4 cups bread flour
5 1/2 tsp. active dry yeast
1 medium egg white
1 1/2 tbsp. water

directions:
Combine all ingredients, except egg white and 1 1/2 tablespoons water, in bread machine in the order recommended by the manufacturer. (Some machines recommend liquid first, whereas others suggest dry ingredients first--be sure to read the manual.) Process on dough cycle. Remove dough and separate into three sections. Lightly spray baking sheet with nonfat cooking spray. Lightly flour smooth surface and roll dough pieces into long, thick rolls. Place on baking sheet and braid pieces, sealing at the ends. Cover and let rise in a warm place until double in size. Combine egg white with 1 1/2 tablespoons water and mix well. Brush over top of dough. Preheat oven to 350 degrees. Bake 45-50 minutes, until golden brown.

Serves: 8

JEWISH

Nutrition per Serving		Exchanges
Calories	159	2 starch
Carbohydrate	31 grams	
Cholesterol	0 milligrams	
Dietary Fiber	2 grams	
Fat	< 1 gram	
Protein	7 grams	
Sodium	288 milligrams	

Shopping List: Egg substitute, eggs, Baking Healthy (Smucker's) bread flour, active dry yeast (for bread machine), vanilla, sugar, salt

CARROT-ZUCCHINI KUGEL

EASY - DO AHEAD - FREEZE

ingredients:
1/2 cup egg substitute
4 large egg whites
1 lb. zucchini, shredded
2 cups shredded carrots
1 medium potato, grated
1 tbsp. onion powder
1/8 tsp. pepper
1/4 tsp. basil
3 tbsp. matzo meal

directions:
Preheat oven to 350°.
Lightly spray a 9x13-inch baking dish with nonfat cooking spray.
Combine all ingredients in a large bowl and mix until blended.
Add extra matzo meal if mixture is too watery.
Spoon into baking dish and lightly spray with nonfat cooking spray.
Bake in preheated oven 45-60 minutes, until golden brown and cooked through.

Serves: 6

Nutrition per Serving

Calories	90
Carbohydrate	16 grams
Cholesterol	0 milligrams
Dietary Fiber	3 grams
Fat	< 1 gram
Protein	6 grams
Sodium	80 milligrams

Exchanges
1/2 meat
2 vegetable
1/3 starch

Shopping List: 4 ounces egg substitute, eggs, 1 pound zucchini, 10-ounce package shredded carrots, 1 potato, matzo meal, onion powder, pepper, basil

CHAROSET

EASY - DO AHEAD

ingredients:
1 large apple, peeled and cored
3 large bananas, sliced
1 cup chopped dates
3/4 cup raisins
1/2 cup orange juice
1 1/2 tbsp. lemon juice
2 tbsp. sugar
1 tsp. cinnamon

directions:
Dice apple and bananas until finely chopped; place in bowl.
Add remaining ingredients to apple mixture and mix well.
If mixture is too watery, add matzo meal, one tablespoon at a time, until thick.
Refrigerate at least 1 hour before serving.
Serve on matzo.

Serves: 8

Nutrition per Serving		Exchanges
Calories	176	3 fruit
Carbohydrate	46 grams	
Cholesterol	0 milligrams	
Dietary Fiber	4 grams	
Fat	< 1 gram	
Protein	1 gram	
Sodium	3 milligrams	

Shopping List: apple, 3 bananas, chopped dates, raisins, 4 ounces orange juice, lemon juice, sugar, cinnamon

CHEESE-NOODLE KUGEL

EASY - DO AHEAD - FREEZE

ingredients:
3 oz. fat-free cream cheese, softened
1/2 cup fat-free cottage cheese
1/4 cup sugar
1/2 cup egg substitute
3 cups yolk-free noodles, cooked and drained
1/4 cup Cornflake Crumbs
1 tbsp. reconstituted Butter Buds

directions:
Preheat oven to 375 degrees.
Lightly spray ring mold with nonfat cooking spray.
Combine cream cheese, cottage cheese, sugar and egg substitute in food processor or blender, and process until blended.
Combine mixture with cooked noodles and toss until mixed.
Spoon into ring mold; sprinkle with Cornflake Crumbs and drizzle with Butter Buds.
Bake in preheated oven for 1 hour, until lightly browned.
Remove from mold; serve hot or cold.

Serves: 6

JEWISH

Nutrition per Serving
Calories	142
Carbohydrate	27 grams
Cholesterol	< 1 milligram
Dietary Fiber	1 gram
Fat	< 1 gram
Protein	8 grams
Sodium	181 milligrams

Exchanges
1 2/3 starch
1/2 meat

Shopping List:
3 ounces fat-free cream cheese, 4 ounces fat-free cottage cheese, 4 ounces egg substitute, yolk-free noodles, sugar, Cornflake Crumbs, Butter Buds

FARFEL KUGEL

AVERAGE - DO AHEAD

ingredients:
1 1/4 cups fat-free chicken broth, divided
1 1/2 cups chopped onions
1 cup chopped celery
1 cup sliced mushrooms
3 1/2 cups farfel
1 tsp. garlic powder
1/4 tsp. pepper
1 cup water
1/2 cup egg substitute

directions:
Preheat oven to 350 degrees. Lightly spray a 9x13-inch baking dish with nonfat cooking spray. Lightly spray a large nonstick skillet with nonfat cooking spray; add 1/4 cup chicken broth and heat over medium-high heat. Add onions, celery and mushrooms, and cook, stirring frequently, until soft. Add farfel; sprinkle with garlic powder and pepper. Pour in remaining chicken broth and water, and mix well. Cook, stirring frequently, until farfel is lightly browned. Remove from heat and stir in egg substitute until blended. Spoon into prepared casserole and bake in preheated oven 55-60 minutes, until golden brown.

Serves: 8

Nutrition per Serving		Exchanges
Calories	262	1 2/3 starch
Carbohydrate	55 grams	5 vegetable
Cholesterol	0 milligrams	
Dietary Fiber	3 grams	
Fat	< 1 gram	
Protein	9 grams	
Sodium	72 milligrams	

Shopping List: 8-ounce package chopped onions. 12 ounces fat-free chicken broth, celery, 1/2 pound sliced mushrooms, farfel (or matzo crackers), 4 ounces egg substitute, garlic powder, pepper

JEWISH

LATKES

EASY

ingredients: 1/2 cup egg substitute
1 small onion, grated
3 large baking potatoes, peeled and grated
3/4 tsp. salt
1/4 tsp. pepper
3 tbsp. Cornflake Crumbs

directions: Combine all ingredients in a medium bowl and mix well.
Lightly spray a large nonstick skillet with nonfat cooking spray, and heat over medium-high heat.
Spoon batter by tablespoons into hot skillet and flatten with back of spoon.
Cook until lightly browned, about 2-3 minutes on each side.
Serve warm, with fat-free sour cream or applesauce, if desired.

Serves: 8 (2 latkes per serving)

Nutrition per Serving		Exchanges
Calories	246	2 1/3 starch
Carbohydrate	54 grams	
Cholesterol	0 milligrams	
Dietary Fiber	6 grams	
Fat	< 1 gram	
Protein	8 grams	
Sodium	658 milligrams	

JEWISH

Shopping List: 3 large baking potatoes, 1 small onion, 4 ounces egg substitute, Cornflake Crumbs, salt, pepper

MAMA'S NOODLE KUGEL

EASY - DO AHEAD

ingredients: 8 oz. yolk-free egg noodles
3/4 cup egg substitute
3/4 cup sugar
1 tbsp. lemon juice
3/4 cup seedless raisins, chopped
1/2 cup fat-free bread crumbs

directions: Preheat oven to 400 degrees.
Lightly spray an 8-inch baking dish with nonfat cooking spray.
Cook noodles according to package directions; drain well.
Combine egg substitute, sugar and lemon juice in a medium bowl, and mix well; add noodles and toss until coated.
Spoon half the noodle mixture into baking dish; top with raisins and remaining mixture.
Sprinkle bread crumbs over top and bake in preheated oven 45 minutes.

Serves: 6

Nutrition per Serving		Exchanges
Calories	328	2 starch
Carbohydrate	72 grams	2 2/3 fruit
Cholesterol	0 milligrams	
Dietary Fiber	3 grams	
Fat	< 1 gram	
Protein	10 grams	
Sodium	113 milligrams	

Shopping List: 8-ounce package yolk-free noodles, 6 ounces egg substitute, sugar, lemon juice, seedless raisins, fat-free bread crumbs

SWEET POTATO TZIMMES

EASY - DO AHEAD

ingredients:
3 cups sweet potatoes, peeled and sliced
3 cups sliced apples (unpeeled)
3/4 cup sliced carrots
1/2 cup pitted prunes, cut in half
2 tbsp. orange juice
3 tbsp. brown sugar

directions:
Preheat oven to 350 degrees.
Lightly spray an 8x8-inch baking dish with nonfat cooking spray.
Layer half of potatoes, apples, carrots and prunes in dish; repeat layering with remaining fruit.
Combine orange juice and brown sugar, and mix until blended; drizzle over fruit.
Cover baking dish with foil and bake for 1 hour, until tender.

Serves: 6

Nutrition per Serving		Exchanges
Calories	185	2 1/3 fruit
Carbohydrate	46 grams	2/3 starch
Cholesterol	0 milligrams	
Dietary Fiber	2 grams	
Fat	< 1 gram	
Protein	2 grams	
Sodium	21 milligrams	

JEWISH

Shopping List: 3 (14-ounce) cans sliced yams (or sweet potatoes), 2 (16-ounce) cans sliced apples (or 3 large apples), 2 carrots, prunes, orange juice, brown sugar

TZIMMES

EASY - DO AHEAD

ingredients: 1 lb. baby carrots*, cut in half
6 medium sweet potatoes*, peeled and chopped
1/2 cup dried apricots
1/4 cup pitted prunes
1 1/2 cups orange juice
1/2 cup brown sugar
1/4 cup honey
3/4 tsp. cinnamon

directions: Preheat oven to 350 degrees. Lightly spray a 9x13-inch baking dish with nonfat cooking spray. Place carrots and sweet potatoes in a large soup pot; cover with water and bring to a boil over high heat. Reduce heat to medium and cook 10-15 minutes, until vegetables are tender. Remove from heat and drain well. Place vegetables in prepared casserole; add apricots and prunes. Combine orange juice, brown sugar, honey and cinnamon in a medium bowl. Mix until sugar is dissolve and ingredients are blended. Pour over vegetables; cover with foil and bake in preheated oven 25-30 minutes. Remove foil and bake an additional 8-10 minutes.

Serves: 6

Nutrition per Serving		Exchanges
Calories	330	1 vegetable
Carbohydrate	82 grams	1 starch
Cholesterol	0 milligrams	4 fruit
Dietary Fiber	5 grams	
Fat	< 1 gram	
Protein	4 grams	
Sodium	65 milligrams	

Shopping List: 1 pound baby carrots*, 6 medium sweet potatoes*, dried apricots, prunes, 12 ounces orange juice, brown sugar, honey, cinnamon

For quick preparation, use frozen baby carrots and canned sweet potatoes. Thaw and drain carrots; drain potatoes and combine remaining ingredients. Do not boil carrots and sweet potatoes.

VEGETABLE LATKES
AVERAGE - DO AHEAD - FREEZE

ingredients: 20 oz. package shredded potatoes
2 cups shredded carrots
1 cup shredded zucchini
1 cup chopped onions
1/2 cup egg substitute
2 tbsp. flour
3/4 tsp. baking powder
3/4 tsp. garlic powder
1/4 tsp. pepper

directions: Preheat oven to 425 degrees. Line baking sheet with foil and lightly spray with nonfat cooking spray. Combine potatoes, carrots, zucchini and onions in a large bowl, and mix well; drain any liquid from bowl. Add remaining ingredients and mix until ingredients are blended. Spoon batter into baking sheet by tablespoons and flatten with the back of a spoon. Bake in preheated oven 15-20 minutes, until golden brown and crisp.

Serves: 6

JEWISH

Nutrition per Serving		Exchanges
Calories	105	1 vegetable
Carbohydrate	22 grams	1 starch
Cholesterol	0 milligrams	
Dietary Fiber	4 grams	
Fat	< 1 gram	
Protein	4 grams	
Sodium	227 milligrams	

Shopping List: 20-ounce package shredded potatoes*, 8-ounce package shredded carrots, 1 large zucchini, 4-ounce package chopped onions (or 1 large onion), 4 ounces egg substitute, flour, baking powder, garlic powder, pepper

Select refrigerated or frozen shredded potatoes (not hash browns). If using frozen, thaw and drain well, before combining with other ingredients.

313

ZUCCHINI PUDDING
EASY

ingredients:
1 medium onion, minced
3 1/2 lb. zucchini, trimmed and diced
1 small carrot, peeled and grated
3 basil leaves, or 1 tsp. dried basil
1 tbsp. fresh parsley
1 tsp. salt
1/4 tsp. pepper
4 tbsp. fat-free Parmesan cheese
1/2 cup egg substitute
1/2 cup fat-free bread crumbs

directions:
Preheat oven to 450 degrees.
Lightly spray a 9x13-inch baking dish with nonfat cooking spray. Lightly spray a large nonstick skillet with nonfat cooking spray and heat over medium-high heat. Add onion and cook until soft. Add zucchini, carrots, basil, parsley, salt and pepper; cook over low heat, stirring often, until zucchini is tender. Remove from heat; add cheese and stir until cheese is melted. Cool mixture 5 minutes. Add egg substitute and mix until completely blended. Pour into baking dish and sprinkle with bread crumbs. Bake in preheated oven 20-30 minutes, until golden brown.

Serves: 6

Nutrition per Serving

		Exchanges
Calories	86	2 vegetable
Carbohydrate	16 grams	1/2 starch
Cholesterol	0 milligrams	
Dietary Fiber	5 grams	
Fat	< 1 gram	
Protein	7 grams	
Sodium	451 milligrams	

Shopping List: 3 1/2 pounds zucchini, 1 onion, 1 carrot, fat-free Parmesan cheese, 4 ounces egg substitute, fat-free bread crumbs, basil, parsley, salt, pepper

APPLE HONEY CAKE
EASY - DO AHEAD - FREEZE

ingredients:
1 cup honey
3/8 cup egg substitute
1/2 cup sugar
1/4 cup brown sugar
1 cup chunky applesauce
2 cups flour
1/2 tsp. baking soda
1 tsp. cinnamon
1/4 tsp. ginger

directions:
Preheat oven to 350 degrees.
Lightly spray large loaf pan (9x5-inch) with nonfat cooking spray.
Combine all ingredients in a large bowl and mix until completely blended.
Pour batter into prepared pan and bake in pre-heated oven 40-45 minutes, until knife inserted in center comes out clean.

Serves: 12

Nutrition per Serving		Exchanges
Calories	231	2 1/2 fruit
Carbohydrate	56 grams	1 starch
Cholesterol	0 milligrams	
Dietary Fiber	1 gram	
Fat	< 1 gram	
Protein	3 grams	
Sodium	51 milligrams	

Shopping List: Honey, egg substitute, chunky-style applesauce (with brown sugar and cinnamon), flour, sugar, brown sugar, baking soda, cinnamon, ginger

JEWISH

BANANA-RAISIN CAKE

EASY - DO AHEAD - FREEZE

ingredients: 3/4 cup Baking Healthy (Smucker's)
1 1/4 cups sugar
1 cup brown sugar
3/4 cup egg substitute
1 1/2 tsp. vanilla
1 tsp. banana extract
1 1/2 cups mashed bananas
3/4 cup hot water
3 cups flour
1 1/2 tsp. baking soda
1 1/2 tsp. baking powder
1 tsp. cinnamon
1 cup raisins

directions: Preheat oven to 350 degrees. Lightly spray tube pan with nonfat cooking spray. Combine Baking Healthy, sugar, brown sugar, egg substitute, vanilla, banana extract and bananas in a large bowl, and mix until completely blended. Add flour, baking soda, baking powder and cinnamon to sugar mixture; gradually add hot water and continue to mix until completely blended. Pour mixture into prepared pan and bake in preheated oven 1-1 1/4 hours, until knife inserted in center comes out clean. Cool 15-20 minutes before removing cake from pan.

Serves: 12

Nutrition per Serving		Exchanges
Calories	347	1 1/2 starch
Carbohydrate	82 grams	4 fruit
Cholesterol	0 milligrams	
Dietary Fiber	2 grams	
Fat	< 1 gram	
Protein	5 grams	
Sodium	179 milligrams	

Shopping List: 6 ounces Baking Healthy (Smucker's), sugar, brown sugar, 6 ounces egg substitute, flour, 4 bananas, raisins, vanilla, banana extract, baking soda, baking powder, cinnamon

DESSERT FRUIT TOPPING

EASY - DO AHEAD

ingredients:
1 large banana, cut into 1-inch pieces
1 cup strawberries, hulled and halved
1/2 cup blueberries
1/2 cup raspberries
1 cup fat-free strawberry-banana yogurt
1 tbsp. vanilla
1/4 cup sugar

directions:
Combine all ingredients in a blender and process until smooth.
Serve over fat-free frozen yogurt, pound cake, honey cake or angel food cake.
Substitute 2 cups of your favorite fruit (cherries, kiwi, blackberries, mangoes, peaches, plums) for banana and berries, for variation.

Serves: 6

Nutrition per Serving		Exchanges
Calories	89	1 1/2 fruit
Carbohydrate	20 grams	
Cholesterol	1 milligram	
Dietary Fiber	2 grams	
Fat	< 1 gram	
Protein	2 grams	
Sodium	25 milligrams	

Shopping List: 1 banana, 1/2 pint strawberries, blueberries, 1/2 pint raspberries, 8 ounces fat-free flavored yogurt, vanilla, sugar

JEWISH

FRITTERS

AVERAGE

ingredients: 2 envelopes (2 1/4 oz.) active dry yeast
1 cup warm water
2 1/2 cups flour
3 tsp. salt
2 tsp. anise seeds
2 tsp. fat-free margarine
1 cup raisins
1 1/2 cups honey
2 tbsp. lemon juice

directions: Dissolve yeast in warm water. Combine flour, salt and anise seeds in a large bowl. Gradually add yeast mixture and margarine, and mix until soft dough forms. Knead dough on lightly-floured surface for 10 minutes, or until dough is smooth. Add raisins and knead until well mixed. Shape dough into ball; place in bowl lightly sprayed with cooking spray. Cover with clean towel and let rise 1 hour, until doubled in size. Remove dough from bowl and flatten on lightly-floured surface until 1/2-inch thick. Let rest, uncovered, 15 minutes. With a sharp, serrated knife, cut dough into 36 diamonds. Spray large nonstick skillet with cooking spray and heat over medium-high heat. Add "diamonds" to hot skillet, four to six at a time, and cook until golden brown on both sides. Heat honey and lemon juice in small saucepan over high heat; let mixture boil 3 minutes. Arrange fritters on serving platter and drizzle with hot honey sauce. Serve warm.

Yields: 36 fritters

Nutrition per Serving		**Exchanges**
Calories	89	1 fruit
Carbohydrate	21 grams	1/3 starch
Cholesterol	0 milligrams	
Dietary Fiber	1 gram	
Fat	< 1 gram	
Protein	1 gram	
Sodium	181 milligrams	

Shopping List: 2 envelopes active dry yeast, flour, fat-free margarine, anise seeds, raisins, honey, lemon juice, salt

SHANA TOVAH HONEY CAKE

EASY - DO AHEAD - FREEZE

ingredients:
1/2 cup egg substitute
3/4 cup sugar
1/2 cup honey
1/2 tsp. vanilla
3 tbsp. Baking Healthy (Smucker's)
3/4 cup skim milk
2 1/2 cups flour
1 tsp. baking powder
1 tsp. baking soda
1 tsp. cinnamon

directions:
Preheat oven to 300 degrees.
Lightly spray an 8x8-inch square pan with nonfat cooking spray.
Combine egg substitute, sugar, honey, vanilla, Baking Healthy and milk in a large bowl; mix until smooth and creamy.
Gradually add flour, baking powder, baking soda and cinnamon; mix until ingredients are blended and smooth.
Pour into prepared loaf pan and bake 1 hour, until knife inserted in center comes out clean.
Remove from oven and let cool on rack 10 minutes. Invert cake onto rack and allow to cool completely.

Serves: 12

Nutrition per Serving		Exchanges
Calories	202	2 fruit
Carbohydrate	46 grams	1 starch
Cholesterol	< 1 milligram	
Dietary Fiber	1 gram	
Fat	< 1 gram	
Protein	4 grams	
Sodium	120 milligrams	

Shopping List: 4 ounces egg substitute, 6 ounces skim milk, Baking Healthy (Smucker's), sugar, honey, flour, baking powder, baking soda, cinnamon, vanilla

MEXICAN

MEXICAN

Fiestas, fun and flavor characterize Mexican culture with the greatest emphasis on FOOD! Preparing and eating certain foods are an important part of Mexican tradition, along with the afternoon siesta. Although women rarely make their own tortillas anymore, fresh breads and cookies are more commonly purchased at the local *panaderia* (bakery), and the siesta has been cut from three hours to two, the tradition of Mexican cooking is still thriving.

5 Basic ingredients in the Mexican kitchen: *tortillas, beans, salsa, fresh vegetables and chili peppers.*

Essentials of Mexican cooking:
1. *Recados* are Mexican spice mixtures used for seasoning meats, fish and poultry before grilling (similar to French *herbes Provence,* Indian *garam masala,* or Chinese *5-Spice Powder*), or flavoring in soups and stews.
2. *Salsa* is the quintessential Mexican condiment used for everything from tortilla chips to baked potatoes. The condiment of the 90's, salsa is a low-calorie, low-fat alternative to mayonnaise, butter, salad dressings or marinades. Why choose salsa over the rest? Count your savings!

2 tbsp. salsa	10-15 calories	0 grams of fat
2 tbsp. butter	200 calories	22 grams of fat
2 tbsp. mayonnaise	220 calories	14 grams of fat
2 tbsp. Italian salad dressing	150 calories	14 grams of fat
2 tbsp. sour cream	100 calories	12 grams of fat

8 Super Ways to Serve Salsa
- dip for fat-free chips, crackers, pita chips or cut-up vegetables
- topping for baked potatoes or other cooked vegetables
- toss with rice or pasta
- pizza topping base
- omelet stuffing or topping
- condiment for sandwiches
- garnish for soup or chili
- salad dressing alternative

3. *Tortillas*, the round, flat unleavened breads made from wheat or corn, are included in almost every Mexican meal. Rolled, folded, baked or fried, sliced into strips, cut in wedges, rolled into cylinders, or folded in half, tortillas are considered **the** staple food of Mexican cuisine.
4. *Beans* or *frijoles* are essential to authentic Mexican cooking. Inexpensive, versatile, loaded with complex carbohydrates, low in fat, full of fiber, nutrient-rich (folic acid, vitamin B6, niacin, thiamin), and high in protein, beans are a healthy addition to any meal.

1 cup cooked beans
- **provides** 20-30% of daily value of iron, plus some zinc, calcium and magnesium
- **contains** less than 1% of calories from fat (compared to 60-85% fat calories in meat)
- **has** 6-7 grams of fiber (compared to one slice of whole wheat bread with 2 grams of fiber)

Other "Beyond Basic" Ingredients

<u>Vegetables:</u> plaintains, avocados (very high in fat), jicama, cactus paddles or nopales (fleshy oval leaves of the pickly peat cactus), tomatillas (resemble green tomatoes with papery husks), tomatoes (both green and red), chickpeas, onions, purple skinned garlic, wild mushrooms, chayote (a native squash).

<u>Chilies:</u> Indisposable to Mexican cooking, chilies are used in both their fresh and dried forms. From mild to spicy-hot there are more than 100 varieties of chilies available. High in vitamins A and C, low in fat and sodium, chilies are the choice for extra flavor and "zip"! Just be sure to select and handle your chilies with care (mild to hot):

1. *Anaheim* - long, narrow, light-green chili that ranges from mild to hot
   Pasados - anaheim chilies dried in the sun
2. *Poblana* - large, dark green chili commonly used in Chili Rellenos
   Ancho - dried version of the red, ripe poblano chili with a mild, spicy, sweet flavor, used in salsa, recados and moles
3. *Jalapeño* - most familiar and popular hot chili
   Chipotle - dried ripe version of a particular type of jalapeño chili, with a smoky, rich flavor

322

4. *Serrano* - small chili that is significantly hotter than the jalapeño
   Arbo - dried version of the ripe serrano chili, with a hot, nutty flavor
5. *Habenero* - the hottest of chilies, it is commonly used in table sauces

Save fat the easy way to get the "least" from your Mexican food:

Instead of	Use	Save
flour tortillas	fat-free flour tortillas	5 grams fat
1/2 cup sour cream	1/2 cup fat-free sour cream	22 grams fat
3 oz. hamburger (lean)	3 oz. fat-free ground turkey	10-12 grams fat
1/2 cup refried beans	1/2 cup fat-free refried beans	1.5 grams fat
1 oz. tortilla chips (fried)	1 oz. baked tortilla chips	5-9 grams fat
1 tbsp. vegetable oil	1 spray nonfat cooking spray	13.5 grams fat

Common Herbs and Spices
- **sweet basil** *albahaca dulce*
- **anise** *anis*
- **savory** *ajedrea*
- **saffron** *azafran*
- **chervil** *cerafolto*
- **chili powder** *chile molido*
- **coriander** *cilantro*
- **cloves** *comino*
- **turmeric** *cucuma*
- **bay leaf** *hojas de laurel*
- **ginger** *jengibre*
- **nutmeg** *nuez moxada*
- **oregano** *oregano*
- **cayenne pepper** *pimienta*
- **allspice** *pimienta dulce*
- **black pepper** *pimienta negra*
- **celery seed** *semillas de apio*
- **thyme** *tomillo*

BLACK BEAN QUESADILLAS
EASY

ingredients: 1 cup fat-free black beans, mashed
2 tbsp. chopped green onions
2 tbsp. chopped red onions
2 tbsp. chopped green peppers
1 tbsp. lime juice
1 tbsp. chopped cilantro
1 crushed garlic clove
4 fat-free flour tortillas
1 cup fat-free Mexican cheese

directions: Combine mashed beans, green onions, red onions, green peppers, lime juice, cilantro and garlic in a medium bowl; mix until blended.
Lightly spray large nonstick skillet with nonfat cooking spray and heat over medium-high heat. Add tortillas one at a time and cook 15 seconds on each side, until softened. Divide bean mixture and cheese among tortillas; fold in half. Respray skillet with cooking spray. Cook filled tortillas 2 minutes on each side, or until cheese is melted.

Serves: 4

Nutrition per Serving		Exchanges
Calories	264	1 meat
Carbohydrate	46 grams	2 starch
Cholesterol	0 milligrams	3 vegetable
Dietary Fiber	5 grams	
Fat	< 1 gram	
Protein	18 grams	
Sodium	684 milligrams	

Shopping List: 15-ounce can fat-free black beans, red onion, green onions, green bell pepper, crushed garlic, cilantro, lime juice, fat-free flour tortillas, 4 ounces fat-free finely-shredded Mexican cheese

MEXICAN

"BROCCOMOLE"

EASY - DO AHEAD

ingredients:
2 1/4 cups broccoli stalks
2 1/4 tbsp. lemon juice
1/4 tsp. ground cumin
1/4 tsp. garlic powder
1/4 tsp. onion powder
1 cup diced tomatoes with green chilies
1 tbsp. chopped green chilies

directions:
Combine broccoli, lemon juice, cumin, garlic powder and onion powder in a food processor and process until smooth. Transfer mixture to medium bowl. Add tomatoes and green chilies; mix lightly. Cover and refrigerate 2-3 hours before serving. Great with fat-free chips, burritos, enchiladas, etc.

Serves: 6

Nutrition per Serving		Exchanges
Calories	18	Free
Carbohydrate	4 grams	
Cholesterol	0 milligrams	
Dietary Fiber	1 gram	
Fat	< 1 gram	
Protein	1 gram	
Sodium	187 milligrams	

Shopping List:
1 1/2 pounds broccoli, 15-ounce can diced tomatoes with green chilies, 4-ounce can chopped green chilies, lemon juice, garlic powder, onion powder, ground cumin

MEXICAN

CRABMEAT QUESADILLAS
EASY - DO AHEAD

ingredients: 3/4 cup fat-free finely-shredded Mexican cheese
1/2 cup fat-free mayonnaise
1/4 cup fat-free sour cream
6 oz. canned crabmeat, drained
1 1/2 tbsp. sliced green onions
1 1/2 tbsp. chopped green chilies
3 whole fat-free flour tortillas
3/4 cup fat-free salsa (optional)

directions: Preheat oven to 425 degrees.
Lightly spray cookie sheet with nonfat cooking spray.
In a medium bowl, combine cheese, mayonnaise, sour cream, crabmeat, onions and chilies; mix until well blended. Divide mixture and spread evenly on tortillas. Fold tortillas in half and arrange in single layer on cookie sheet. Bake in preheated oven 7-10 minutes, until cheese is melted and cooked through. Remove from oven and let stand 2-3 minutes, until cheese is melted and cooked through. Remove from oven and let stand 2-3 minutes; cut each tortilla into thirds and serve with salsa, if desired.

Serves: 6

Nutrition per Serving		Exchanges
Calories	151	1 vegetable
Carbohydrate	23 grams	1 starch
Cholesterol	35 milligrams	1 meat
Dietary Fiber	2 grams	
Fat	< 1 gram	
Protein	13 grams	
Sodium	802 milligrams	

Shopping List: 3 ounces fat-free shredded Mexican cheese, 4 ounces fat-free mayonnaise, 2 ounces fat-free sour cream, 6-ounce can crabmeat, green onion, 4-ounce can chopped green chilies, fat-free flour tortillas (burrito size), 6 ounces salsa

FIERY CAJUN SHRIMP

EASY

ingredients: 1 cup reconstituted Butter Buds
1/4 cup Worcestershire sauce
2 tbsp. ground pepper
1/2 tsp. rosemary
1 tsp. liquid hot pepper sauce
1 tsp. salt
2 small cloves garlic, minced
Juice of 1 lemon
2 lb. shrimp
1 lemon, sliced

directions: Preheat oven to 400 degrees. Lightly spray a 9-inch baking dish with nonfat cooking spray. Combine Butter Buds, Worcestershire sauce, pepper, rosemary, pepper sauce, salt, garlic and lemon juice in a medium bowl; mix well. Place shrimp in baking dish and top with sauce mixture. Arrange lemon slices on top and bake in preheated oven 15-20 minutes, until shrimp are cooked through.

Serves: 6

Nutrition per Serving		Exchanges
Calories	144	3 meat
Carbohydrate	11 grams	1/2 starch
Cholesterol	47 milligrams	
Dietary Fiber	1 gram	
Fat	< 1 gram	
Protein	22 grams	
Sodium	836 milligrams	

Shopping List: 2 pounds fat-free shrimp, 1/2 pound fat-free margarine, Worcestershire sauce, 1 lemon, liquid hot pepper sauce, pepper, rosemary, salt, garlic

MEXICAN

GRILLED VEGETABLE RELISH ON BAKED YAM CHIP

DIFFICULT - DO AHEAD

ingredients:
1/2 red bell pepper
1/2 yellow bell pepper
1 medium yam, cut in 1/8-inch thick rounds
1 eggplant, sliced 1/4-inch thick
1 zucchini, sliced 1/4-inch thick
1 yellow squash, sliced 1/4-inch thick
1 red onion, sliced 1/4-inch thick
6 stalks asparagus, blanched and sliced thin
1 portabello mushroom cap, stem and "lungs" removed
1/4 cup balsamic vinegar, divided
Ground black pepper

directions:
Preheat broiler on high heat. Line baking sheet with foil and lightly spray with nonfat cooking spray. Arrange pepper halves on baking sheet and broil until charred black. Turn broiler off and heat oven to 275 degrees. Under running water, remove charred skin and julienne peppers, setting aside for garnish. Arrange yam slices on baking sheet and bake 40 minutes, until crisp; turn slices several times. Prepare grill on medium-high heat. Brush all vegetables with balsamic vinegar and sprinkle with black pepper. Grill vegetables 2 minutes on each side; arrange on platter, cover and refrigerate 20 minutes. Dice vegetables and toss with a splash of balsamic vinegar. Top each yam chip with vegetable relish and roasted bell peppers.

Serves: 6

Nutrition per Serving

Calories	115	
Carbohydrate	26 grams	
Cholesterol	0 milligrams	
Dietary Fiber	1 gram	
Fat	< 1 gram	
Protein	4 grams	
Sodium	168 milligrams	

Exchanges
4 1/2 vegetable

Shopping List: 1 yam, 1 eggplant, 1 zucchini, 1 yellow squash, 1 red onion, 1 portabello mushroom, 1/2 pound asparagus, red bell pepper, yellow bell pepper, 2 ounces balsamic vinegar, ground black pepper

MEXICAN

MEXICAN PINWHEELS

EASY - DO AHEAD

ingredients:
16 oz. fat-free cream cheese, softened
3/4 cup sliced black olives
4 oz. can diced green chilies
1 green onion, sliced
1/8 tsp. seasoned salt
1/8 tsp. chili powder
12 fat-free flour tortillas
Fat-free salsa

directions:
Combine cream cheese, olives, chilies, onions, seasoned salt and chili powder in a medium bowl and mix until completely blended. Spread mixture on tortillas; roll up tortillas and wrap with plastic wrap. Refrigerate tortilla rolls overnight. Just before serving, cut tortillas into 1/4-inch slices; serve with salsa.

Serves: 12

Nutrition per Serving		Exchanges
Calories	76	1/2 starch
Cholesterol	0 milligrams	1 vegetable
Carbohydrate	14 grams	1/2 meat
Dietary Fiber	1 gram	
Fat	< 1 gram	
Protein	5 grams	
Sodium	375 milligrams	

Shopping List: fat-free flour tortillas, 16 ounces fat-free cream cheese, 4 ounces diced green chili peppers, 6-ounce can sliced black olives, green onion, chili powder, seasoned salt, fat-free salsa

MEXICAN

PAPAYA TOMATILLO SALSA

EASY

ingredients:　1 large papaya, peeled, seeded and diced
2 medium tomatillos, diced
1/2 small red onion, diced
2 red jalapeño peppers, seeded and diced
4 green onions, diced
1/4 bunch cilantro, cleaned and chopped
1/4 cup orange juice
Salt
Pepper

directions:　Combine all ingredients in a medium bowl and mix well. Serve with chicken, fish, or fat-free tortilla chips.

Serves: 4

Nutrition per Serving		Exchanges
Calories	47	1/2 fruit
Carbohydrate	11 grams	1/2 vegetable
Cholesterol	0 milligrams	
Dietary Fiber	3 grams	
Fat	< 1 gram	
Protein	2 grams	
Sodium	5 milligrams	

Shopping List:　1 large papaya, 2 tomatillos, red onion, 2 red jalapeño peppers, green onions, fresh cilantro, orange juice, salt, pepper

MEXICAN

ROASTED TOMATO SALSA
EASY - DO AHEAD

ingredients:
12 vine-ripened tomatoes
2 medium yellow onions, diced
6 cloves garlic
2 jalapeño chilies
1/2 bunch cilantro
1/2 cup V8 juice*
Salt and pepper, to taste

directions:
Preheat oven to 425 degrees.
Lightly spray large roasting pan with nonfat cooking spray. Arrange tomatoes, onions, garlic and jalapeño chilies in pan and bake 45 minutes, until tomatoes are browned. Remove from oven and cool to room temperature.
Spoon vegetables into food processor; add cilantro and process until chopped. Gradually add juice until salsa is desired consistency.

Serves: 24

Nutrition per Serving

		Exchanges
Calories	21	1 vegetable
Carbohydrate	5 grams	
Cholesterol	0 milligrams	
Dietary Fiber	1 gram	
Fat	< 1 gram	
Protein	1 gram	
Sodium	42 milligrams	

MEXICAN

Shopping List: 12 vine-ripened tomatoes, 2 yellow onions, garlic, 2 jalapeño chilies, fresh cilantro, 4 ounces V8 tomato juice (*or tomato juice), salt, pepper

SNOW CRAB SLAW
WRAPPED IN JICAMA
AVERAGE

ingredients: 1/2 small head green savoy or napa cabbage, julienned
1 small red onion, peeled and julienned
1 small red bell pepper, seeded and julienned
1 small poblano or anaheim chili, julienned
1 small leek
4 cups boiling water
1/8 cup seasoned rice vinegar
1/8 cup fat-free plain yogurt
Juice of 1 lime
Salt and pepper, to taste
2 tbsp. sugar
4 oz. fat-free crabmeat
1 small jicama, peeled and sliced into 1/16-
inch-thick rounds (about 24)

directions: Combine cabbage, onion, bell pepper and chili in
a large bowl; toss to mix. Blanch 2 outer leaves of
leek in boiling water 1 minute. Remove from water; submerge in ice
bath for 5 minutes. Remove from ice and pat dry. Lay on cutting
board and slice 1/8-inch lengthwise strips (about 24). Combine
vinegar, yogurt, lime juice, sugar, salt and pepper in a small bowl;
mix until blended. Add crabmeat and sauce to julienned vegetables;
toss until ingredients are mixed. To prepare, lay leek strings out;
position 1 jicama round on top. Top jicama with generous amount
of slaw; roll jicama around slaw; secure with leek tie.

Serves: 12 (2 per serving)

Nutrition per Serving		Exchanges
Calories	44	2 vegetable
Carbohydrate	10 grams	
Cholesterol	6 milligrams	
Dietary Fiber	1 gram	
Fat	< 1 gram	
Protein	2 grams	
Sodium	112 milligrams	

Shopping List: 1 jicama, 1 small leek, small head green savoy or napa
cabbage, red bell pepper, red onion, poblano or anaheim
chili, 1 lime, 4 ounces fat-free crabmeat, seasoned rice
vinegar, fat-free plain yogurt, sugar, salt, pepper

TORTILLA PINWHEEL WITH SUN-DRIED TOMATO CREAM CHEESE AND FRESH VEGETABLES

AVERAGE - DO AHEAD

ingredients:
2 oz. sun-dried tomatoes (not oil-packed), finely chopped
1 cup fat-free cream cheese, softened
Black pepper, toasted and cracked
4 (8-inch) fat-free flour tortillas
1 small zucchini
1 small yellow squash
1 small carrot
1/2 small red onion

directions:
Combine chopped tomatoes, cream cheese and pepper in a medium bowl; mix until blended. Spread cream cheese mixture liberally on one side of each tortilla.

Peel zucchini and squash about 1/8-inch thick, reserving skins and discarding the rest. Julienne squash skins, carrot and red onion. Layer julienne vegetables on one end of each tortilla and roll into tight cylinders. Slice in 3/4-inch pieces with a sharp knife, discarding the ends.

Yields: 3 dozen

Nutrition per Serving		Exchanges
Calories	23	1 vegetable
Carbohydrate	5 grams	
Cholesterol	0 milligrams	
Dietary Fiber	< 1 gram	
Fat	< 1 gram	
Protein	1 gram	
Sodium	80 milligrams	

Shopping List: fat-free flour tortillas, 8 ounces fat-free cream cheese, 2 ounces sun-dried tomatoes (*not oil-packed*), 1 carrot, 1 zucchini, 1 yellow squash, small red onion, black pepper

CHICKEN CORN CHOWDER

EASY - DO AHEAD

ingredients: 3 quarts fat-free chicken broth
16 oz. yolk-free noodles
2 cups fat-free chicken tenders, cooked and diced
1/2 tsp. nutmeg
2 (17 oz.) cans fat-free cream-style corn

directions: Pour chicken broth into large soup pot and bring to a boil over high heat. Add noodles, chicken, nutmeg and corn; cook, stirring occasionally, for 10 minutes, until noodles are tender. Serve hot.

Serves: 10

Nutrition per Serving		Exchanges
Calories	190	1 meat
Carbohydrate	35 grams	2 starch
Cholesterol	21 milligrams	
Dietary Fiber	2 grams	
Fat	< 1 gram	
Protein	12 grams	
Sodium	909 milligrams	

Shopping List: 6 (16-ounce) cans fat-free chicken broth, 8-ounce package yolk-free noodles, 1 1/4 pounds fat-free chicken tenders, 2 (17-ounce) cans fat-free cream-style corn, nutmeg

CHICKEN TORTILLA SOUP
AVERAGE - DO AHEAD

ingredients:
2 ears corn
2 jalapeño chilies, seeded and diced
1 medium red onion, diced
2 roma tomatoes, diced
3/4 lb. fat-free chicken tenders, cooked and diced
8 cups fat-free chicken broth
Fat-free corn tortillas (red, yellow and blue), julienned
1/2 bunch cilatnro
1/4 cup lime juice

directions:
Grill or roast corn and shave kernels off cob. Combine corn, jalapeños, onions, tomatoes, chicken and broth in a large soup pot; bring to a boil over high heat. Immediately reduce heat to low and simmer 1 hour. Preheat oven to 400 degrees. Line baking sheet with foil and lightly spray with non-fat cooking spray. Arrange tortilla strips on baking sheet and bake 10-12 minutes, until crisp. Just before serving, add cilantro and lime juice to soup; cook until heated through. Garnish with tortilla strips and serve.

Serves: 8

MEXICAN

Nutrition per Serving

Calories	165
Carbohydrate	21 grams
Cholesterol	36 milligrams
Dietary Fiber	3 grams
Fat	< 1 gram
Protein	20 grams
Sodium	601 milligrams

Exchanges
1 vegetable
2 meat
1 starch

Shopping List: 3/4 pound fat-free chicken tenders, 4 (16-ounce) cans fat-free chicken broth, 2 ears of corn, 2 jalapeño chilies, 1 red onion, 2 roma tomatoes, small bunch cilantro, fat-free corn tortillas (if available, use red, yellow and blue), lime juice

SPICY SHRIMP SOUP

EASY

ingredients: 2 cups canned puréed tomatoes
1/2 lb. diced red potatoes
1 tbsp. onion powder
1/2 tsp. garlic powder
1/2 tsp. ground cumin
1/2 tsp. dried oregano
1/2 tsp. pepper
2 cups clam juice
2 cups fat-free chicken broth
1 lb. fat-free frozen shrimp (raw)

directions: Lightly spray a large saucepan with nonfat cooking spray.
Add tomatoes, potatoes, onion powder, garlic powder, cumin, oregano and pepper; heat over medium heat. Add clam juice and chicken broth; bring to a boil over medium-high heat. Reduce heat to low, cover and simmer until potatoes are tender, about 10-15 minutes. Add the shrimp and cook until shrimp are pink and cooked through. Serve immediately.

Serves: 6

Nutrition per Serving		Exchanges
Calories	137	3 vegetable
Carbohydrate	24 grams	1/2 starch
Cholesterol	9 milligrams	1/2 meat
Dietary Fiber	1 gram	
Fat	< 1 gram	
Protein	11 grams	
Sodium	1125 milligrams	

Shopping List: 16-ounce can puréed tomatoes, 8 ounces red potatoes, 16 ounces bottled clam juice, 16 ounces fat-free chicken broth, 1 pound fat-free frozen shrimp (raw), onion powder, garlic powder, ground cumin, dried oregano, pepper

MEXICAN COLESLAW

EASY - DO AHEAD

ingredients:
5 cups shredded red and green cabbage mix
1/2 cup shredded carrots
1/2 cup shredded jicama
1 cup fresh cilantro leaves, minced
1 tbsp. water
1 tbsp. sugar
1/4 cup lime juice
1/8 tsp. pepper
1/8 tsp. cumin powder

directions:
In a large bowl, combine cabbage, carrots, jicama and cilantro; toss until well mixed.
In a small bowl, combine water, sugar, lime juice, pepper and cumin; mix until blended. Pour over cabbage mixture and toss until mixed. Cover with plastic wrap and refrigerate 2-4 hours before serving.

Serves: 6

Nutrition per Serving

Calories	43	
Carbohydrate	10 grams	
Cholesterol	0 milligrams	
Dietary Fiber	3 grams	
Fat	< 1 gram	
Protein	1 gram	
Sodium	24 milligrams	

Exchanges
2 vegetable

Shopping List: 16-ounce package shredded cabbage mix, 8-ounce package shredded carrots, jicama, fresh cilantro leaves, lime juice, sugar, pepper, cumin powder.

MEXICAN

SOUTHWEST COOL SLAW
AVERAGE - DO AHEAD

ingredients:
1 small head green cabbage, shredded
1/2 small head purple cabbage, shredded
1 small red onion, julienned
2 jalapeño peppers, julienned
1 small red bell pepper, seeded and julienned
1 large carrot, julienned
1/2 cup fat-free plain yogurt
1/4 cup cider vinegar
1/4 cup sugar
1 tsp. ground cumin
Salt and pepper, to taste

directions:
Combine all vegetables in a large mixing bowl. In a separate bowl, combine yogurt, vinegar, sugar, cumin, salt and pepper; whisk until completely blended. Pour dressing over slaw and toss until well mixed. Cover and refrigerate at least 1 hour before serving.

Serves: 6

Nutrition per Serving

		Exchanges
Calories	80	3 vegetable
Carbohydrate	19 grams	
Cholesterol	< 1 milligram	
Dietary Fiber	3 grams	
Fat	< 1 gram	
Protein	3 grams	
Sodium	117 milligrams	

MEXICAN

Shopping List:
1 small head green cabbage, 1 small head purple cabbage, 1 small red onion, 2 jalapeño peppers. 1 small red bell pepper, 1 large carrot, 8 ounces fat-free plain yogurt, cider vinegar, sugar, ground cumin, salt, pepper

CHICKEN CHIMICHANGA

DIFFICULT - DO AHEAD - FREEZE

ingredients:
1 lb. fat-free ground chicken
1 1/2 tbsp. onion powder
1 tsp. garlic powder
1/8 tsp. ground cumin
1/2 tsp. chili powder
4 oz. chopped green chili peppers
1 cup fat-free finely-shredded Mexican cheese
6 fat-free flour tortillas (burrito-size)
Fat-free salsa (optional)

directions:
Lightly spray a large nonstick skillet with nonfat cooking spray and heat over medium-high heat. Add chicken, onion powder, garlic powder, cumin and chili powder to skillet and cook, stirring frequently, until chicken is no longer pink. Remove from skillet and drain well. Return chicken to skillet; add chili peppers and cheese to chicken; mix well. Spoon 1/4-1/3 cup chicken mixture down the center of each tortilla. Fold the sides of tortilla and roll up from the bottom to seal. Secure tortilla rolls with wooden toothpick and lightly spray with nonfat cooking spray. Lightly spread large nonstick skillet with cooking spray and heat over medium-high heat. Add chimichangas to skillet and cook until both sides are browned and crisp. Keep warm in oven, or cool and package for freezing. Serve with salad, if desired.

Serves: 6

MEXICAN

Nutrition per Serving

		Exchanges
Calories	44	2 vegetable
Carbohydrate	40 grams	2 meat
Cholesterol	28 milligrams	2 starch
Dietary Fiber	3 grams	
Fat	< 1 gram	
Protein	23 grams	
Sodium	800 milligrams	

Shopping List: 1 pound fat-free ground chicken, 4 ounces fat-free finely-shredded Mexican cheese, 4 ounces green chili peppers, fat-free flour tortillas, garlic powder, chili powder, ground cumin, onion powder, fat-free salsa (optional)

CHILI RELLENO CASSEROLE

AVERAGE - DO AHEAD

ingredients:
12 oz. whole green chili peppers, drained
1 cup evaporated skim milk
2 tbsp. egg substitute
3 large egg whites
1/3 cup flour
1/8 tsp. pepper
4 cups fat-free finely-shredded Mexican cheese
1 cup fat-free salsa

directions:
Preheat oven to 350 degrees. Lightly spray a 1 1/2-quart casserole with nonfat cooking spray. Wearing gloves or plastic wrap to protect hands, carefully cut the peppers in half lengthwise. Remove the seeds and rinse peppers; drain until dry. Combine evaporated milk, egg substitute, egg whites, flour and pepper in a food processor or blender and process until smooth; set aside. To assemble casserole: arrange half the chili peppers on bottom of casserole; top with 1 1/2 cups cheese and half the egg mixture. Repeat layers with remaining chili peppers, 2 cups cheese and remaining egg mixture. Pour salsa over the top and bake in preheated oven 30 minutes. Remove from oven; sprinkle with remaining cheese and bake an additional 20-25 minutes, until a knife inserted in the center comes out clean. Serve immediately.

Serves: 6

Nutrition per Serving

		Exchanges
Calories	189	1 vegetable
Carbohydrate	18 grams	2 meat
Cholesterol	4 milligrams	1 milk
Dietary Fiber	1 gram	
Fat	< 1 gram	
Protein	29 grams	
Sodium	1410 milligrams	

Shopped List:
12-ounce can whole green chili peppers, 8-ounce can evaporated skim milk, egg substitute, large eggs, flour, 16 ounces fat-free finely-shredded Mexican cheese, 8 ounces salsa, pepper

CITRUS SAGE CHICKEN BREASTS

EASY

ingredients:
2 lb. fat-free chicken breasts
6 oz. can lemonade concentrate, thawed
1/3 cup honey
1/2 tsp. lemon juice
1 tsp. dried crushed sage
1/2 tsp. dried crushed thyme
1/2 tsp. dry mustard

directions:
Preheat oven to 350 degrees.
Lightly spray a 9x13-inch baking dish with nonfat cooking spray. Arrange chicken breasts in baking dish.
Combine remaining ingredients and mix until blended. Pour 1/2 the mixture over chicken and bake in preheated oven 20 minutes. Turn chicken over and cover with remaining sauce. Bake 15-20 minutes longer, until chicken is cooked through and no longer pink.

Serves: 8

Nutrition per Serving		Exchanges
Calories	197	3 1/2 meat
Carbohydrate	22 grams	1 1/3 fruit
Cholesterol	56 milligrams	
Dietary Fiber	1 gram	
Fat	< 1 gram	
Protein	26 grams	
Sodium	232 milligrams	

MEXICAN

Shopping List:
2 pounds fat-free chicken breasts, 6-ounce can lemonade concentrate, honey, lemon juice, dried crushed sage, dried crushed thyme, dry mustard

PASTA CHILI

EASY

---

ingredients:
1 tbsp. fat-free chicken broth
1 onion, chopped
1 clove garlic, peeled and minced
1 lb. fat-free beef crumbles
2 tsp. chili powder
1 cup fat-free pasta sauce
1/2 tsp. basil
1/2 tsp. oregano
1/2 cup chopped green pepper
8 oz. fat-free pasta (rotini, rotelle or pasta twists), cooked and drained
1 cup fat-free finely-shredded Cheddar cheese

directions:
Lightly spray large nonstick skillet with nonfat cooking spray; add chicken broth and heat over medium-high heat. Add onion and garlic; sauté until translucent. Add beef crumbles and cook until browned. Stir in chili powder, pasta sauce, basil, oregano and green pepper; simmer 10 minutes, stirring occasionally. Add cooked pasta to beef mixture and toss lightly until mixed and heated through. Remove pan from heat; sprinkle cheese over pasta mixture. Cover pan and let stand 5 minutes, until cheese is melted. Serve immediately.

Serves: 4

Nutrition per Serving

Calories	367
Carbohydrate	51 grams
Cholesterol	0 milligrams
Dietary Fiber	7 grams
Fat	< 1 gram
Protein	36 grams
Sodium	1029 milligrams

Exchanges
4 vegetable
3 meat
2 starch

Shopping List: 8 ounces fat-free pasta, 1 pound fat-free beef crumbles, 8 ounces fat-free pasta sauce, 4 ounces fat-free finely-shredded Cheddar cheese, fat-free chicken broth, 1 onion, green bell pepper, garlic, chili powder, basil, oregano

HOT TAMALE TORTILLA PIZZAS

EASY - DO AHEAD

ingredients: 6 (8-inch) fat-free flour tortillas
15 oz. spicy refried beans
1 1/2 cups fat-free finely-shredded Mexican cheese
2 tbsp. chopped green chilies
1 cup corn kernels, drained
3 tbsp. chopped green onions
1 1/2 cups chopped tomatoes, well drained
3/4 cup fat-free salsa

directions: Preheat oven to 425 degrees.
Line baking sheet(s) with foil and spray with non-fat cooking spray. Arrange tortillas in a single layer on baking sheet(s). Spread each tortilla with refried beans; sprinkle 2 tablespoons cheese on each tortilla. Top with chilies, corn, green onions, tomatoes and remaining cheese. Bake in preheated oven 10-12 minutes, until tortilla is crisp and cheese is completely melted. Serve with salsa.

Serves: 6

Nutrition per Serving		Exchanges
Calories	288	4 vegetable
Carbohydrate	52 grams	2 starch
Cholesterol	1 milligram	1 meat
Dietary Fiber	6 grams	
Fat	< 1 gram	
Protein	21 grams	
Sodium	1593 milligrams	

Shopping List: fat-free flour tortillas, 15-ounce can fat-free spicy refried beans, 4-ounce can chopped green chilies, 8-ounce can corn kernels, 6 ounces fat-free finely-shredded Mexican cheese, green onions, 2 small tomatoes, fat-free salsa

MEXICAN

MEXICAN OMELET

AVERAGE

ingredients:
3/4 tsp. fat-free chicken broth
1 cup finely-chopped onions
2 tbsp. chickpeas
1/2 cup diced green bell pepper
1/2 cup diced red bell pepper
1 cup sliced mushrooms
1/4 cup egg substitute
6 whole egg whites
1/8 tsp. dry mustard
1/8 tsp. turmeric
1/8 tsp. chili powder
1/2 tsp. garlic powder
1/4 cup fat-free finely-shredded Cheddar cheese

directions:
Lightly spray large nonstick skillet with nonfat cooking spray. Add chicken broth to skillet and heat over medium-high heat; stir in onions, chickpeas, green peppers, red peppers and mushrooms. Cook until tender. Remove from skillet; wipe skillet dry and spray again with cooking spray. In a medium bowl, combine egg substitute, egg whites, mustard, turmeric, chili powder and garlic powder; mix until ingredients are blended. Pour egg mixture into skillet and cook over medium heat until eggs are set. Fill with vegetable mixture, sprinkle with cheese, fold over, and cook until cheese is melted and omelet is heated through.

Serves: 2

MEXICAN

Nutrition per Serving		Exchanges
Calories	149	3 vegetable
Carbohydrate	16 grams	2 meat
Cholesterol	0 milligrams	
Dietary Fiber	1 gram	
Fat	< 1 gram	
Protein	20 grams	
Sodium	372 milligrams	

Shopping List:
2 ounces egg substitute, large eggs, chopped onions, chickpeas, green bell pepper, red bell pepper, 4 ounces sliced mushrooms, fat-free chicken broth, 1 ounce fat-free finely-shredded Cheddar cheese, dry mustard, turmeric, chili powder, garlic powder

RASPBERRY CHIPOTLE GLAZED CHICKEN

AVERAGE

ingredients: 1 lb. fat-free chicken breasts
1/2 cup sugar
1 cup raspberry beer
1/4 cup puréed chipotle chilies

directions: Lightly spray large nonstick skillet with nonfat cooking spray and heat over medium-high heat. Cook chicken until browned, about 4 minutes on each side. Add sugar to skillet and cook until caramelized; deglaze with beer. Add chilies to chicken mixture, cover and cook over low heat until a syrupy glaze is formed and coats the chicken.

Serves: 4

Nutrition per Serving		Exchanges
Calories	309	2 vegetable
Carbohydrate	27 grams	5 meat
Cholesterol	96 milligrams	1 starch
Dietary Fiber	< 1 gram	
Fat	< 1 gram	
Protein	46 grams	
Sodium	488 milligrams	

Shopping List: 1 pound fat-free chicken breasts, 8 ounces raspberry beer, sugar, chipotle chilies

MEXICAN

345

SWEET AND CITRUS SHRIMP

EASY

ingredients:
1/3 cup tequila
3 tbsp. lime juice
3 tbsp. water
3 tbsp. chopped cilantro
1 1/2 tbsp. sugar
1 1/2 lb. fat-free frozen (uncooked) shrimp, thawed and drained

directions:
In a small bowl, combine tequila, lime juice, water, cilantro and sugar; mix until blended.
Lightly spray a large nonstick skillet with nonfat cooking spray and heat over medium heat. Pour tequila mixture into pan; stir in shrimp and cook until pink and opaque. Remove shrimp from pan and place on serving platter.
Increase heat to high and bring liquid to a boil. Cook 3-5 minutes, stirring constantly. Pour sauce over shrimp and serve immediately.

Serves: 6

Nutrition per Serving		Exchanges
Calories	149	1 1/3 fruit
Carbohydrate	19 grams	2 meat
Cholesterol	13 milligrams	
Dietary Fiber	0 grams	
Fat	< 1 gram	
Protein	12 grams	
Sodium	748 milligrams	

Shopping List: 3 ounces tequila, 1 1/2 ounces lime juice, 1 1/2 pounds fat-free frozen (uncooked) shrimp, cilantro, sugar

MEXICAN

VEGETABLE BURRITOS
EASY - DO AHEAD

ingredients:
1/3 cup lime juice
2 tbsp. white wine vinegar
1 tbsp. honey
2 tsp. Dijon mustard
1 tsp. ground cumin
1/2 tsp. garlic powder
1 tbsp. diced jalapeño peppers
16 oz. corn kernels, drained
15 oz. fat-free black beans, drained
1 lg. cucumber, peeled, seeded and chopped
3 green onions, sliced thin
2 tsp. cilantro
3/4 cup diced tomatoes with green chilies
6 fat-free flour tortillas

directions:
In a medium bowl, combine lime juice, vinegar, honey, mustard, cumin, garlic powder and diced jalapeños; mix until blended. Pour mixture into large Ziploc bag. Add corn, beans, cucumber, green onions and cilantro to marinade; toss to coat. Refrigerate 1-2 hours. Scoop vegetable mixture out of marinade and place in a large bowl. Add tomatoes and toss to mix. Divide mixture evenly among tortillas; roll up and serve.

Serves: 6

MEXICAN

Nutrition per Serving
Calories	294
Carbohydrate	63 grams
Cholesterol	0 milligrams
Dietary Fiber	9 grams
Fat	< 1 gram
Protein	13 grams
Sodium	730 milligrams

Exchanges
3 vegetable
3 starch

Shopping List: 16-ounce can corn kernels, 15 ounces fat-free black beans, 15-ounce can diced tomatoes with green chilies, 1 cucumber, green onions, fat-free flour tortillas, 3 ounces lime juice, 1-ounce white wine vinegar, Dijon mustard, honey, ground cumin, garlic powder, cilantro, canned jalapeño peppers

VEGETARIAN BURRITOS
EASY - DO AHEAD

ingredients: 6 fat-free flour tortillas
1 1/2 cups fat-free cooked rice
3/4 cup fat-free black beans, rinsed and drained
1/3 cup diced green chilies
1/3 cup corn kernels, drained
1 tbsp. onion powder
2 tsp. dried parsley
1/2 tsp. pepper
1 cup fat-free finely-shredded Mexican cheese
1 1/2 cups shredded lettuce
3/4 cup fat-free salsa

directions: Preheat oven to 350 degrees.
Wrap tortillas in foil and heat in oven 5-10 minutes, until heated through.
In a large bowl, combine rice, beans, chilies, corn, onion powder, parsley and pepper; toss until mixed. Divide rice mixture among tortillas and top each with shredded cheese, lettuce and salsa. Roll tortillas up and serve immediately.

Serves: 6

Nutrition per Serving		Exchanges
Calories	340	4 vegetable
Carbohydrate	71 grams	3 starch
Cholesterol	1 milligram	
Dietary Fiber	4 grams	
Fat	< 1 gram	
Protein	16 grams	
Sodium	716 milligrams	

Shopping List: fat-free flour tortillas, fat-free rice, fat-free canned black beans, 4-ounce can diced green chilies, 8-ounce can corn kernels, 6 ounces fat-free salsa, 4 ounces fat-free finely-shredded Mexican cheese, 8-ounce package shredded cheese, dried parsley, pepper, onion powder

MEXICAN

BANANA BLACK BEAN RELISH

AVERAGE - DO AHEAD

ingredients:
1 cup rice vinegar
1 mango, diced
1/2 cup dry black beans
1 medium banana, peeled and diced into
 1/4-inch cubes
1 small papaya, peeled and diced into 1/4-inch
 cubes
1/2 medium red onion, peeled and diced into
 1/8-inch cubes
6 green onions, sliced 1/8-inch thick
1 small red bell pepper, diced into 1/8-inch cubes
1/2 bunch fresh cilantro leaves, chopped
Salt and pepper

directions:
Combine rice vinegar and mango in a medium bowl; mix well. Cover and refrigerate 48-72 hours. Cover black beans with salted water in a large soup pot; bring to a rolling boil for 45-60 minutes, until beans are cooked al denté. Combine cooked beans, banana, papaya, red and green onions, bell pepper and cilantro in a large bowl; toss until mixed. Add mango vinegar, salt and pepper; mix well. Serve as a side dish or garnish for fish or chicken.

Serves: 8

MEXICAN

Nutrition per Serving		Exchanges
Calories	57	1 vegetable
Carbohydrate	101 grams	1/2 fruit
Cholesterol	0 milligrams	
Dietary Fiber	15 grams	
Fat	< 1 gram	
Protein	20 grams	
Sodium	24 milligrams	

Shopping List: 8-ounce bag dry black beans, 1 banana, 1 papaya, red onion, green onions, red bell pepper, fresh cilantro, 8 ounces rice vinegar, mango, salt, pepper

BELL PEPPER SAUCE

AVERAGE

ingredients: 2 red or yellow bell peppers
1/2 white onion, chopped
1/2 celery stalk, chopped
1/2 carrot, peeled and chopped
1/2 c. fat-free vegetable broth
1 1/2 cups fat-free mocha mix nondairy creamer
Salt and pepper

directions: Roast peppers over gas burner or broil in oven, turning frequently, until charred. Run under cold water and peel away charred skin; discard skin. Stem, seed and chop peppers.
Lightly spray large nonstick skillet with nonfat cooking spray and heat over medium-high heat. Add onion, carrot and celery to skillet and cook, stirring frequently, until soft. Add peppers and cook 2 minutes longer. Pour vegetable broth into skillet and cook over low heat 5 minutes. Transfer mixture to food processor or blender and purée until smooth. Add mocha mix and blend to desired consistency. Season with salt and pepper, to taste.

Serves: 8

Nutrition per Serving		Exchanges
Calories	42	2 vegetable
Carbohydrate	9 grams	
Cholesterol	0 milligrams	
Dietary Fiber	< 1 gram	
Fat	< 1 gram	
Protein	1 gram	
Sodium	53 milligrams	

Shopping List: 2 large red or yellow bell peppers, 1 onion, carrot, celery, 8 ounces fat-free vegetable broth, 12 ounces fat-free mocha mix nondairy creamer, salt, pepper

CILANTRO-PESTO VEGETABLES

EASY - DO AHEAD

ingredients: 1 1/2 cups chopped fresh cilatnro, washed and destemmed
3 garlic cloves
1/4 cup fat-free chicken or vegetable broth
1/4 cup fat-free Parmesan cheese
4 medium zucchini, quartered lengthwise
4 medium yellow squash, quartered lengthwise

directions: Combine cilantro, garlic, chicken broth and Parmesan cheese in a food processor or blender and purée until pasty. Prepare grill with medium-high fire. Grill vegetables until tender; brush with pesto dressing.

Serves: 4

Nutrition per Serving		Exchanges
Calories	82	3 vegetable
Carbohydrate	16 grams	
Cholesterol	0 milligrams	
Dietary Fiber	6 grams	
Fat	< 1 gram	
Protein	6 grams	
Sodium	110 milligrams	

Shopping List: 4 medium zucchini, 4 medium yellow squash, 2 ounces fat-free chicken or vegetable broth, 1 ounce fat-free Parmesan cheese, fresh cilantro, garlic

MEXICAN

ENCHILADA SAUCE

EASY - DO AHEAD

---

ingredients:　　2 tbsp. cornstarch
1/4 cup cold water
1 cup tomato sauce
1 1/2 cups water
1 1/2 tbsp. onion powder
1 1/2 tsp. garlic powder
1 tbsp. chili powder
1/2 tsp. ground cinnamon
1/2 tsp. dried oregano

directions:　　Combine cornstarch and cold water in a small bowl. Mix until cornstarch is dissolved and mixture is blended.
Combine remaining ingredients in a large saucepan. Bring to a boil over high heat. Reduce heat to low, cover and simmer 30 minutes. Add cornstarch mixture and cook, stirring constantly, until sauce thickens.
Store in refrigerator up to 2 weeks. Serve over your favorite burritos, enchiladas or chimichangas.

Serves: 8

Nutrition per Serving		**Exchanges**
Calories	26	1 vegetable
Carbohydrate	6 grams	
Cholesterol	0 milligrams	
Dietary Fiber	< 1 gram	
Fat	< 1 gram	
Protein	< 1 gram	
Sodium	197 milligrams	

MEXICAN

Shopping List:　　8 ounces tomato sauce, cornstarch, onion powder, garlic powder, chili powder, ground cumin, dried oregano

MEXICAN RICE
EASY

ingredients: 1 cup brown rice (raw)
1 1/2 tsp. onion powder
1/2 tsp. garlic powder
2 cups fat-free chicken broth
3/4 cup fat-free salsa
4 oz. diced green chilies
1/4 tsp. cumin
1/8 tsp. pepper

directions: Lightly spray large nonstick skillet with nonfat cooking spray and heat over medium-high heat. Add rice, onion powder and garlic powder to skillet and cook, stirring frequently, until rice is lightly browned. Add chicken broth, salsa, chilies, cumin and pepper to skillet; mix well. Bring to a boil over high heat. Reduce heat to low, cover and simmer 40-45 minutes, until all the liquid is absorbed.

Serves: 6

Nutrition per Serving
Calories	128
Carbohydrate	27 grams
Cholesterol	0 milligrams
Dietary Fiber	2 grams
Fat	< 1 gram
Protein	3 grams
Sodium	495 milligrams

Exchanges
2 vegetable
1 starch

MEXICAN

Shopping List: brown rice *(do not use instant rice)*, 16 ounces fat-free chicken broth, 6 ounces fat-free salsa, 4 ounces diced green chili peppers, cumin, pepper, onion powder, garlic powder

MEXICAN VEGETABLE MEDLEY

EASY - DO AHEAD

ingredients: 1 1/2 tbsp. + 1/4 cup fat-free chicken broth, divided
1 medium onion, sliced
1 tsp. minced garlic
2 cups frozen corn kernels
2 cups canned, diced tomatoes, drained
1/8 tsp. ground cumin
1/4 tsp. pepper

directions: Lightly spray a large nonstick skillet with nonfat cooking spray. Pour 1 1/2 tablespoons chicken broth into skillet and heat over medium heat. Add onion and garlic; cook until vegetables are tender, about 2-3 minutes. Add corn, tomatoes, remaining chicken broth, cumin and pepper; cook over medium-high heat 1 minute. Reduce heat to low and cook 5-8 minutes, just until vegetables are tender. Stir in cilantro and serve.
Mexican Vegetable Medley can be refrigerated and served cold; or reheated before serving.

Serves: 6

Nutrition per Serving		Exchanges
Calories	79	2 vegetable
Carbohydrate	19 grams	1/2 starch
Cholesterol	0 milligrams	
Dietary Fiber	2 grams	
Fat	< 1 gram	
Protein	3 grams	
Sodium	265 milligrams	

Shopping List: fat-free chicken broth, 1 onion, minced garlic, 10 ounces frozen corn kernels, 28-ounce can diced tomatoes, fresh cilantro, cumin, pepper

PAELLA

EASY

ingredients:

2 1/4 cups + 1 tbsp. fat-free chicken broth, divided
2 cups frozen pepper strips
1 1/2 cups chopped onions
1 1/2 tsp. minced garlic
3 3/4 cups crushed tomatoes, undrained
14 ounces artichoke hearts, drained
2 cups frozen corn kernels
1 cup frozen peas
3/4 tsp. dried thyme
1/8 tsp. saffron
1 1/2 cups couscous

directions:

Lightly spray large nonstick skillet with nonfat cooking spray. Add 1 tablespoon chicken broth and heat over medium-high heat. Add peppers, onions and garlic to skillet; cook 2-3 minutes, until vegetables are softened. Add tomatoes, artichokes, corn and peas; bring to boil over high heat. Reduce heat to low and simmer 5-10 minutes, until vegetables are tender. Add remaining chicken broth, thyme and saffron. Bring to a boil over high heat; add couscous. Remove skillet from heat, cover. Let stand 10 minutes, until couscous is softened. Fluff with fork just before serving.

Serves: 6

MEXICAN

Nutrition per Serving		Exchanges
Calories	338	4 vegetable
Carbohydrate	74 grams	3 starch
Cholesterol	0 milligrams	
Dietary Fiber	12 grams	
Fat	< 1 gram	
Protein	13 grams	
Sodium	847 milligrams	

Shopping List: 2 (16-ounce) cans fat-free chicken broth, 16 ounces frozen pepper strips, 16 ounces chopped onions (packaged or frozen), minced garlic, 2 (28-ounce) cans crushed tomatoes, 14-ounce can artichoke hearts, 16 ounces frozen corn kernels, 10 ounces frozen peas, dried thyme, saffron, couscous

RED BEANS AND CHILIES

EASY - DO AHEAD

ingredients:
1 tbsp. vegetable broth
1 cup chopped onion
1/2 tsp. minced garlic
4 cups tomatoes with green chilies
2 tbsp. diced green chilies
1 1/2 tbsp. chili powder
1/4 tsp. cumin
1/4 tsp. oregano
3 cups canned pinto beans, drained

directions:
Lightly spray large saucepan with nonfat cooking spray. Pour vegetable broth into pan and heat over medium-high heat. Add onions and garlic; cook until soft. Stir in tomatoes, green chilies, chili powder, cumin and oregano; mix lightly. Reduce heat to low and simmer 15 minutes; stir in beans and cook 5-6 minutes, until heated through. Serve as a side dish, rolled in tortillas, or in taco salad shell.

Serves: 6

Nutrition per Serving

		Exchanges
Calories	135	2 vegetable
Carbohydrate	27 grams	1 starch
Cholesterol	0 milligrams	
Dietary Fiber	2 grams	
Fat	< 1 gram	
Protein	7 grams	
Sodium	1205 milligrams	

MEXICAN

Shopping List: vegetable broth, 28-ounce can pinto beans, 2 (15-ounce) cans tomatoes with green chilies, 4-ounce can diced green chilies, 1 large onion, minced garlic, chili powder, cumin, oregano

REFRIED BEANS

EASY - DO AHEAD

ingredients:
1 tbsp. vegetable broth
3/4 cup chopped onions
1 tsp. minced garlic
3 cups canned pinto beans, drained
15 oz. can tomatoes with green chilies
1/2 tsp. cumin
3/4 tsp. chili powder
1/8 tsp. cayenne pepper

directions:
Lightly spray large saucepan with nonfat cooking spray. Pour vegetable broth into pan and heat over medium-high heat. Add onions and garlic; cook until soft. Add beans, tomatoes, cumin, chili powder and cayenne pepper; mash with fork until slightly chunky. Reduce heat to low and simmer 10 to 15 minutes, until heated through.

Serves: 6

Nutrition per Serving		Exchanges
Calories	114	1 vegetable
Carbohydrate	22 grams	1 starch
Cholesterol	0 milligrams	
Dietary Fiber	5 grams	
Fat	< 1 gram	
Protein	2 grams	
Sodium	795 milligrams	

Shopping List: vegetable broth, 1 medium onion, minced garlic, 2 (15-ounce) cans pinto beans, 15 ounces tomatoes with green chilies, cumin, chili powder, cayenne pepper

MEXICAN

SPANISH RICE
EASY - DO AHEAD

---

ingredients:
3/4 lb. fat-free ground turkey
1 1/2 tbsp. onion powder
1 cup frozen pepper strips, thawed, drained
    and chopped
3 cups water
1 1/2 cups tomato sauce
1 1/2 cups fat-free rice (raw)
3 tbsp. Worcestershire sauce
1 tsp. chili powder
1/2 tsp. dried thyme
1/4 tsp. cayenne pepper

directions:
Lightly spray large nonstick skillet with nonfat cooking spray and heat over medium-high heat. Add turkey, onion powder and peppers to skillet and cook, stirring frequently, until meat is cooked through and peppers are tender. Add water, tomato sauce, rice, Worcestershire sauce, chili powder, thyme and cayenne pepper to skillet; bring to a boil over high heat. Reduce heat to low, cover and simmer 30 minutes, until rice is tender.

Serves: 6

Nutrition per Serving		Exchanges
Calories	236	2 vegetable
Carbohydrate	45 grams	2 starch
Cholesterol	20 milligrams	1/2 meat
Dietary Fiber	1 gram	
Fat	< 1 gram	
Protein	12 grams	
Sodium	1077 milligrams	

Shopping List:
3/4 pound fat-free ground turkey, 16 ounces frozen pepper strips, 12 ounces tomato sauce, fat-free rice, Worcestershire sauce, chili powder, onion powder, dried thyme, cayenne pepper

MEXICAN

CHEESE AND CORN TORTE

EASY - DO AHEAD

ingredients: 4 (8-ounce) packages fat-free cream cheese,
softened
1/4 pound fat-free margarine
2 cups fat-free sour cream
1 1/2 cups sugar
7 tbsp. cornstarch
1 tbsp. vanilla
2 cups cream-style corn
2 tbsp. lemon juice
1 1/4 cups egg substitute

directions: Preheat oven to 350 degrees.
Lightly spray a 9x13-inch baking dish with nonfat
cooking spray.
Combine cream cheese and margarine in medium
bowl and mix until creamy. Add sour cream,
sugar, cornstarch, vanilla, corn and lemon juice;
mix well. Stir in egg substitute and mix until
blended. Pour batter into baking dish and bake 1
hour. Turn oven off and leave dish inside for
another hour (*do not open oven door!*). Remove from
oven and let cool for 2 hours; refrigerate until
ready to serve.

Serves: 12

MEXICAN

<u>**Nutrition per Serving**</u>		<u>**Exchanges**</u>
Calories	238	1 milk
Carbohydrate	45 grams	1 fruit
Cholesterol	0 milligrams	1/4 meat
Dietary Fiber	< 1 gram	1 starch
Fat	< 1 gram
Protein	15 grams
Sodium	685 milligrams

Shopping List: 4 (8-ounce) packages fat-free cream cheese, fat-free
margarine, 16 ounces fat-free sour cream, 16-ounce can
cream-style corn, 10 ounces egg substitute, sugar, cornstarch, vanilla, lemon juice

EMPANADAS DE FRUTA
EASY - DO AHEAD

---

ingredients:

6 cups flour
1 tsp. salt
3/4 cup + 1 tbsp. sugar, divided
3/4 cup Lighter Bake
1/4 cup egg substitute
1 1/2 cups water
20 oz. dried fruit
8 oz. raisins
1/2 tsp. cloves
1 tsp. cinnamon
1/2 tsp. nutmeg

directions:

Combine flour, salt, 1 tablespoon sugar and Lighter Bake in a large bowl; mix well. Combine egg substitute and water in a small bowl and mix well; pour into flour mixture and mix until dough becomes soft, but not sticky. Divide dough into 12 equal pieces; roll into 5-inch circles (1/8-inch-thick) on lightly-floured surface. Combine dried fruit, raisins and water in medium saucepan; cook over low heat until fruits become tender and softened. Stir in 3/4 cup sugar, cloves, cinnamon and nutmeg. Spoon fruit filling onto half of each dough circle; fold dough and press edges to seal. Lightly spray large nonstick skillet with nonfat cooking spray and heat over medium-high heat. Cook fruit-filled empanadas in skillet until golden brown on both sides.

Serves: 12

MEXICAN

Nutrition per Serving		Exchanges
Calories	562	1 1/2 starch
Carbohydrate	47 grams	7 1/2 fruit
Cholesterol	0 milligrams	
Dietary Fiber	7 grams	
Fat	< 1 gram	
Protein	9 grams	
Sodium	206 milligrams	

Shopping List: flour, sugar, Lighter Bake, egg substitute, 20 ounces dried fruit (of choice), 8 ounces raisins, cloves, nutmeg, cinnamon, salt

FRESH FRUIT PALETTES

EASY - DO AHEAD

ingredients: 2 bananas, peeled and sliced
2 mangoes, sliced
1/2 cup chopped pineapple
3/4 cup strawberries
1/3 cup orange juice

directions: Combine all ingredients in a food processor or blender and process until smooth. Pour into mold and freeze until firm.

Serves: 4

Nutrition per Serving		Exchanges
Calories	147	2 1/2 fruit
Carbohydrate	37 grams	
Cholesterol	0 milligrams	
Dietary Fiber	4 grams	
Fat	< 1 gram	
Protein	2 grams	
Sodium	3 milligrams	

Shopping List: 2 banana, 2 mangoes, pineapple, strawberries, orange juice

MEXICAN

MEXICAN MOCHA COFFEE

EASY

ingredients: 4 cups brewed coffee
1/2 cup Kahlua
1/4 cup lite chocolate syrup
1/2 cup fat-free Cool Whip
Cinnamon

directions: Pour coffee into 4 mugs. Add 2 tablespoons Kahlua and 1 tablespoon chocolate syrup to each cup and mix well. Top each cup with 2 tablespoons Cool Whip and sprinkle with cinnamon.

Serves: 4

Nutrition per Serving		Exchanges
Calories	178	2 starch
Carbohydrate	31 grams	
Cholesterol	0 milligrams	
Dietary Fiber	0 grams	
Fat	< 1 gram	
Protein	1 gram	
Sodium	20 milligrams	

Shopping List: coffee, Kahlua (or coffee-flavored liqueur), lite chocolate syrup, 4 ounces fat-free Cool Whip, cinnamon

MEXICAN

SPICY MEXICAN DRINK
EASY - DO AHEAD

ingredients:
2 tbsp. chopped green onions
1/2 cup chopped cucumber
1/2 cup low-sodium tomato juice
1/2 cup chopped green bell pepper
1 tsp. tarragon vinegar
1/2 tsp. garlic powder
1/8 tsp. cayenne pepper
1/8 tsp. pepper
1 stalk celery, cut in half

directions:
Combine all ingredients except celery stalks in food processor or blender, and process until smooth. Pour into pitcher, cover and refrigerate several hours before serving. Garnish with celery sticks before serving.

Serves: 2

Nutrition per Serving

Calories	29	
Carbohydrate	7 grams	
Cholesterol	0 milligrams	
Dietary Fiber	2 grams	
Fat	< 1 gram	
Protein	1 gram	
Sodium	25 milligrams	

Exchanges
1 vegetable

Shopping List: green onions, 1 cucumber, 4 ounces low-sodium tomato juice, 1 green bell pepper, garlic powder, tarragon vinegar, cayenne pepper, pepper, celery

MEXICAN

HOLIDAY
MENUS

HOLIDAY MENUS

JANUARY

Chinese New Year

Chinese New Year begins on the first full moon after January 21, and lasts for fifteen days. Customs include paying off debts, buying new clothes, cleaning the house and enjoying family feasts with traditional Chinese fare.

Appetizers: Chinese Egg Rolls*
Garlic Cheese Wonton Chips

Entrée/Sides: Orange Chicken*
Steamed Rice
Vegetable Medley Stir-Fry*

Desserts/Drinks: Mango Sorbet*
Orange Ginger Cookies*
Hot Tea

FEBRUARY

Valentine's Day

The celebration of Valentine's Day (February 14th) began years ago in ancient Rome. The ancient festival and celebration of fertility honored two Roman gods, Juno and Pan. Create a romantic atmosphere and enjoy an Italian feast fit for the gods!

Appetizers: Crab-Stuffed Artichoke Hearts*
Caesar Salad*

Entrée/Sides: Spicy Angel Hair Pasta Puttanesca*
Parmesan Breadsticks*

Desserts/Drinks: Chocolate Chip Biscotti*
Espresso

MARCH

St. Patrick's Day

Green, shamrocks, leprechauns, and Irish Potato Stew symbolize the celebrations of St. Patrick's Day--a holiday that began when Irish slave raiders captured a 16-year-old Celtic pagan. After his escape, he went to Spain to become a priest and changed his name to Patrick. Eight years later, he returned to Ireland to convert the pagans to Christianity. St. Patrick's Day honors the patron saint of Ireland with overflowing food, drinks and GREEN!

Appetizers: Spinach Dip with fat-free chips
Celery, stuffed with fat-free cream cheese
with chives

Entrée/Sides: Chilled Cucumber Soup*
Potato Stew*

Desserts/Drinks: Fat-free lime sherbet
Irish coffee

APRIL

Easter

Celebrated by many cultures around the world, Easter is based on a religious observance, but would not be complete without the traditions of fun and food. Try a Greek celebration for something new!

Appetizers: Chili Minted Meatballs*
Stuffed Cucumber Slices*

Entrée/Sides: Green salad with Minted Yogurt Dressing*
Lemony Chicken Vegetable Kabobs*
Lemon Skillet Rice*

Desserts/Drinks: Fat-free Carrot Cake
Sparkling water with lemon

HOLIDAY MENUS

MAY 5th

Cinco De Mayo

The 5th of May, Cinco De Mayo, is a celebration of freedom and liberty. A fiesta to commemorate the day 4,000 Mexican soldiers smashed the French and traitor Mexican army at Pueblo, Mexico. What better way to party than to bring on traditional Mexican food, drinks, music and more--bring on the family and friends.

Appetizers: Broccomole* with fat-free chips
                         Mexican Pinwheels*

Entrée/Sides: Sweet and Citrus Shrimp*
                         Mexican Rice*
                         Cilantro-Peso Vegetables*

Desserts/Drinks: Empanadas de Fruta*
                         Sparkling water with lime

JULY 4th

Independence Day

On July 4th, America celebrates its freedom from England with picnics, parties, parades and fireworks. Why not share the celebration with the French who celebrate the beginning of the First Republic on the fourteenth of July? Keep the red, white and blue, but give it the flavor of France.

Appetizers: Eggplant Caviar*
                         Fat-free crackers

Entrée/Sides: Red Cabbage-Carrot Slaw*
                         Dijon Grilled Chicken*
                         Potatoes Cinderella*

Desserts/Drinks: Fat-free frozen vanilla yogurt with fresh
                            berries
                         Diet colas/sparkling water

SEPTEMBER

Rosh Hashanah

Rosh Hashanah marks the beginning of the Jewish High Holy Days and serves as the Jewish New year--a time for family and friends to gather together to share the traditional customs, prayers and food. On this holiday, food represents the sweetness of the New Year--right from apples dipped in honey through dessert.

Traditional Rosh Hashanah Menu:

> Apples with honey
> Challah*
> Grandma's "Get-Well" Chicken Soup* with
>   matzo balls
> Honey-Dijon Chicken*
> Cheese-Noodle Kugel*
> Steamed broccoli
> Fresh fruit platter
> Apple Honey Cake*

OCTOBER

Oktoberfest

Do you think Crown Prince Lultpold I and Princess Theressa of Bavaria ever imagined their wedding on October 17, 1810, would become a traditional two-week festivity filled with beer, wine, and gargantuan servings of food? In Munich, Germany, close to one million people gather to consume 10 million pints of beer, 750,000 spit-roasted chickens, and more than 800,000 wursts and sausages. Keep your Oktoberfest celebration on the healthy living side--eat, drink and enjoy without all the calories and fat!

Appetizers: Fat-free Bavarian pretzels
                       Sauerkraut Balls*

Entrée/Sides: Cucumber Salad*
                       Paprika Chicken*
                       Dumplings*
                       Sweet and Sour Red Cabbage*

Desserts/Drinks: German Apple Cake*
                       German Beers and Wines
                       Hot Apple Cider*

NOVEMBER

Thanksgiving

Thanksgiving--the time to get together with family and friends and EAT! Turkey, stuffing, sweet potatoes, cranberry sauce, and pumpkin pie fill the bill--they also fill you up with lots of calories and fat. How about starting new traditions with a healthier menu fare? Make it a healthy-living "around the world" celebration and start some new traditions!

Appetizers: Grilled Vegetable Relish on Yam Chips*
                     Spicy Pumpkin Soup*

Entrée/Sides: Tandori Turkey Breast*
                     Honey-Baked Onions*
                     Whole Cranberry Sauce
                     Garlic Mashed Potatoes*

Desserts/Drinks: Sour Cream Apple Pie*
                     Hot Mulled Cranberry Drink*

DECEMBER

Christmas

A time for joy, goodwill towards men, and parties with lots of food! Keep all the ingredients for a very Merry Christmas--just eliminate some of the fat and calories. Healthy Living--the best gift you can give yourself and others!

Appetizers: Liptauer Cheese Spread*
                     Fat-free crackers

Entrée/Sides: Swiss Rosemary Chicken*
                     Potatoes Au Gratin*
                     Honey Dijon Asparagus*

Desserts/Drinks: Fat-free hot chocolate
                     Anise Biscotti*
                     Chocolate Chip Biscotti*

HOLIDAY MENUS

Chanukah

Chanukah, the Festival of Lights, *is an eight-day celebration to com-memorate the victory of the Jewish Maccabees as they reclaimed their Temple from the Greeks. The Chanukah table usually includes deep-fried foods representing the "miracle of the oil" that burned for eight days. Get rid of the oil, but keep the flavor and tradition with a healthier menu.*

Appetizers: Challah*

Entrée/Sides: Cucumber and Pepper Salad*
                     Baked Fish Roll-Ups*
                     Latkes*

Desserts/Drinks: Fritters*
                     Flavored Seltzer Water

COOKING
GLOSSARY

COOKING GLOSSARY

ADOBADO

a paste or sauce made from chilies, vinegar, and other seasonings

ADOBO SAUCE

Mexican sauce that is dark red and rather spicy; made from ancho or guajillo chilies, herbs and vinegar

ADZUKI BEANS

small reddish brown beans

AIL

French word for "garlic"

AJO

Spanish word for "garlic"

AL DENTÉ

describes the correct degree of doneness for pasta and vegetables, meaning "to the bite"

AL FORNO

Italian term that describes a dish cooked in the oven

ALLSPICE

a fragrant berry that comes from an evergreen pimento tree and tastes like a combination of cinnamon, cloves and nutmeg

A LA, AU, AUX

French terms meaning "served with" or "served in the manner of"

ANISE SEEDS

seeds of the anise plant with a licorice-like flavor; popular addition to Italian biscotti

ANTIPASTO

Italian word for an assortment of appetizers, including cold cuts, olives, pickles, peppers, vegetables and cheese

ARROWROOT

a starch that is similar in appearance and qualities to corn-starch; used as a thickening agent for puddings, sauces and other cooked foods, arrowroot should be mixed with a cold liquid before being heated or added to hot mixtures

ARROZ

Spanish word for "rice"

ARUGULA

also known as rocket and Italian cress, a popular Mediterra-nean salad green--most often used in salads, but can be added to soups and pasta dishes

AUBERGINE

French word for "eggplant"

AU GRATIN

any dish that has a browned covering of bread crumbs (usually mixed with butter or cheese--prepare fat-free au gratin with fat-free cheese, fat-free margarine or Butter Buds)

BAGUETTE

a long, narrow, cylindrical loaf of French white bread

BAKE

cook with dry heat as in an oven

BARBECUE

using hot coals to cook on a grill

BASIL

popular Italian herb with pungent aroma and flavor--great with tomatoes, other vegetables, chicken--classic herb for making pesto sauce

BASTE

to brush or spoon food as it cooks with marinades, cooking juices or melted fat (*not used in fat-free cooking*); this not only prevents foods from drying out, but also adds flavor and color

BAY LEAF

sharp and pungent leaves that are frequently used to add flavor to meat and poultry dishes, soups and stews, and tomato sauces--always remove bay leaves from the dish before serving

BEAN CURD (*Also known as* **dou foo** *or* **tofu**)

made from yellow soybeans, bean curd is a popular source of protein in Asian cooking

BEAT

to mix vigorously, in order to blend foods to smooth texture or increase the air in the food

BLANCH

immersing a food into boiling water, usually to remove the skin off of fruit and vegetables

BLEND

combine two or more ingredients with a blender, beater or spoon and mix thoroughly

BLINTZ

Jewish crêpes or thin, flat pancakes rolled around a filling of cheese, potatoes or fruit

BOIL

heat a liquid to its boiling point, when bubbles break the surface; "boil" can also refer to cooking foods in a boiling liquid

BOK CHOY

Chinese white cabbage with a light, fresh, and mustard taste that requires little cooking; commonly used in stir-fries and soups, bok choy is also know as Chinese Chard

BOUILLON

a clear soup made from beef, vegetable or chicken broth

BRAISE

food (meats or vegetables) is browned (*for fat-free methods, brown foods in fat-free broth, wine, fruit juice, or water*) and then cooked over low heat, tightly covered, for a long period of time

BREAD CRUMBS
made by removing the crust from bread and leaving it unwrapped to dry at room temperature for several hours; grind in blender and add desired seasonings for special flavor--essential ingredients for stuffings and coatings (1 slice bread = 1/2 cup soft bread crumbs)

BROIL
cook food directly above or under a heat source--food can be broiled in the oven or on the grill

BROTH
a light soup made from simmering fish, chicken or vegetables in water.

BRUSH
apply a liquid, glaze or sauce to the surface of food with a pastry brush

CAPERS
small round green buds picked from a Mediterranean bush and packed in brine; common addition to Italian dishes with a tangy flavor

CARAMELIZE
to melt granulated sugar over a medium heat until a brown syrup forms

CELLOPHANE NOODLES
made from mung beans, these noodles are almost white when dry, and become translucent when cooked

CHALLAH
special kind of Jewish bread (sweet, golden and made from eggs) used for Sabbaths and holidays

CHERVIL
mild anise flavor that goes with seafood and chicken

CHILI POWDER
made from dried red chilies, also known as **cayenne pepper**, widely used in spicy dishes for its pungent and aromatic flavor

CHIFFONADE
a French word that refers to a way of cutting herbs and lettuces into thin strips or shreds

CHINESE BLACK MUSHROOMS
an edible fungi that grow on dead tree trunks; these need to be soaked in water and destemmed before using them

CHIVES
member of the onion family, should be added at the end of cooking process to retain flavor

CHOP
cut food into uneven and bite-size pieces, using a knife or food processor

CHOWDER
a thick, creamy soup usually made from fish, seafood, vegetables, potatoes, onions and milk

CHUTNEY
a sweet and spicy preserve of fruit, vinegar, sugar and spices that is used in Indian cooking; American chutneys are less spicy and sweeter than Indian versions

CODDLING
cooking in water that is kept just below the boiling point

COMPOTE
a chilled dish of fresh or dried fruit that has been slowly cooked in sugar syrup and spices

CONDIMENT
substances used to make foods more appetizing, such as ketchup, mustard, chutney or relish

COQUILLE
a dish cooked in a scallop shell

CORIANDER
also known as cilantro or Chinese parsley

COOKING GLOSSARY

CORNSTARCH
a fine, powdery gluten-free flour used as a thickening agent in sauces, puddings, etc.

COULIS
a thick sauce that gets much of its body from puréed fruits or vegetables

CRÉPE
a very thin pancake of French origin

CRUSHED RED PEPPER
sold as dried flakes, crushed red pepper is made from the seeds and membranes of the red chili pepper--use sparingly in cooked dishes

DEGLAZE
to dissolve cooking juices and particles of food by adding liquid and stirring (liquid is added to pan in which food has already been cooked and particles of food remain)

DEVEIN
to remove the blackish-grey vein from the back of a shrimp, use a deveiner or the tip of a sharp knife to devein shrimp

DICE
cut food into tiny (1/8-1/4-inch) cubes which are, more or less, even in size

DILL
goes with cucumber, yogurt, fish

DIM SUM
Cantonese term that refers to an array of dishes, including shrimp balls, dumplings, steamed buns and Chinese pastries

DRAIN
place food in a colander to remove any liquid

DREDGE
lightly coat food with flour, bread crumbs or cornmeal to provide a crunchy coating; breaded foods are dredged twice before cooking (dredged in flour, dipped in egg, dredged in breading)

ESCAROLE
salad green with a firm, crisp texture and a slightly bitter flavor--often mixed with other greens in chilled and wilted salads--flavorful addition to soups

FALAFEL
Middle Eastern specialty made of highly-spiced ground garbanzo beans; most often served in pita bread as appetizer or entrée

FENNEL
bulb-shaped vegetable with celery-like stems and a licorice-like taste--can be used raw in salads or cooked in soups and stews--fennel seed seasoning adds a licorice-like flavor to Italian sausage, stuffings and meat dishes; sprinkle fennel on pizza for sausage flavor without the fat

FILLET
to cut away the bones from meat or fish; a thin boneless strip of meat, poultry or fish

FIVE SPICE POWDER
a combination of star anise, Szechwan peppercorns, cinnamon, fennel and cloves that have been stir-fried and ground to a fine powder; commonly found in Asian cooking

FOLD
to combine a lighter mixture (i.e., beaten egg whites) with a heavier mixture, or lightly mix ingredients (i.e., raisins, chocolate chips) into batter or dough

FONDUE
a cheese dip for small pieces of bread

GARAM MASALA
Indian spice blend which may include cumin, fennel, coriander, cloves, cardamom, cinnamon, saffron, black pepper, chilies and caraway; also used as a condiment added to the dish at the end of cooking

GARBANZO BEANS
a firm-textured bean with a slightly nutty flavor; also known as chick-peas

GARLIC
essential ingredients in many international and American recipes; generally peeled, and then crushed or minced to release flavors

GARNISH
a decorative, edible addition to dishes

GNOCCHI
Italian dumplings made from potatoes or flour, most often cooked in boiling water

GRAPE LEAVES
lightly flavored green leaves of a grapevine used to wrap ingredients (i.e. Greek Dolmathes)

GRATE
to coarsely shred a large piece of food by using a grater or food processor fit with the appropriate blades (i.e., cheese, vegetables)

GRILL
to cook over hot coals or other heat source, so outside of food is browned and juices are sealed inside

GRIND
reduce food to very small pieces by running through a grinder; food can be ground from fine to coarse texture

HERBS
usually grown in the Northern Hemisphere; leaves, roots, flowers and seeds are used fresh or dried, and best when added near the end of cooking (use 4 times the amount of fresh herbs as dried; 1 teaspoon dried = 4 teaspoons fresh)

HERBES de PROVENCE
a mix of dried herbs grown in Southern France, used for seasoning meat, sauces and salad dressing; premixed packages include marjoram, rosemary, summer savory and thyme

HOISIN
dark, red Chinese sauce made from fermented mashed soybeans, salt, sugar, garlic and chili peppers; it is a thick, rich sauce used as a flavoring in sauces, marinades and dipping sauces

HORS D'OEUVRES
a selection of different canapés and appetizers

ITALIAN PARSLEY
flat-leaf parsley with a stronger flavor than the curly variety

ITALIAN SEASONING
dried blend of several Italian herbs, including basil, oregano, thyme and rosemary

JICAMA
a large, light-brown root often called a "Mexican potato", with a sweet, nutty taste and crispy, crunchy texture; jicama can be eaten raw or cooked

JULIENNE
to cut food into matchstick-size pieces with a sharp knife or mandolin

KIRSCH
clear brandy distilled from cherry juice and pits of the German kirsch ("cherry") and wasser ("water")

KOSHER SALT
coarse-grained and additive-free salt; substitute half the amount of Kosher salt for table salt

KNEAD
to mix or work a dough until it is smooth and elastic; kneading can be accomplished by hand or machine, to hold in gas bubbles and allow the dough to rise

KUGEL
a type of Jewish "pudding", usually made of noodles, eggs, and fruit or potatoes, eggs and onions; served as a side dish or dessert

LATKES
culinary symbol of Hannukah, made from shredded potatoes or vegetables and cooked as pancakes

COOKING
GLOSSARY

LEEK

a vegetable that looks like an overgrown green onion, with a sweet, mild onion flavor--serve raw in salads or cooked in sauces, soups, side dishes, frittatas, and other dishes

LEGUMES

beans, peas, and lentils

LEMON GRASS

also called citronella, lemon grass is a member of the mint family and is widely used in Asian cooking; remove from food before serving

MACERATE

to soak fruit in liquid (alcohol, liqueur, wine, brandy or sugar syrup) to absorb the liquid's flavor and draw out natural juices

MARINADE

a meat tenderizer or flavor enhancer

MARINATE

to soak food (meat, fish, vegetables) in a seasoned liquid for a specified period of time; marinating adds flavor and tenderizes food

MARJORAM

delicate herb that is related to oregano and commonly used in Italian cooking

MARSALA

Italian wine with a rich, smoky flavor, ranging from dry to sweet; a popular cooking wine in Italy

MASA HARINA

Spanish word that refers to flour made from dried masa (corn kernels cooked in lime water); the traditional dough used to make corn tortillas

MASH

to crush food into a smooth texture, using a ricer, masher, food mill or processor

MATZO MEAL
crumbs of matzo (unleavened bread)

MINCE
to cut food into very small uneven pieces, smaller and finer than diced food

MINESTRONE
a thick Italian vegetable soup

MIREPOIX
a classic French seasoning that includes onion, celery and carrot, often used to season stews and soups

MIRIN
a sweetened non-alcoholic Japanese cooking wine made from rice

MISO
bean paste that is made of fermented soybeans and grains; high in protein

MIX
combining ingredients by stirring

OREGANO
powerful herb used to season pizzas, Italian dishes, tomato sauces, beans, soups and stews

ORZO
tiny pasta that is a good substitute for rice

OYSTER SAUCE
made by mixing fermented oyster with water and salt; this sauce has a special seafood flavor; popular in Asia as a condiment and seasoning

PAELLA
national rice dish of Spain; flavored with saffron

PARBOIL
partial cooking of food in boiling water and then completing the cooking by some other method (baking, grilling, etc.)

PARE

to remove the thin outer layer of foods with a paring knife or vegetable peeler

PEEL

to remove the rind or skin from fruits or vegetables with a knife or vegetable peeler

PHYLLO

paper-thin flour and water pastry, most commonly used in Greek cuisine

POACH

to cook food in a gently-simmering liquid, just below the boiling point

POLENTA

staple food of northern Italy made from cornmeal (cooked with liquid until mushy) to which cheese is usually added; served as a first course, side dish, or breakfast food

PORTABELLO MUSHROOM

large mushrooms with a meaty taste; these mushrooms have flat caps with exposed gills

POUND

place meat or poultry between two pieces of plastic or waxed paper and pound with mallet until thin; this tenderizes certain cuts of meat by breaking down the muscle

PURÉE

to process food with a food processor, blender, or pressed through a sieve, until completely smooth

QUESADILLA

Mexican dish made from two flour tortillas that are filled with cheese and cooked until cheese is melted

RADICCHIO

slightly bitter-tasting green; a member of the chicory family and used in salads

RAGOUT
French term which means stew, usually made of meat or poultry, and rather thick

REDUCE
to boil down a liquid in order to concentrate its flavor and thicken its consistency

RELISH
a flavored blend of sweet pickles and spices

RICE NOODLES
a type of thin, dried thread made from rice starch, commonly used in Chinese cooking

ROAST
to cook food in the oven in an uncovered pan

ROSEMARY
available as fresh or dried herb, with a flavor that goes well with potatoes, bean soups, meat or chicken

ROTELLE
wagon-wheel shaped pasta

SAFFRON
highest-priced spice in the world, with a bright orange-yellow color; substitute turmeric, if desired

SAGE
pale green fuzzy leaf that complements most stuffings and bean soups

SAUTÉ
to cook food quickly in a skillet over direct heat; most foods are sautéed in some form of fat, but for healthier choices, sauté foods in fat-free broth, wine or fruit juice

SEAR
to brown meat or fish quickly over very high heat, in a skillet, under the broiler, or in a hot oven; juices are sealed in, under a crisp outer layer

SEASON
> to add flavor to foods

SEMOLINA
> coarsely-ground, or cracked, wheat often used in making pastas

SHALLOTS
> member of the onion family, shallots have a mild onion flavor with a hint of garlic--commonly used in salads, sauces and dressings

SHRED
> to cut food into thin strips with a grater or food processor

SIFT
> to pass through a sieve to remove lumps

SIEVE
> to strain liquids or food through a sieve or strainer

SIMMER
> to cook food in liquid over low heat until tiny bubbles break the surface

SKEWER
> pointed rods used to spear small pieces of food

SNOW PEAS
> young, flat, green pea pods eaten whole, with only the stems and strings removed

SOY SAUCE
> made by mixing steamed, fermented soybeans and black beans with salt and water; sold as dark, light, regular, or low-sodium

SPAGHETTI SQUASH
> large, yellow or tan-skinned member of the squash family that can be baked or steamed; cooked flesh resembles strands of spaghetti

SPICE

almost always grown in the Southern Hemisphere, and the parts used are the nuts, fruits, seeds and bark; the best flavor comes from spices that are ground and heated

STAR ANISE

fragrant spice used in Chinese cooking

STEAM

to cook food on a rack or in a steamer basket over boiling liquid in a covered pan; best cooking method for retaining nutrients

STOCK

a strained liquid made from simmering chicken, meat or fish bones in water with herbs, seasonings and vegetables

TABBOULEH

Middle Eastern food that consists of bulgur wheat mixed with tomatoes, onions, parsley, mint, olive oil and lemon juice; served hot or cold

TAMARI

similar to soy sauce, but thicker; substitute soy sauce in equal measures

TAMARIND SEEDS

also known as Indian date, tamarind is used to season chutneys, curry dishes and pickled fish

THYME

available fresh or dried, thyme adds flavor to dried beans, stuffings, tomato dishes, eggplant, onions and green beans

TOMATILLO

small green tomato-like vegetable with an outer papery husk used to make salsa verde and other dishes

TORTE

German word for cake, made with little or no flour

TORTILLA

a thin, round Mexican flat bread made from corn or flour

COOKING GLOSSARY

International Index

INDEX

INDEX

INDEX

INDEX

ALAN SKVERSKY

Alan Skversky, a native Philadelphian and graduate of the Culinary Institute of America, held various positions at some of Philadelphia's finest establishments, including the Bellevue Stratford Hotel and San Marco Restaurant, and met the challenge of co-owning a restaurant before moving to the Valley of the Sun to accept a position with the highly acclaimed Hops! Bistro & Brewery. He credits his mother's cooking talents with sparking his interest in becoming a chef.

Since his arrival, Skversky has made quite an impact on the culinary scene in Arizona. Working in a micro brewery has allowed Alan the opportunity to be at the forefront of an emerging culinary trend - beer cookery, which is becoming popular all over the country. In fact, Skversky has enjoyed the honor of being asked to speak on this subject at the NRA Food Show in Chicago in May, 1996. Beer guru Candy Schermerhorn has called him "a beer savvy chef".

Alan came across Jyl Steinback quite by accident when looking to change his eating habits in order to lose weight and be more health-conscious. While browsing in the bookstore for nutritional information, he noticed one of Jyl's first books and was hooked. He was most impressed by the simplicity and ease of preparation of the recipes and the variety therein. Realizing that Jyl was from Scottsdale, he called the FAT FREE Living office and asked for a meeting. As they say, it's all in the timing; Jyl was about to embark on this book "FAT FREE Living from Around The World", and Alan was asked to participate. Since following Jyl's eating life-style, and with exercise, Alan has lost a total of 40 pounds and feels terrific!

Chef Skversky is an active member of the ACF and frequently participates in social and charitable culinary events. He is the food columnist for Southwest Brewing News and is frequently called up for his beer recipes for ice creams and desserts, some of which have been published in cookbooks. Look for him at Kitchen Classics where he conducts cooking classes, teaching everything from basic salads to more classic entrées and desserts. Alan resides in Scottsdale with his wife, Sandee, four sons, Brian, Jonathan, Robert and Evan, and new daughter, Kendall.